THIS GRACIOUS SEASON

Barry Bonds and the Greatest Year in Baseball

By Josh Suchon

Foreword by Bob Nightengale

WINTER PUBLICATIONS

ISBN #:   Hardcover   0-9718729-0-2
              Softcover   0-9718729-1-0

Book cover design by EMAGINE Companies

Cover Photo & Interior art by Brad Mangin

Author photography courtesy of Kevin Lock

Print management by httprint. Printed in the U.S.A.

To order additional copies of this book, contact:
WINTER PUBLICATIONS, Inc.
www.winterpublications.com
orders@winterpublications.com

Dedicated to my late grandmother Jewell Ashworth, for taking me to spring training games as a teen-ager and always inspiring me to follow my dreams.

ACKNOWLEDGMENTS

Remember the title of John Madden's first book ("*Hey, I Wrote A Book!*")? That's how I feel. This book was a wild idea that came to me one day, dismissed as quickly as I thought of it. A couple weeks later, during a radio interview I did, Greg Papa asked me on the air if I'd considered writing a book about the season. Then the idea took off.

The biggest thanks go to Barry Bonds. It was an honor and privilege to watch his 2001 season on a daily basis. I thank Barry for his patience in individual interviews with myself, and the multitude of group interviews he did throughout the season, and believe I speak for my journalistic colleagues in thanking him on their behalf. Barry was also gracious enough to allow me to watch an offseason workout one day and went over a few items with me to ensure complete accuracy. Thanks to Bonds' assistant, Steve Hoskins, for his help in keeping the lines of communication open. This book is unauthorized, but I believe this is a book Barry would want on his bookshelf at home. Readers should know that I did not write this book with the idea of making Barry look good or bad. I simply wrote what I witnessed and lived for one year.

Without my agent and publisher Eric Winter, I'd never be where I am and never would have started writing this book. We first met when Eric was a senior and sports editor of *The Daily Aztec* in 1993. Eric hired me, then a sophomore, to cover the San Diego State baseball team as the beat writer. We've remained close friends to this day. I consider him the big brother I never had. Eric brought everyone together on this project. His connections, enthusiasm and will are the reason this book was published.

My mom and dad taught me so many things. How to play baseball, how to keep score, the love of the game, believing in myself, daring to dream and following through on dreams. I love you both. The entire family on both sides were so supportive and their enthusiasm around the holidays were an inspiration. Now go tell all your friends to buy a copy of this book, will ya?

Special thanks to my fellow Giants beat writers: Nick Peters of *The Sacramento Bee*, Joe Roderick of the *Contra Costa Times*, Henry Schulman of *The San Francisco Chronicle*, Jeff Fletcher of the *Santa Rosa Press Democrat* and Dan Brown of the *San Jose Mercury News*. The overwhelming majority of quotes in this book came from questions asked by one of those five gentlemen or myself. I thank them for showing me the ropes as a rookie beat writer in 2000 and the camaraderie of working as competitors during the 2001 season. I know that I'm going to forget a deserving sportswriter in this next listing, but thanks to Jeff Bradley, Howard Bryant, Bruce Jenkins, Tim Keown, Brian Murphy, Dave Newhouse, Rob Neyer, Bob Nightengale, Richard Obert, Monte Poole, Ray Ratto, Jason Reid, Mark Saxon, John Shea (another Aztec), Art Spander and Carl Steward. I did my best to give proper reporting credit whenever a statement wasn't made to myself or a group of reporters and apologize in advance if any quotes were used without proper attribution.

Thanks to Blake Rhodes of the Giants media relations staff for always knowing a statistic that I couldn't find for this project, and his tireless work during every season. Additional thanks to the entire Giants organization, including Brian Sabean, Ned Colletti, Peter Magowan, Larry Baer, Bob Rose, Jim Moorehead, Maria Jacinto, Matt Hodson, Luis Torres, Karen Sweeney and Ilene Snider.

Manager Dusty Baker is a beat writer's dream. I thank for him being the man he is, and his cooperation, along with his coaching staff, and all the players on the Giants, in particular Shawon Dunston, Eric Davis and Rich Aurilia. Trainer Stan Conte is another quality human who always makes my job easier by explaining medical stuff in a way I can understand. From other teams, I'd like to send a thank you to Tony Gwynn (another Aztec), who was incredibly gracious with his time, plus Gary Sheffield and Luis Gonzalez.

Many assisted in editing this book. Dr. Andrea Goodman, Tom Davis, Rudy Klancnik and Marissa Contreras (another Aztec) ensured the grammar was correct, the book flowed, and it would captivate a reader, regardless of their baseball knowledge.

A big thanks to Emagine Media's Don Richmond and Gretchen Gordon, who have become good friends, for their overall art design and leadership. Same goes to Brad Mangin, whose amazing art can be seen on the cover and throughout this book. Long-time friend Kevin Lock (another Aztec) somehow coaxed a decent enough picture of me for the back sleeve. Early guidance through the publishing smoke was given by Mark Porter and Jack Walklet at HTTPRINT. A final thanks to my sports editor at *The Oakland Tribune*, Jon Becker, for his friendship, loyalty and support.

CONTENTS

FOREWORD

By Bob Nightengale

Ok, I'll admit it.

I like the guy.

Actually, I like the guy a lot.

I know I'm not supposed to admit to such an abhorrent opinion. There are hundreds of sportswriters across the country that will think I'm certifiably nuts for liking the guy, let alone being able to stand him.

Sorry, but he really is one of my favorite interviews, and persons, in all of baseball.

No, I'm not talking about Josh Suchon, who brings us this terrific new book, but I'm talking about the subject:

Yep, Barry Lamar Bonds.

Bonds indeed can be a complex man, and his mood swings can change as quickly as the wind at ol' Candlestick, but you know something?

That's what makes him so damn appealing.

You never know what you're going to get from one day to the next talking to Bonds, but always, always, expect the unexpected. He'll make you laugh one minute, curse the next, and have you looking up to the high heavens for help during every interview.

Yet, his greatest characteristic, and perhaps the one that his teammates detest the most, is his brutal honesty.

You want to know the truth? Then don't be afraid to ask the question.

You ask a candid question, you're going to get a candid answer.

Bonds has always been that way ever since I've known him back in the late 80's. I can't remember the first time I met him, but always, he was a terrific interview. He'll tell you what he thinks of his teammates. He'll tell you what he thinks of any of his peers. And if he can't talk candidly, he'll give you that smirk, raise his eyebrows, and say, "Next question."

He was that way when I frequently approached him when he played for the Pittsburgh Pirates. He was that way when I interviewed him while lying sprawled on his bed at the '92 winter meetings, waiting for Peter Magowan to provide a personal contract so that he could sign with the San Francisco Giants. He was that way when I've dined with him at his favorite spring-training restaurant in North Scottsdale.

And he was that way all last season when I saw him the first week of spring training, caught up with him in June in St. Louis, and spent the last month of the season following him.

Oh, it's not that I was planning to spend the last two months of the season on the road, following Barry one month, and jumping to the playoffs and World Series the next, but when you're watching history unfold before your eyes night after night, why complain?

Watching Bonds night after night, you secretly rooted for the guy to break the record, only because you know the rest of the country was rooting against him.

America loved it in '98 when Mark McGwire and Sammy Sosa put on a home-run derby for the ages. They went mano y mano through the heart of the summer. It no longer became a sports story. It was national news. Dan Rather and Peter Jennings were talking about it nightly, not just Dan Patrick and Peter Gammons.

Now, just three years later, Bonds was alone in the national spotlight. McGwire and Sosa were chasing the ghost of Roger Maris. What was Bonds chasing? McGwire's shadow?

You couldn't help but feel sorry for Bonds. Here he was, producing the finest offensive season in baseball history, and it was as if a nation yawned. Oh, sure, McGwire's record was just three years old. And certainly, after the horrifying events of Sept. 11, we didn't have quite the same passion for sports, let alone an individual record.

Still, there was such a drastic difference in attention. When I covered McGwire during his record-breaking run, the St. Louis Cardinals' clubhouse was a mob scene. It was elbow-to-elbow in the press box, let alone near McGwire's locker.

Yet, with Bonds, it was so different. The local Bay Area media was out in force, but the hysteria was missing. Most of the national media didn't even start arriving until Bonds already had 67 home runs. And when he set the record one night, and then broke it the next, no one bothered to stick around for the final two games of the weekend. Everyone caught the first flight out as if it was a nuisance to watch history be made.

It made no sense, but then again, it didn't make much sense that Bonds wasn't an unanimous MVP. It made no sense that Bonds' only free-agent contract offer was from the Giants. It made no sense that Bonds was nowhere to be found on the talk-show circuit, or advertising trail. You didn't see his face on a national commercial until the Super Bowl.

But you think Bonds cared?

Uh-uh.

He actually worried more about whether anyone cashed in on his record-breaking year.

"I know one casino had me at 3-million-to-1 odds," Bonds told me the final week of the season. "Sammy [Sosa] was 500,000-to-1. Someone had to bet on me, didn't they?"

Maybe the only one who really did was Suchon.

It was his idea to do the book. And he was going to do it his way, just like Bonds would want. He didn't go over it with Bonds. He didn't even ask for permission. He was just going to write it, whether Bonds wanted it done or not.

That's why Bonds can't help but respect Suchon for his efforts. Bonds loves rebels. He loves people who stand up to their beliefs. He may not agree with you, and might actually detest your profession, but stand up to the man, and he'll always respect you.

That's why it was so refreshing watching Bonds this past year. He didn't change. He'll be the first to tell you that. No sir, it was everyone else who changed around him. Bonds knew that if he changed, he couldn't look at himself in the mirror. He'd be a phony. If people wanted to jump on his bandwagon, he left an open invitation. If they wanted to ignore him, hey, it's their prerogative.

People jumped on, liked what they saw, and there were more complimentary and flattering stories on Bonds in one summer than he received in his life.

He still laughs about that, feeling good that he never changed, but everyone around him did.

If nothing else, everyone came to the same realization that all of his peers in the game have known for quite awhile: We're watching one of the greatest players in the history of baseball, and if we wait too long to appreciate his talents, he'll be gone forever, and we'll be left wondering where he went.

"People talk about Babe Ruth and this guy or that guy," Atlanta Braves outfielder Gary Sheffield says. "But to me, Barry is not only the greatest player in the game, but he might be the greatest in the history of the game.

"He's been the best player in this game for a long time, but no one ever acknowledged it."

Now, in the first book written about Bonds, Suchon is letting us sit down and watch the show most of America missed. He tells us in his own words what it was like as a Giants' beat writer to witness history, taking us right through the season, from the first day of spring training to the final day of the year.

We found out what it was like being in the clubhouse every day and being around Bonds through the course of the season. You feel as if you're re-living history, as if you're the one talking to Willie Mays, sitting in the dugout listening to Giants manager Dusty Baker, and in the stands cheering next to Bonds' family.

This is a book, filtered through the eyes of the people who lived it, and watched it being lived. No punches are pulled. Nothing is out-of-bounds. And everything is fair game.

And when you are finished reading, you know what?

You will feel as if you never missed the show, after all.

Who knows, if you're not careful, your emotions may get carried away and you'll start liking Barry.

But like him or hate him, you'll definitely love the book.

BOB NIGHTENGALE
USA Today Baseball Weekly

To see this gracious season.
All o'er joy'd,
Save these in bonds: let them be joyful too.

William Shakespeare
Act V, Scene 5
Cymbeline

THIS GRACIOUS SEASON

Barry Bonds and the Greatest Year in Baseball

INTRODUCTION

MY LAPTOP WAS always down. It was a decision I made at the start of the 2001 season, knowing that Barry Bonds was six away from reaching the magical milestone of 500 career home runs. Every player in baseball history who has hit 500 homers, and is eligible for the Hall of Fame, has been immortalized in Cooperstown, New York.

I didn't want to miss anything Barry Bonds did because you never know what he might do next. It first hit me when I heard an interview Bonds did with ESPN early in the season. Bonds wasn't sure what he would say at the Hall of Fame induction speech he will undoubtedly be making in the future, except to tell people, "you missed the show."

So, at my suggestion, myself and a couple other beat writers who cover the San Francisco Giants decided that whenever Bonds was up to bat, our laptops would be down.

We wouldn't read the paper. We wouldn't read the game notes. We wouldn't surf the Internet. We wouldn't type our stories. We wouldn't transcribe interviews. We wouldn't eat or drink. We would rarely even talk. We would simply take advantage of our (near) front-row seats and watch history.

It seemed a little silly when Bonds was in a 0-for-21 slump eight games into the season. But then Bonds hit No. 496, 497, 498 and 499 in a four-day stretch and you could just sense this was history in the making. Even in the eighth inning of a night game and facing a tight deadline, I stopped everything I was doing when Bonds came to the plate against Terry Adams of the Los Angeles Dodgers.

I didn't miss the show that night. Watching Bonds' 500th leave the bat, soaring into the pitch-black sky, this white object heading toward the San Francisco Bay, I tell you it was a thing of beauty.

By then, it became habit. The laptop was down when Bonds batted. As Bonds continued to punish baseball after baseball over fences throughout North America, it became an obsession. The laptop would always, always be down.

It's the wisest decision I've ever made in my journalistic career.

In fact, on the final day of the 2001 regular season, as the crowd of reporters was leaving Bonds' locker, I walked up to him and told him, "I'm proud to say that I didn't miss the show."

Barry smiled. I think he respected that.

CHAPTER 1

On the Mark

October 4, 70th Homer

"I can't even express those feelings. I think some of them got some cheap shots in on my ribs. So many years of frustration, I guess. They kind of got it out on me."

Barry Bonds,
on his teammate reaction at home plate after hitting No. 70

"GIVE OUR DADDY A CHANCE" was the hand-written message that 11-year-old Shikari Bonds wrote and held up for the television cameras. On the verge of breaking the most glamorous record in all of sports, her father was a baseball hostage. In his last 18 plate appearances over nearly four games, needing just one home run to tie the single-season record, Barry Bonds had seen 64 pitches and 51 were balls.

For six months, the baseball world debated if Barry Bonds could break Mark McGwire's single-season, home-run record. If the rest of baseball would give him a chance to break the record. If the public would care about this record getting broken just three years after a magical summer produced such good will for the game. If the public would embrace the man pursuing the record. And if the man himself would embrace the pursuit.

Was this the answer? Sixty-four pitches and fifty-one balls?

It was October 4, 2001, a day the British government released a document that Prime Minister Tony Blair said "leaves absolutely no doubt that (Osama) bin Laden and his network are responsible" for the September 11 attacks.

In Moscow, 76 people died as a Russian airliner exploded over the Black Sea, renewing terrorism fears. In Washington, President Bush unveiled a $3 billion plan to help people who lost their jobs in the terrorist attacks. In Florida, a 63-year-old man was hospitalized with inhalation anthrax, starting weeks and weeks of fear of the next potential terrorist threat to the country.

Back in Houston, a sold-out ballpark was booing its home team for a strategy designed to help them win baseball games and make the playoffs. The objects of the home crowd's scorn were the pitchers of the Houston Astros baseball team, a former pitcher named Larry Dierker who manages them, a former pitcher named Burt Hooton who is the pitching coach and the catchers who were calling the pitches.

The previous 14 plate appearances in Houston had produced these astounding numbers: eight walks, a hit-by-pitch, two singles, three outs. The walks came with the bases empty and runners on base. With the score tied and with a seven-run lead.

Were the heartfelt boos, the veins bulging in fans' faces, the expletives being shouted from the stands and the sympathy of hundreds of sportswriters — the same sportswriters who have never cared much for Barry Bonds — providing the answer about whether America cared or not? It sure seemed that way.

Like anything else in this country — whether it's OJ or Jon Benet or "Survivor" or terrorism or a home-run record — this story had to be magnified; we had to look ourselves in the mirror a couple dozen times and debate this into the broadest picture possible.

What does the story say about us as people? What does the act of hitting a baseball over a fence and our fascination with this act say about us? Why do we care? Do we care? If it does mean anything, why does it mean so much?

Men and women are still combing through concrete and debris at what used to be the World Trade Center, people are scared to get on airplanes, the economy is plummeting, families have been ruined forever, that quiet neighbor always working in his basement suddenly has our minds wondering, and we're supposed to care about a home run record?

Somebody on television is asking if homers can help cure a nation and we're supposed to take him seriously?

Puh-leeze.

Right?

Or maybe, just maybe, if you can call it a distraction, if you needed a break from the images of airplanes being used as bombs of mass destruction, maybe a baseball player doing the most primitive and natural act — hitting an object as far as humanly possible, as frequently as possible — and making a run at the most storied record in professional sports, is precisely what we needed to give our minds a breather from the unbelievable visuals on our news every day.

From a weekend in mid-May, when Bonds first launched himself to the lead story of SportsCenter with a dizzying home-run pace, we knew that if he ever got close to the record, it wasn't going to be like 1998. Not enough time had passed. It was too fresh in our minds. We'd been there; we'd cheered that. Regis wouldn't be there early in the morning. Koppell wouldn't be there late at night. Now, with the world changed forever, the heavyweights of the news world had a real news story to cover.

This was a story for baseball seamheads and Americans who wanted an escape. As time passes and *if* Bonds' record lasts more than a couple of years, it will be remembered for its amazing place in history as much as the amazing season by the individual.

Yeah, maybe, but this is Barry Bonds, for crying out loud. Right?

Barry Bonds is going to heal us?

Forget the name for a moment. Erase everything you've ever heard for a moment about Barry Bonds. Wipe it all from your brain. Pretend you never heard his name and somebody is describing the actions and words of an unknown person. And ask yourself what you would think of a person who did the following:

* Pointed to the sky to thank God after each home run.
* Stayed away from drugs and cigarettes and rarely touched alcohol.
* Played through pain and did not complain or make excuses.
* Hugged and kissed his wife and children after memorable moments.
* Hit 22 homers after 43 games and said something like, "To talk about it on May 21st is ridiculous. I could get hit by a truck tomorrow. Then what? 'He was on his way, but damn, he got hit by a car.'"
* Hit 38 homers in 72 games, arrived in the city of the record-holder McGwire and said something like, "I don't want his record. I want his (World Series) ring. Well, I don't want his ring. I want my own."
* Hit 53 homers in 121 games and said something like, "I love this game, I love to win. I've come up short a lot of times. I hope I can just carry this on, all the way through. That's on my mind more than anything. I've been able to help teams win divisions. I need to help a team win a World Series."
* Hit 66 homers in 150 games and said something like, "If I do it, I'll be excited. Don't worry. I won't hold back. I guarantee that. But right now, I'm on a quest to win a championship. If it means to hit home runs to help this

team, then that's my job. If it means take a walk and get on base, that's my job. I'm not gonna come out of my game for this record."

* Hit 69 homers in 156 games, got within one of the record and said something like, "I think everyone needs to understand, Mark McGwire set the table. He's the first one and it's his record and he needs to be recognized for his record. Mark deserves that respect. He has put new hype on this thing and he deserves every amount of respect for being the man."

* And, what if, after seeing 51 balls out of 64 pitches over nearly four games, when his daughter was making a new hand-held sign in the ballpark begging to "PLEASE PITCH TO OUR DADDY" and his son was near tears at what he was witnessing, he said something like this to both the media and his children: "The main thing is winning. Keep winning and keep rolling and if Jeff Kent and the rest of them keep doing their job, eventually they are going to have to come at you."

Well, ladies and gentlemen, perhaps it's time you met Barry Bonds.

"I know there will be people who will say, 'well, yeah, he said all the right things, but we know who the real Barry is," admitted Giants owner Peter Magowan. "But I think he has changed and I think, frankly, that his marriage has a lot to do with it. He's got a lovely wife and wonderful kids. He's a very good father, and he loves his children. They give him a lot of pleasure."

Barry Bonds is not perfect.

He is far from perfect.

Barry Bonds can be a real pain in the ass.

This book is not about a misunderstood man. You will not read the word misunderstood again in this book.

This is a story about an extraordinary baseball player having an extraordinary baseball season, interrupted and impacted by an extraordinary time in America, how he dealt with the extraordinary attention he brought on himself, how it changed him, how it changed the people around him and how he rarely got a chance to enjoy any part of the season.

"When you've had everything in your career but winning it all, what else can you desire for?" Giants manager Dusty Baker said. "He's had MVPs, he's had home-run titles, he's had 400 stolen bases, 500-something home runs. After awhile, what does a rich man who has all the riches crave? Wisdom."

It can only happen with Barry Bonds. Only with this complex individual can the reaction of fans and his own teammates become a part of the story. Everybody cheered Mark McGwire in 1998. But how would everybody react in 2001?

The answer was coming quickly and dramatically.

It came in the ninth inning of that same October 4 game, with the Giants leading 9-2 over the Astros, Bonds leading off the inning and the Astros no longer having any motive for continuing to pitch around him. They simply *had* to throw him a strike.

The manager, Larry Dierker, summoned a hard-throwing, left-handed rookie named Wilfredo Rodriguez. He was making his second appearance in the major leagues.

Bonds patiently waited in the on-deck circle as Enron Field stirred with anticipation. Rodriguez completed his eight warm-up pitches. Catcher Tony Eusebio threw down to second and walked to the mound.

"I told him not to leave it over the plate," Eusebio said. "I told him to try to calm down, and if you feel you've got your fastball, go right after him."

In anticipation, the Enron Field sellout crowd of 43,734 started up the chant, "Bar-ry, Bar-ry, Bar-ry, Bar-ry, Bar-ry."

Bonds walked to the plate, looking calm and relaxed as ever. The first pitch was a 95-mph fastball. Bonds took a mighty swing and missed. Rodriguez, a native of Venezuela, briefly clinched his face. The crowd oooh'd and ahhh'd in anticipation. Flashbulbs were going off from the time Rodriguez's delivery started until after the ball whizzed past Bonds' bat and landed in Eusebio's glove.

Sensing the kid was going after him and throwing awfully hard, Bonds zoned in a little more and geared himself up.

The flashbulbs continued and Bonds watched a 96-mph fastball sail high out of the strike zone. It was now obvious that Rodriguez was going after Bonds. This was a hard-throwing rookie, without great control, who wasn't going to work the corners and must have had his blood pumping faster than at any other moment in his life.

Bonds knew this was his chance. The Los Angeles Dodgers were the team in town next. If the Astros wouldn't pitch to him, would the hated rivals ever pitch to him?

It was now or never for the record.

Rodriguez cocked and fired a 94-mph fastball to Bonds. At 9:21 p.m. CT, Bonds' maple bat connected with the pitch.

> *"The 1-1, there it goes! There it goes! Mark McGwire has a*
> *co-owner of the home run throne! Number 70 for Bonds!"*

> — Charlie Steiner, on ESPN Radio

Once it left the bat, there was never a doubt. This homer was crushed. Another Bonds Bomb. The estimated distance was 454 feet. It landed in the second deck at Enron Field and was caught by Charles Murphy of Houston. Bonds flipped the bat to the side and put his hands up in the air. He rounded first base with his index finger in the air. He pumped his fist.

Nikolai Bonds, the nine-year-old son and batboy, was the first one there, jumping up and down deliriously on his way to the plate.

Bonds' teammates, in an emphatic answer to the questions of how they would react to his triumphant moment, sprinted toward the plate and joyfully hugged and mobbed their teammate.

"I can't even express those feelings. I think some of them got some cheap shots in on my ribs," Bonds said laughing. "So many years of frustration, I guess. They kind of got it out on me."

Bonds received the biggest hugs from Baker and his two best friends on the team, fellow outfielders and late-30-somethings Shawon Dunston and Eric Davis.

"It's awesome," Dunston said. "I was a teammate of Mac's and now Barry. We always see Hank Aaron's home runs. You see Babe Ruth home runs and Roger Maris and Mac's and now Barry's. You just want to pinch yourself that you are really here. I'm just so happy for Barry. He deserves it."

There was a lot of controversy back on April 17 about the reaction, or lack thereof, by Bonds' teammates after he hit the 500th homer of his career. In the nearly six months that had passed, Baker had noticed some changes between Bonds and his teammates.

"But it was also much more significant," Baker said. "There's been, what, 15 people who have hit 500 homers, right? Well, only Big Mac ever hit 70 before. It was so much more significant and climactic because of the suspense leading up to it."

The Enron Field crowd stayed on its feet and continued cheering. Bonds' wife Liz cried in the stands. So did daughters Shikari and Aisha and their friends. The crowd brought Bonds out for one curtain call. And then another curtain call.

The inning ended and Bonds went to the outfield. The guys in the bullpen came out and mobbed him, hugging and congratulating him.

"Home plate is really good," Bonds said. "But then when the guys came from the bullpen, I think that really, really touched me even more."

Like a basketball coach milking every moment, Baker then brought in a defensive replacement for Bonds in left field — so his star could receive one more round of applause as he left the field.

Bonds did an interview on the field with ESPN and local rights-holding station KTVU after the game ended. He then walked toward the interview room. He was greeted by his wife and daughters before he got there. They hugged and kissed. Shikari was still so emotional, she couldn't stop crying and buried her head in her dad's stomach, her arms around his waist, as she walked to the podium with him.

"You guys are going to make me start to cry," Bonds told his family, before facing a packed interview room of reporters. "Wow. Two fastballs. It was electrifying. It came with a victory and that's what made it really special. We have our work cut out for us, we are trying to get to the postseason. You know, this team is gutting it out, really, really pushing hard. We got a lot of key hits in a lot of key situations, and we played very well this series as a team."

Back in the Giants clubhouse, the rookies found outrageous outfits replaced their normal clothes in their lockers — the customary attire for the final road trip of the regular season — and it was a scene that's hard to describe.

Pitcher Ryan Jensen walked around in a pink tutu. Reliever Chad Zerbe had some green lizard costume on. Catcher Edwards Guzman sported a yellow-feather jumpsuit. Pitcher Kurt Ainsworth paraded around in a skin-tight, all-black silk bodysuit worthy of a diva.

You had Jeff Kent — the villain of this drama for his biting criticism in a magazine article a month earlier — sitting on a couch, watching the replays on a TV, eating an ice cream cone and talking glowingly about Bonds. You had rookies getting dressed, veterans taking pictures, clubhouse workers quickly packing things up and loading them onto the truck, the traveling secretary reminding everybody when the bus was leaving, and players trying to find words to explain what they'd seen their teammates accomplish the past 159 games.

Bonds patiently answered the questions back in the interview room as his son Nikolai joined him at the podium with Shikari.

* Relief of hitting it? "You know, I have a lot of respect for Mark McGwire. To me, it's an honor to have this opportunity to share this with him because he's such a great home-run hitter. He's always established power and strength. He put the home run record at where it is and I will always respect that. But I want three more victories. I want the playoffs."

* Anger at the walk with an 8-1 score? "Robby Thompson was at first base and really upset because it wasn't really a close game. Everyone could understand if the situation was a close game."

* Knew it was gone immediately? "I was happy that I made contact because, you know, it's hard to just take pitches all the time and you really don't have an opportunity to swing. You feel like you're losing your swing a little bit. When you get the opportunity to swing the bat a lot, you can get your timing and you can stay consistent. It's hard. It's a really hard thing."

* What he'll remember most from the night? "Probably Robby Thompson's frustration at first base (laughter). It takes a lot to make Robby mad and I think that's the first time I've really seen him upset."

How we ever got to this place is beyond the scope of unbelievable.

Barry Bonds had never hit 50 homers in a season in his lifetime. And now he had 70 with three games left in the season to set a new record.

Barry Bonds never liked doing interviews with the media. And now he was doing meaningful interviews before *and* after almost every game.

Barry Bonds was never liked on the road, usually booed, and content with his status as a loner in his own clubhouse. And now he was wildly cheered on the road, accepted in his own clubhouse, and Jeff Kent was making genuine statements like, "we're riding the adrenaline rush" of Barry's chase.

His teammates, and the nation, just couldn't help it. We didn't think it would happen. We didn't think we would care if it did happen. But we couldn't help it. Records are made to be broken and damn how long ago the record was set. You can't deny history. And once we get close to history, we want to see it, we want the athlete to have a legitimate chance to do it — and we want to be part of history.

How we got to this night couldn't happen overnight.

And it didn't.

This is the story of how it happened.

CHAPTER TWO

State of the Barry

Spring Training, February 10-April 1

"They know, I don't believe that for one minute. If they do not want me to be here — at this point in my career and after what I've done for this organization — let me know. I'm a man. I can deal with it. So I can at least tell my family. All I want to do is be able to tell my family if I'm going to be here or I'm not going to be here. I think I deserve that much."

Barry Bonds

SOME PLACES JUST inspire optimism. Scottsdale Stadium, the spring training home of the San Francisco Giants, is one of them. Built in 1956, remodeled in 1993, it's like a mini-Camden Yards in the Arizona desert with its intimate setting, and mix of older design with new features. It doesn't have bleachers. The outfield area is a grassy hill, perfect for sunbathing and baseball viewing. You couldn't design a more intimate, relaxing and beautiful place for a team to prepare for a baseball season.

Back in San Francisco, it's raining. In places like Milwaukee, it's still snowing. In Scottsdale, it's shorts and sandals weather. The grass just seems greener here. The crack of the wooden bat seems more resounding. The pop of the catchers glove a little louder.

But today is February 20, 2001, and even the Scottsdale weather, even the picturesque mountains in the horizon, even the sights and sounds from a baseball diamond, could not inspire optimism.

Barry Bonds reported to camp this morning. His arrival changed the atmosphere. A camp that was relaxed is now filled with tension. Everybody knows why. When the superstar arrives to spring training, it's always news. Barry Bonds is no different. Bonds' first day at camp is always a "State of the Barry Address" with the media. If something is on Barry's mind, he's going to make it clear.

The previous year, Barry stated his desire to reach the career home run total of his Godfather, the great Willie Mays, who hit 660. Other years, it was Barry's goal to win a fourth Most Valuable Player award or extend his contract or become more of a movie star.

This year, everyone knows what the topic will be. Bonds has one year remaining on his contract. On December 8, 1992, Bonds signed a six-year contract that returned him to his hometown of San Francisco. Prior to the 1997 season, Bonds signed a two-year extension for 1999 and 2000 with a club option for the 2001 season. On July 30, 1998, the Giants exercised their 2001 option.

Now it's the final year. And the team hasn't tried to negotiate a new contract yet. The Giants don't know what the market is for an outfielder who will turn 37 during the season — even an outfielder with three Most Valuable Player awards, even an outfielder with 494 career homers, even an outfielder coming off a season when he just hit a career-high 49 home runs.

Exactly one month ago, the stage for this morning was set. A story appeared in the *Contra Costa Times* under the headline, "Lack of Loyalty Bugs Bonds" that had KNBR-AM, the flagship radio station of the Giants, buzzing with calls and opinions.

"I don't know what to think," Bonds calmly told *Times* beat writer Joe Roderick. "I mean, if I get an answer like what you're saying, 'we'll see how things go during the course of the season,' I guess that kind of hurts my feelings a little bit and makes me feel not wanted, if you have to wait and see. How long have I been here, eight years, and I have to 'wait and see?' I'm just going to play. That's what I've always done. It hurts my feelings, from what you've said their statement was. That hurts, to think I'm not wanted."

General manager Brian Sabean was furious when I called him for a reaction. Before he could even begin answering my questions, Sabean launched into an obscenity-laced tirade at the author of the story. It was Sabean's belief that a statement he'd made, three months earlier, was taken out of context and used unfairly as the basis for the entire article.

The comment was made on October 10, two days after the Giants were defeated, three games to one, in the best-of-five National League Division Series by the New York Mets. Sabean ate lunch with myself and the other five traveling beat writers and we talked about the team's offseason agenda. Near the end, I asked Sabean if he plans on working out an extension to Bonds' contract in the upcoming offseason. Sabean said it "was not a pressing issue. He's signed and that's good for the ballclub and good for him. It's not something I've thought about."

In recent years, a sentiment around baseball general managers is that you must sign your superstar player before he enters the final year of his contract — or you trade him to ensure that you get something for him.

"I don't buy into that logic," Sabean said. "Now, if we go into the tank, the dynamics change. If you're an underachieving team stuck with a hell of a player that you can move, then it's different. Teams make a bigger deal about that stuff than they should. If Barry is a free agent at the end of next season, we don't resign him, and we don't get anything in return, that's not going to concern me."

Sabean never said that he didn't want Bonds back. He just said it wasn't a pressing issue, he didn't subscribe to the notion of "I've got to get somebody for my big guy," as he put it, and his offseason priorities were on other players.

Three months later, Sabean suddenly had a firestorm on his hands because of an article that he felt unfairly categorized his, and the Giants, feelings about Bonds.

Sabean finally calmed down and gave me his response to this latest article.

"I've never said we didn't want Barry or want Barry back," Sabean said. "It's obvious what Barry's contributions and loyalties have been to our organization — above and beyond the call of duty. But given today's landscape, how do we quantify Barry's worth as we go forward? I'm literally in a quandary. We don't have all the answers right now. And when you don't have all the answers, you better proceed conservatively."

These were the questions to which Sabean didn't have the answers: What length contract is Bonds seeking? Is he seeking Manny Ramirez ($20 million annually) money or Alex Rodriguez money ($25 million annually)? What will the Giants payroll be in 2001? And 2002? And 2003? And 2004? How would a $15-20 million salary to one player (Bonds) skew the entire payroll when the next-highest salary is $8 million? And what impact will the presence of Bonds' notorious agent, Scott Boras, create to the situation?

Sabean said he was open to a contract discussion in spring training. However, "the last thing we want to do is engage in something that becomes counterproductive because you can't get something done and it's construed the wrong way," he said. "Then you hold that against each other. Or the player becomes unhappy or pissed off. That's the last thing we want to do."

Meanwhile, as I talked with Sabean on the phone, the KNBR phone lines were heating up. After we hung up, I listened intently to gauge the fan reactions. Some said to trade Bonds. Some said to let Bonds go. Some said to give Bonds whatever he wants financially.

Suddenly, out of nowhere, host Bob Fitzgerald said, "We have a call from a Barry in San Francisco. Barry, what would you like to talk about?"

It was Barry Bonds.

"This guy should be sued," were the first words out of Bonds' mouth. Bonds was angry. His friends were listening to the radio station and told him what was happening. Bonds took the unusual approach of calling KNBR himself.

"I have never once, ever, made any negative comments about the Giants organization," Bonds said. "Nor did I make any inquiries toward the Giants, like, if they don't sign me, I'm upset. I'm not upset about anything. The only thing I want to do is win a World Series ring, OK? That's it."

Bonds said *if* what the reporter told him Sabean said was accurate — making it clear Bonds was skeptical — then it would hurt his feelings.

"It hurt my feelings that (Sabean) would feel that way about me personally, but that's OK," Bonds said. "I'm not mad at him. If that's his opinion, that's his opinion. I don't know if that was his opinion because it was written through an article."

The phone call turned into an interview and lasted 20 minutes. Bonds was bitter and didn't hold back his emotions.

"Every question toward me is always, 'well, you're getting older.' Well, I'm playing like I'm 25, OK?" Bonds said. "I don't play like I'm 36. I play and I dedicate myself to this game. And I love this game. And I can't force anybody to do anything. And I'm not going to force (the Giants). And I'm not going to beg anybody. I want to play the game. Whether it's here in San Francisco, that would be my ideal choice. But if it's not here in San Francisco, those are not my choices, (so) don't sit there and make quotes and statements like I'm upset. I'm more upset that people would say I'm upset, then me being upset. I want to play baseball as long as God is going to let me play this game of baseball. And I'm going to play this baseball to the best of my capabilities. Not every day is a good day. But I've had some pretty good years."

Then came a line that was classic Bonds because of its frankness.

"I hear this all the time, 'He's arrogant, he's this . . . , "Bonds said. "I'm not arrogant. I'm good. There's a difference. I'm a good baseball player."

Bonds was asked if being a free agent would motivate him to have a better year.

"No. I'm going to have a good year because Barry Bonds is a good baseball player," Bonds said. "I've had guaranteed contracts and I've played good anyways. I could have sat on my butt. My contracts were guaranteed."

By this time, Bonds had calmed down. At first, he was bordering on hysteria. He was so upset and talking so fast, he couldn't string words together continuously. By now, he'd calmed down and was talking normally.

"I'm sorry that I had to get on the phone like this," Bonds said. "It just irks me when people call me up and say, 'Barry read this article and listen to what people are saying about you on KNBR.' Sure, you're not going to please the world, which is fine. But there doesn't have to be a reason to start something, when there's nothing there to start."

When Bonds walked into the clubhouse, he didn't make eye contact with anybody. The year before, he walked into the clubhouse and did a lap, saying hello to all his teammates and introducing himself to the rookies. The expression on his face was emotionless. Bonds was with Steve Hoskins, his longtime friend and personal assistant. Bonds changed into shorts and a Giants T-shirt and went onto the field. He jogged with head trainer Stan Conte and went through a small workout.

As Bonds finished his workout, Giants public relations man Blake Rhodes approached Steve and had a brief conversation. They agreed that Bonds would talk to the media. It took place behind home plate at Scottsdale Stadium with Bonds standing against the chain-link fence backstop.

Sweat was still pouring off his shaved head.

It started slow. The eight print reporters didn't know what type of mood Bonds was in. Everybody knew the topic would eventually turn to his contract. The question was when. And which reporter would initiate the conversation. Bonds was asked about his family and his offseason workouts. He mumbled a few short responses. He wasn't initially in a chatty mood.

Finally, Bonds brought up the contract himself. The entire interview was intense because of the look in Bonds' eye and the anger in his voice. At one point, Bonds said he doesn't hold grudges. He pointed at Roderick and said, "If I did, I would punch you."

Then he looked at beat writer Henry Schulman of the *San Francisco Chronicle* and said, "and I'd have punched you a long time ago."

"A deal doesn't have to be done," Bonds told the group. "I just want some form of communication. If it's just dead silence, all my questions are answered."

It was suggested to Bonds that the Giants don't know how much they can offer him because of their payroll and other concerns.

"They know, I don't believe that for one minute," Bonds said. "If they do not want me to be here — at this point in my career and after what I've done for this organization — let me know. I'm a man. I can deal with it. So I can at least tell my family. All I want to do is be able to tell my family if I'm going to here or I'm not going to be here. I think I deserve that much."

Bonds was asked if he'd accept less money to remain a Giant.

"I don't want Alex Rodriguez money," Bonds said. "I just want what I work for. I'd rather be on a contending team. You have to be willing to give up a little to stay on a team, or be with a ballclub, so if they can get help, they'll do it . . . I want to make sure there is a commitment to winning. And then I'll be willing to work out anything."

"I think it's only fair to the city," Bonds continued. "San Francisco is a big-market city. How can you not have a contending team? I can understand a small city. But I can't understand that in a big city. It just doesn't make any sense."

Bonds consistently reiterated his desire to remain in San Francisco, while staying skeptical it would happen.

"I've been here my whole life," he said. "I came back home. I'm pretty lucky. But I look at it this way: Why should I be any different from the way my godfather (Willie Mays) was sent out, the way Matt Williams was sent out, the way the rest of them were sent out? It's just unfortunate. But we'll see. Time will tell. Nobody knows what will happen. It's up to my agent. And it's up to them."

Bonds was finished. But the drama was just beginning. The beat writers then walked upstairs to the front office. We had to get Sabean's opinion and reaction. And everybody knew this wasn't going to be pretty.

Bob Rose, the Giants' vice president of communications, informed Sabean there was a group of reporters waiting to speak with him. About five minutes later, Rose told the writers to meet Sabean outside on the patio.

Except for one. Sabean was still so furious at Joe Roderick, he wouldn't allow him to be part of the interview.

The group gathered outside. The reporters were unsure of just how pissed Sabean would be. I opened my mouth first. I didn't even complete a sentence and Sabean went ballistic.

His expletive-laced tirade lasted a good 2-3 minutes. Nobody said a word. Sabean just ranted and cursed. All the reporters just waited until he was done. Outbursts like this aren't uncommon from Sabean. He averages one per spring training.

The year before, it was when former Giants outfielder Kevin Mitchell, clearly not in playing shape, showed up at camp unexpectedly and announced he was interested in a comeback. Manager Dusty Baker, a friend of Mitchell, said he thought Mitchell could still hit. Of course, the reporters had to ask Sabean if he was interested in signing Mitchell. Sabean screamed obscenities for a couple minutes. Once on the record, Sabean explained the Giants weren't interested.

These outbursts are partly spontaneous and partly calculated. By reacting with such anger at the mere mention of the topic, Sabean was sending a message to the writers to avoid this topic in the future. He was making it clear he did not want Bonds' contract to hover over camp for six weeks. He did not want to be giving daily updates on Bonds' contract situation. It was real simple to Sabean. They were not negotiating now. They would take their chances to sign him in the offseason. Any attempts to make this a daily drama would be shot down with an angry reaction.

Finally, Sabean had cursed his peace. He took a deep breathe. A smirk came across his face and he told the group he was ready to answer any question.

"There's never been an issue where we've said we don't want Barry back," Sabean said. "Unequivocally, we want Barry back. The obvious problem, as we stand here today is, it's easier said than done. I don't have the answers to the questions that need to be answered. How many years? How much money?

"If (Bonds) needs me to sit down in front of his face and say we want him back, I'm not opposed to that."

Sabean's reluctance to negotiate, it was later explained to me privately, was based on how the Alex Rodriguez contract played out the previous spring training with agent Scott Boras.

The Seattle Mariners went into spring training negotiating with Boras in good faith. The Mariners made their ultimate best offer, beyond what they really wanted to spend, and then Boras/Rodriguez walked away from the bargaining table. The two sides agreed to not talk contract until the end of the season. Seven months later, the Mariners final offer was used as the opening bid in the offseason sweepstakes. It was too rich for Seattle's blood. Eventually, Boras convinced the Texas Rangers to bid against themselves and they ended up signing Rodriguez for a professional sports record 10 years and $252 million.

"We make offers to sign people," Sabean told the group, from the patio outside his office. "We don't make offers to not get something done. I know it's always incumbent on the team to get something done in the end. I've said, since day one, we want the player back. But for all purposes, for all people, it will probably be better served to do it at the end of the year — when I know exactly what we are up against for 2002 and into the future."

Sabean said that Bonds is just one piece of the championship-team puzzle.

"We also need to look at other people," Sabean said. "Barry is the most important piece. But we also need to figure out Shawn Estes when he gets eligible for free agency. Jeff Kent is coming up (on free agency). I'm in charge of putting together the best possible and deepest roster. We don't have a $100 million payroll. We won't next year. We probably won't have a $75 million payroll next year. It will be a lot closer to what it is this year (mid-$60 million). I'm juggling a lot of balls. Unequivocally, we want the player back. That's the easiest answer at this point."

Sabean also knew that Boras' presence makes it extremely difficult. Seven months prior, the Giants signed their closer, Robb Nen, to a four-year contract in the middle of the season that was far below what Nen could have commanded as a free agent on the open market. Sabean wasn't expecting Boras to do that again with Bonds.

"That's not Scott's style," Sabean said. "Scott kicked and moaned when Robb Nen wanted to get a contract done. Scott is about market value. Arguably, Barry will be the premiere free agent out there. I find it hard to believe that Scott Boras and Barry Bonds would contact us and do the type of deal that Robb Nen did — which, in the end, was well-below market value."

News of the Sabean explosion circulated quickly around the Arizona desert. Copies of a tape recording of Sabean's outburst were in high demand. One reporter played the tape by telephone back to his office in the Bay Area, where co-workers gathered over a speaker phone and laughed. Reporters from teams all over the Cactus League asked who had a copy to hear it themselves.

Before the day was over, Oakland Athletics general manager Billy Beane called Sabean, jokingly, and asked if Bonds was available in a trade.

Even Sabean, a few days later, asked reporters if anybody still had a copy of the tape. He listened to it, along with a couple of friends who were in town, and laughed hysterically at himself.

Barry Lamar Bonds was born on July 24, 1964 in Riverside, California to Bobby and Pat Bonds. In the hospital that day to hold him, among others, was longtime family friend Dusty Baker and his father.

Baker's father was the Little League coach of Bobby. Bobby's mother used to baby-sit a young Dusty Baker. When Dusty got older, he followed around his dad and Bobby to Pony League games, high school football games and track meets.

"Bobby was four years older than me and he was my childhood hero," Baker told me. "I played four sports because Bobby did. I did the long jump because Bobby did. I played football because Bobby did. I wanted to be just like Bobby."

The day of Bobby Bonds' tryout (and subsequent signing) with the San Francisco Giants in 1964, Baker was in the outfield shagging baseballs. His hero was Tommy Davis of the Los Angeles Dodgers, but that was the first day Dusty started to like the Giants.

A job transfer moved the Baker family to Sacramento before Dusty's junior year in high school. He was drafted in the 26th round of the 1967 draft by the Atlanta Braves and reached the majors very briefly in 1968, the same year as Bobby Bonds made his debut.

Baker had cameo appearances with the Braves the next two seasons and came up to the majors to stay in the 1971 season. His mentor on the team was

Hank Aaron. The day Aaron broke the all-time homer record in 1974, Baker was in the on-deck circle. Baker was traded to the Dodgers before the 1976 season and spent eight seasons with the team, earned two all-star game appearances, played in four playoff series and was a member of the 1981 world-championship team.

His divorce from the Dodgers was bitter and Baker still has hard feelings to this day. Baker played the 1984 season with the Giants and the final two years of his career with the Oakland Athletics, plagued by knee problems, but still convinced he had productive years left in his body. He finished his career with quite respectable numbers: .280 average, 242 homers and 1,013 RBIs.

Baker took one year off from baseball and returned as the Giants first-base coach in 1988, then batting coach the next five seasons under manager Roger Craig. Despite no previous managing experience — other than one brief season in the Arizona Fall League — Baker became the 34th manager in Giants franchise history on Dec.16, 1992, eight days after Barry Bonds signed the contract that returned him home.

Baker is one of just two managers Barry Bonds has ever had in the majors. They aren't as close as you might assume. Their relationship is complex. They respect each other, but they have much different personalities. Any clashes are never public, except for the time Bonds told Baker he could, "kiss my ass." Some believe Baker has never forgiven him for that statement.

Bonds never said so publicly, but those close to him disclosed he was disappointed that Baker publicly endorsed Jeff Kent as the league Most Valuable Player in 2000 — instead of endorsing Bonds or instead of simply saying you could vote for either and not go wrong.

The statistics broke down this way:

Player	AVG	R	H	2B	HR	RBI	BB	OB	SLG
Bonds	.306	129	147	28	49	106	117	.440	.688
Kent	.334	114	196	41	33	125	90	.424	.596

"Barry was our homer man," Baker said. "But Jeff was our RBI man."

All six of the Giants traveling beat writers, including myself, thought Kent was the MVP. Any of the Giants who were asked, including black players (Ellis Burks) and white players (J.T. Snow), thought Kent was the MVP.

Still, Bonds felt slighted.

He had support from Total Baseball, the final word on statistical data and analysis. Total Baseball determined that Bonds was the best player in the National League an amazing eighth time in 2000. The other years were 1990, 1991, 1992, 1993, 1995, 1996 and 1998. Bonds won three MVPs in those years and finished second in the voting by baseball writers in 1991 to Terry Pendleton, whose numbers weren't close to Bonds'.

For perspective, Ted Williams was the American League's best player six times. Stan Musial was the NL's best player four years. Total Baseball calculated that Bonds has given his teams more career wins (89.4) than any player in history except Babe Ruth, Willie Mays, Nap Lojoie and Ty Cobb. With two more productive seasons, Bonds could vault into second, trailing only the Bambino.

Baker is a three-time Manager of the Year and considered by many the best in the business. He is the ultimate players' manager. He's faithful to a fault. He's a tremendous communicator. If a player is slumping, Baker will bring him food and have it waiting in his locker. The message is clear: *"I'm thinking of you. Eat your food. Get strong. The hits will start coming."*

Every year, at least one player signs with the Giants simply because of their desire to play for Baker. Giants broadcaster Mike Krukow calls Baker, "a bilingual black man who the white guys can relate to."

Baseball writers also love interviewing Baker. There is no better storyteller. He broke into the league with the Atlanta Braves. Aaron was his role model and mentor. There are few men as deep and spiritual and positive than the man born Johnnie B. Baker, Jr.

It was during a typical 8 a.m. interview session with reporters one morning when Baker was asked if a player — pardon the cliche — can "step it up" in the final year of a contract. Only Baker can start talking and end up using the space program as an analogy for a player stepping it up in the final year of his contract — and make it work. His entire lengthy response was Baker at his best, making him a beat writer's dream:

"You prepare more in the offseason, physically and mentally," Baker said. "It's almost to the point where, if you are not signed, it's all encompassing and it's your total focus. Hell yeah, you can step it up. I stepped it up. Anybody I know who is any good and can handle pressure stepped it up. You step it up by, say . . . Luke Appling used to tell me, 'don't give away at-bats.' Well, in your option year, you aren't going to give away at-bats as often. The good hitters probably give away 25-50 at-bats (a season), maybe. The bad hitters give away 100. When I say give them away, say you are 3-for-3. Instead of going for 4-for-4, you're going for the home run, figuring you already have three hits, and you pop it up. Or you swing at bad pitches because the score is lopsided, one way or the other. And those add up. One here. One there. In your option year, runner at third, less than two outs, you're going for RBIs, you really concentrate on getting that run home. Instead of taking that close pitch, you foul it off, then bam, get another and you have a sac fly. There's a number of ways to step it up. Per at-bat. Per inning.

"Nobody can do it every single at-bat," Baker continued. "I don't care who you are. You can't tell me you work as hard if you're a lot more secure than if you don't have a job and then you'll work your ass off to keep that job. A hungry man works harder. You know how hard it is to concentrate on every at-bat, every day, in the field, every pitch? Some days, you don't feel like playing. Some days, you don't feel like going to work. Some days, it's easier than other days. You're right on top of it, bam. Other days, you can't do (squat). That's how it is.

"I've only seen a couple players who can turn it on and get ready. Oh yeah, Barry is one. Rickey (Henderson) is another one."

Baker was asked if it's a scary thought, Bonds in a contract-drive season.

"I'd like to see it," Baker said. "It's not scary. No matter what, the whole thing is Barry's health. If Barry's healthy, he's going to get it. You can count on it. That's fact."

The year before, Baker was in the final year of his contract. It was Baker's decision not to negotiate with the Giants until after the season. Baker led the Giants to a division title and won a manager of the year award. That's a pretty good example of a manager "stepping it up" in the final year of his contract.

"It seems like it always works out for me that year," Baker said. "I have faith. As long as you are not afraid of the unknown. And I'm not afraid of the unknown. Like those dudes who go into space. Either you handle it, or die. If they handle it, they come home. If they don't, they die. Barry's a grown man. Barry's been through this before. If he doesn't want to talk about it, you leave him alone."

———•◦•◦•———

Even if they won't admit it, surely the Bonds contract was a topic on the minds of other players. In fact, during one workout at nearby Indian School Park, a Giants player brought up the topic in an informal conversation with a beat writer.

The players take: "I think Barry is going to whine about his contract all season and have a terrible year."

In the days that followed, Barry Bonds wasn't talking about anything. At least, not with the media. Word, as it always does, spread fast among reporters to not even bother trying. Bonds had denied a couple of reporters' interview requests. He would give you that look that said, "don't bother. I'm not talking to you." If the reporter persisted, Bonds would shake his head, tell him "no" or barely even acknowledge the reporter's existence.

Bonds wasn't happy with the media. So he wasn't talking.

It was actually good news to us beat reporters. One less person to worry about interviewing. Bonds wasn't in a good mood anyway. If Bonds wasn't talking, we didn't have to keep asking stupid questions about stupid contracts — since it was clear nothing was going to be done.

The problem with Bonds not talking is the national media wasn't reporting the story very accurately. Either they weren't reading the Bay Area media's stories very closely, or they were letting Bonds' reputation get in the way of their thinking.

Whether it was ESPN, *USA Today* or the *Associated Press* — whose stories then go to hundreds of newspapers around the country — Bonds was being lumped together with the malcontents of spring training: Gary Sheffield and Frank Thomas.

This was not only wrong.

This was incredibly unfair to Bonds.

Here's a quick review:

* Bonds showed up to camp on time. He told reporters he wanted to know whether he would return to the Giants next season or not. He wanted to see his agent and the Giants talk about a contract. He wanted to stay with the Giants. He didn't demand a trade. He didn't walk out of camp and demand more money. He didn't ask for Alex Rodriguez money. He didn't make it an issue every day.

* Thomas boycotted the Chicago White Sox camp for six days at the start of spring. He considered himself grossly underpaid (at $9 million annually) compared to Rodriguez and wanted a new contact — despite having six years left on his contract. He finally returned to camp and said it wasn't about the money.

* Sheffield arrived to the Los Angeles Dodgers camp late. He ripped management. He ripped his teammates. He demanded a trade. He wanted a new contract. Before long, Sheffield fired his agent and hired Scott Boras.

Is it any wonder Bonds was pissed at the media?

On February 23, Scott Boras arrived in Scottsdale. His arrival was based, in part, on the numerous calls Boras he was getting from journalists in other markets about Bonds. There was a feeling that Bonds might become available in a trade.

Enough words had been spoken through newspapers. Boras wanted to talk with the Giants executives himself.

Boras met Sabean and assistant general manager Ned Colletti at Indian School Park, site of the Giants minor league complex. It was supposed to rain that day. Instead, the sun came out for a meeting that could best be described as peace talks. The three men went to a picnic table, away from reporters and fans, and talked for about 45 minutes.

In late September, nearly six months later, what was discussed at this meeting would become a source of great disagreement among the people involved.

But, at the time, this is what Boras told reporters:

"We had a very amicable and mutual discussion," Boras said. "We expressed our interest to stay in San Francisco. And Brian and Ned expressed their interest in Barry remaining. We talked about a lot of foundational things. The player's interest and the team's interest in the player. The question, in the end, do you have to go to the next step? Our goal is to play baseball. We have a contract for another year — and we're going to certainly fulfill that. From that stand-point, it's something where we wanted to communicate our willingness to try and work through this."

Boras was asked if contracts were discussed.

"No contract form," he answered. "We just talked about some of the important things from our side about the relationship Barry's had with the city and franchise. Making sure the club knows those elements are important. Sometimes, I don't know where that perception comes from, when I'm involved in negotiations, the orientation is always to the optimum . . . We know we have a contract. We just expressed that Barry would like to continue and further his relationship. We're prepared to do it. But the decision is solely up to the club."

About 30 minutes later, it was Sabean's turn.

"The tone of the meeting was exactly what Boras just stated," Sabean said. "We went to great lengths to explain to him, first hand, what we've said publicly and further reiterated: how much we value the player and his contributions past and present. That was, by and large, the tone. More than that, it was him taking the liberty, first hand, why he thought we might want to enter some type of train of thought now, rather than later. We took a lot of time explaining what our fears were in doing that.

"At the end of the day, I appreciate that they were that open," Sabean continued. "Scott is a smart guy. He's been doing this a long time. It was almost, it had an air of diplomacy to it. In my mind, it was a clear-the-air type of issue. The player has made comments. We've made comments. Now it's all laid out. There's not anything left to chance in terms of reading something or interpreting something or not understanding the tone of what our thoughts are."

Peter Magowan is credited with saving baseball in San Francisco.

In December 1992, the Giants were on the verge of moving to Tampa Bay. Magowan grew up in New York as a diehard Giants fan. His family moved to San Francisco about the same time the Giants moved west in 1958. He is a 1964 graduate of Stanford with a degree in American literature. He received his master's degree in politics, philosophy and economics from Oxford University.

He also completed two years of additional postgraduate work at the Johns Hopkins School of Advanced International Studies.

And he's always been a baseball fan.

Magowan was the chairman and CEO of Safeway, Inc., a grocery store chain, and decided to get involved when the Giants were nearing a move to Tampa Bay. In an 11th-hour effort, Magowan organized a group of local investors who purchased the Giants for substantially less money than the group in Florida was going to spend.

Before the sale was even finalized, Magowan shocked the baseball community by signing Barry Bonds to a six-year, $43.75 million contract that made him the highest paid baseball player at the time — even though Magowan's group hadn't been officially approved as the team's new owners.

"We went through a lot of hassles to get him here," Magowan told me in a lengthy interview near the end of spring training. "(Former owner) Bob Lurie didn't want us to sign him. The commissioner, president of the National League, lawyers for the National League, a lot of people tried to undo the contract that we signed. They were all concerned that if the Giants' (new) ownership group was not approved as owners, Bob Lurie didn't want to be stuck with this $43 million obligation to Barry. Whereas, I would think anybody would want to be stuck with a contract that obligates the best player in the game to being a Giant for at least six years. But that wasn't the way other people looked at it.

"What I think they expected us to do as new owners was watch other people sign other players," Magowan continued. "We were supposed to learn how to do it. And maybe 4-5 years later, they would let us sign a regular player. But nobody wanted us to sign the best player in the game, when we were just coming into the game. But we needed to do something to get interest to revitalize the Giants. And that first year, we drew 2.6 million. That was the best year of attendance the Giants ever had (at Candlestick Park). I think Barry had a lot to do with it. So did winning 103 games. I'm not saying it's the only thing. We had a lot of other players on that team the fans liked, such as Matt Williams and Will Clark and Robby Thompson. But those same guys were on the team the previous years, too. Barry made quite a change."

To this day, it's the only contract Magowan has ever negotiated.

"I think it's one of the best things we've ever done as owners of the Giants, to get him on the team," Magowan said. "I said, at the time, to his agent (Dennis

Gilbert), I felt Barry was the best player in the game, and the best player should be the best paid. And I think what happened in the last eight years proves that prediction was correct. He has been, in the '90s, the best player in the game.

"I think Barry did a lot to revitalize our fortunes when we took over," Magowan continued. "The team was headed for Tampa, only drew a million-five the year before, there wasn't much interest in the Giants. We needed something to get ourselves jump-started and when he came over, we won 103 games and we didn't make many other changes in the team that year. We've never won 103 before. And never since. And he was the MVP that year. And last year, eight years later, he's the runner-up MVP. He's been a great player, he's played every day, he's played hurt. He's contributed mightily to the Giants won-loss record over these eight years, which is the third best in the National League."

Magowan wasn't just interested in Bonds because he was the best player in the game.

"When we first starting talking to his agent, Dennis Gilbert, we thought this guy would really be a great fit with us," Magowan said. "His godfather is Willie Mays. His father was a great star for the Giants. He grew up at Candlestick. We would be bringing him home. This would be a huge shock to the baseball world, if we landed him. And we just wanted (Gilbert) to know, we have very sincere interest in doing this and we can be very competitive in our offer. I think the Giants had something like four people playing left field in 1992: Cory Snyder, Tiny Felder, Chris James and somebody else I can't remember. Then (shortstop Jose) Uribe was at the end of his contract. (Pitcher) Scott Garrelts was through. So we could get Barry Bonds basically onto the team without spending any more money — by saying goodbye to all these other guys. That was the other thing. We fit him onto our payroll."

The Giants won 103 games in Bonds' first season, but they didn't make the playoffs. The Atlanta Braves won 104 games and the Giants were eliminated on the final day of the season. Bonds won the Most Valuable Player, a third in four years, to join seven other Hall of Famers with three MVP awards. He batted .336 with 46 homers, 123 RBIs, led the league in slugging and on-base percentage, won his fourth straight Gold Glove and was the leading vote-getter at the all-star game. In the final 16 games of the season, when the Giants had no margin for error in chasing the Braves, Bonds hit .333, slugged .860, hit six homers, seven doubles and had 21 RBIs.

The following season, Bonds suffered bone spurs in his right elbow, but kept playing. When the strike wiped out the final seven weeks of the year, Bonds was on pace for even greater power numbers: a pace of 52 homers and 114 RBIs. The Giants were 3.5 games out of first when the strike hit.

The next two seasons, the team was besieged with injuries and finished 11 games out of first in 1995 and 23 out in 1996. Bonds still produced at the same level. He hit 33 home runs and stole 31 bases in 1995, his third 30-30 season. Then in 1996, he hit 42 home runs and stole 40 bases, joining Jose Canseco as the only men in baseball history to accomplish the 40-40 feat (Alex Rodriguez has since become the third).

"(Financially) we were fine until we got into trouble in '95 and '96, in the aftermath of the strike," said Magowan, who was busy working on a new downtown ballpark that seemed an impossible dream in those lean years. "The attendance had sunk way back down again and too much of our payroll was going to two players."

Bonds and Matt Williams were making up 40 percent of the payroll. It was on the final day of the 1996 season that general manager Bob Quinn retired and his assistant Brian Sabean was elevated to the top position.

Sabean was a rising star in the front office ranks. He spent eight years with the New York Yankees, holding increasing positions of responsibility, including scouting director and vice president of player development/scouting.

Sabean never gets any credit for it, but it was his drafting and signing of players — such as shortstop Derek Jeter, catcher Jorge Posada, closer Mariano Rivera, reliever Ramiro Mendoza and starter Andy Pettitte — that laid the foundation for the start of the Yankees dynasty in 1996.

Or it was his drafted and developed players — such as Russ Davis, Sterling Hitchcock, Carl Everett, Hal Morris, Brad Ausmus, Roberto Kelly and Bob Wickman — who were used as trade bait to land key veteran players such as first baseman Tino Martinez, outfielder Paul O'Neill, starter David Cone and second baseman Mariano Duncan.

The previous four years, Sabean was the Giants' senior vice president of player personnel and assistant general manager. He was raised in the win-now Yankees' culture and his fearless instincts would be put to the test immediately. Sabean quickly identified that either Bonds or Williams must go. They were simply making too much money and not enough was available to improve the rest of the team.

Sabean chose the highly popular Williams.

Even Baker wondered what Sabean was thinking. Baker and Williams had become extremely close friends, starting when Baker was the Giants batting coach and mentored the young Williams. They fished together. They talked about life. They were the closest of friends. And now Williams was traded.

The fans were livid. Sabean sent Williams to the Cleveland Indians for a package of second baseman Jeff Kent, shortstop Jose Vizcaino and rubber-armed reliever Julian Tavarez. The talk-show circuits lit up in furious outrage that Williams was traded. The columnists weren't much kinder to Sabean.

In a memorable moment, a fed-up Sabean said on KNBR, "I'm not an idiot. I know what I'm doing."

Sabean, indeed, knew what he was doing. Kent hit 29 homers and drove in 121 runs. Tavarez provided a crucial arm out of the bullpen. Vizcaino solidified the infield. More importantly, there was flexibility in the payroll and Sabean added first baseman J.T. Snow (who he originally drafted with the Yankees) and outfielder Darryl Hamilton.

When the Giants hit a lull in late July, Sabean pulled off another block-buster — because there was room in the budget — by acquiring starting pitchers Wilson Alvarez and Danny Darwin, plus much-needed closer Roberto Hernandez for six minor league prospects.

Bonds was his usual self, hitting 40 homers, driving in 101 runs, stealing 37 bases, scoring 123 runs — despite being walked 145 times (34 intentional). The Giants outlasted their hated rivals, the Dodgers, and clinched the National West division on the second-to-last day of the season. Bonds climbed on top of the dugout and hugged fans in celebration.

Now, in 2001, the Giants were starting to get close to a similar predicament as after the 1996 season. Between Bonds' $10.3 million and Robb Nen's $6.6 million, 26 percent of the team's $66 million payroll in 2001 was going to two players. Factor in Kent's $6.0 million and Snow's $5.75 million and 43 percent of the payroll was going to four players.

Meanwhile, player salaries — led by Alex Rodriguez's $25 million and Manny Ramirez's $20 million — were continuing to explode. If Bonds was signed for even a bargain-like $16 million a season for 2002, then he and Nen (who was due a raise to $8 million) would make up 36 percent of the payroll. Add in Kent's $6 million, and three players would be earning 45 percent of the payroll.

"And that's the concern now," Magowan said. "We don't want to get back into that situation again. Because it's pretty hard to field a good team, when you have two great players, but who are you going to play them with?"

Magowan reiterated to me there wasn't anything new about Bonds' contract. Then he launched into a lengthy explanation anyway and used the Florida Marlins as a primary example of what not to do.

"We'd like to have Barry back," Magowan said. "But there's so many things we have to have answers to. Other players that are expensive and important to the Giants and how it all fits into the budget number we have to live with. We're going to be disciplined enough to have a budget. Some teams don't have one. I don't want to see happen to the Giants what happened to Florida. Yeah, you want a World Series and I'd love to win a World Series. I had 10 goals when we bought the Giants. We've fulfilled nine of them and the 10th one we have not fulfilled is a World Series. I'd love to win a World Series. Anybody who knows me knows how competitive I am.

"But I don't want to do it the way it was done in Florida (in 1997)," Magowan continued. "They lost $37 million. And then what happened? The owner put the team up for sale. The team was completely split up. And now, nobody goes to their games. Their future is in question. Maybe they will get their stadium. Maybe they won't. All of that is a direct result of losing too much money. We've done our share of losing. We lost $100 million to get in a position to build this ballpark. We're on the hook for $170 million in mortgage. I don't think it's unreasonable for the partners who ask me to manage this franchise so that it does not lose money. We're not trying to make money. But we don't have to lose money. We have to fit in what Barry's needs might be, what Kent's needs are going to be, what (Shawn) Estes' and other players who are getting better and better and will need more money. How it all fits in to put the best team on the field."

Barry Bonds didn't conduct another interview the rest of spring training. The Giants and Boras never talked again.

As the Giants broke training camp in beautiful Scottsdale, Arizona, Bonds was six homers away from the 500-homer club and reporters couldn't even ask him about that upcoming historic milestone.

Whatever Bonds was feeling, he kept inside.

His motivations seemed pretty clear though.

He was in the final year of a contract.

People thought he was getting old.

He was disappointed his manager and teammates endorsed Kent for MVP the previous year.

And he was feeling underappreciated.

CHAPTER THREE

The House Built for Bonds

April 2-15, Home Runs 1-5

"You get a little bit nervous. It seems like you're always out there on center stage. You're out there all by yourself, alone. Now I've probably figured out why I don't hit in the playoffs."

Barry Bonds

PACIFIC BELL PARK celebrated its first birthday on Monday, April 2, 2001. The $357 million ballpark by the bay was hailed a miracle by some people, most notably the people who made it possible. Politics in San Francisco are unconventional by nature and there was no way this liberal city would ever use taxpayer money to build a new ballpark to be used by million-dollar players.

When the Giants moved west from New York in 1958, they played two seasons at Seals Stadium on 15th and Bryant, a ballpark previously used by the San Francisco Seals of the old Pacific Coast League. The Giants moved into Candlestick Park for the 1960 season — total cost, just under $15 million — and then-California governor Richard Nixon called it, "the finest ballpark in America."

From day one, however, Candlestick Park and its legendary wind and fog was a nightmare. One game against the Dodgers was delayed 24 minutes by a thick fog. Legends of the wind's power have been exaggerated over the years, too. The most notable is the story of pitcher Stu Miller getting "blown off" the mound by wind during his windup at the 1961 all-star game that resulted in a balk that gave the American League the go-ahead run in the top of the ninth inning. In reality, the wind pushed him and that made him stop his delivery for the balk. He then walked off the mound.

Nonetheless, anybody who spent a night under two blankets sipping hot chocolate and absolutely freezing in the middle of summer can testify to how miserable a place it was to watch a baseball game. A typical July night at Candlestick would remind people why Mark Twain once (allegedly) uttered the famous line, "the coldest winter I ever spent was the summer I spent in San Francisco."

Candlestick Park was enclosed in 1972 and the hope was it would cut down on the wind. It did. But only a little. It remained bitterly cold and unpleasant for everybody involved. Opposing teams dreaded coming to Candlestick. It wasn't uncommon for a player to conveniently get ejected in the first inning of a night game when the fog was thick and the wind whipping uncontrollably. The better Giants teams were wise to utilize this home-field advantage. However, it was a nightmare for fans and a major deterrent in convincing paying customers to spend an afternoon, let alone an evening, watching a ballgame.

The Giants tried numerous different ideas over the years to make a difference. Artificial turf was installed in 1971 (so the wind wouldn't blow as much dirt) and later removed after 1978. The team shifted most of its games to afternoon starts for a couple of years in the mid-'80s, figuring enough people would play hooky from work or school to catch a game in a better climate. When she was mayor of San Francisco, now-senator Diane Feinstein proposed putting a dome on Candlestick — an idea that quickly fizzled.

None of these ideas worked very well. The Giants drew 1,795,356 fans their opening season in 1960, but would never reach that level again until their 1987 division-championship season. Attendance hit a low of 818,697 in the 100-loss season of 1985 (an average of 10,363) and what had always been obvious — the Giants needed a new ballpark — was now undeniable.

On four separate occasions, the Giants put a measure on the ballot for a new ballpark. In 1987 and 1989, it was in San Francisco. A third try was south in the growing city of San Jose. A fourth and final was in 1992 in Santa Clara County. On all four, the citizens voted it down.

Giants fans might have wanted a ballpark. But they weren't going to pay for it with taxpayer dollars.

The inability to secure funding for a new ballpark was the primary reason a frustrated Bob Lurie put the team up for sale. When Peter Magowan and his group of partners purchased the Giants in December 1992, he invested money into Candlestick, adding left-field bleachers that were closer to the playing field, improving the food with the popular garlic fries and burritos, wearing buttons that proclaimed "we're listening" and adding some features like a fog horn to blow after Giants home runs to give a more San Francisco feel.

The new owners broke even during the 103-win season of 1993 — aided by the arrival of superstar free agent Barry Bonds — and drew a record 2,606,354 fans. However, the owners claimed a $5 million operating loss in the strike-marred 1994 year and more than $45 million in losses over the next four years. Magowan and his trusty right-hand man Larry Baer, the chief executive officer, were working feverishly behind the scenes to organize plans for a downtown ballpark that wouldn't become the fifth victim at the voting polls — and would double their revenue streams.

In December, 1995, the Giants announced plans for the first privately financed major league ballpark since Dodger Stadium in 1962. It would be built in the neglected China Basin area, south of Market Street and along the waterfront in downtown San Francisco. It still needed voter approval because it still involved some taxpayer money. Four months later, after a major grass-roots campaign aimed at educating voters, the measure was approved by 67 percent — a landslide by any city's measures.

Pacific Bell, the local telephone company, paid $50 million for the naming rights for 24 years. Another $122 million came from other sponsorships, pouring rights, concession rights and the selling of controversial charter seat licenses — a fee customers had to pay for the ability to have lifetime rights to the best 15,000 seats. The Giants were also on the hook for $170 million from a bank loan, on which they would have to make $20 million payments annually for 20 years. San Francisco mayor Willie Brown leased 13 acres of waterfront property, located at Third and King Streets, to the Giants for the site of the new ballpark.

The groundbreaking was December 11, 1997, four months after the Giants completed the improbable worst-to-first turnaround season — engineered by Brian "I'm not an idiot" Sabean, managed by Dusty Baker (who won his second Manager of the Year award) and starring Barry Bonds.

To celebrate the groundbreaking, Bonds took batting practice from pitcher Shawn Estes to show off the defining image of the ballpark — home runs that land in the San Francisco bay. The ballpark was designed by HOK Sports, who revolutionized ballparks with its design of Camden Yards in Baltimore. The dimensions called for a cozy 307 feet down the right-field line — the shortest porch in the National League — and perfect for power-hitting lefties like Bonds. It took a few swings, but it wasn't long before Bonds, after taking off the jacket from his sharp beige suit and tie, started launching a half-dozen baseballs from the approximate place where home plate would be, into the water.

Many immediately started calling it "The House Built for Barry Bonds."

However, the address unveiled that day by Magowan made it clear the new ballpark would always belong to Willie Mays, the greatest Giant of them all and the godfather of Barry Bonds. Magowan told a crowd estimated at 7,000 the ballpark's address would be "1 Willie Mays Plaza" — it was later changed to "24 Willie Mays Plaza" — and a statute of Mays would greet visitors. A choked up Mays couldn't hold back the tears.

One more significant item from groundbreaking day: It was just past noon, in the middle of December, it was so warm that people were sweating and there was no wind. Clearly, this would be different than Candlestick.

Pacific Bell Park hosted its first real game on April 11, 2000 against — who else? — the archrival Los Angeles Dodgers.

Barry Bonds had the first RBI, a double in the first inning that scored Bill Mueller. Bonds also hit the first Giants home run in the third inning. Kevin Elster, a journeyman shortstop, hit the first home run and added two more homers as the Dodgers won, 6-5, before a sellout crowd of 40,930. The weather was a balmy 65 degrees at first pitch and increased throughout the game.

The next 80 regular-season games, and two postseason games, would have the exact same attendance of 40,930. Every game was sold out. The Giants had only drawn over 2 million fans on two prior seasons and they drew 3,315,330 fans in their new ballpark.

On May 1, Bonds hit the first homer into the bay that was named "McCovey Cove" after the beloved former Giants first baseman Willie McCovey. Joseph Figone, a former Giants groundskeeper, snatched the ball out of the water with a fisherman's net while driving his boat, nearly ramming into another boat in the scramble.

"Yeah, man, that wasn't cool, that was dangerous," Bonds said. "What if he rammed into his engine and it blew up or something?"

Pitchers feared and critics scoffed the ballpark would become a launching pad because of the dimensions. However, the ballpark proved fair for hitters and pitchers. Crosswinds off the arcade and nearby Lefty O'Doule Bridge knocked down many flyballs — especially those hit by right-handed batters. Only three righties, Chicago's Sammy Sosa, Oakland's Miguel Tejada and the Giants' Ellis Burks, hit opposite-field homers the entire first season.

Bonds had six "Splash Hits" into McCovey Cove during the season, the only Giants player to do it. Los Angeles' Todd Hundley and Arizona's Luis

Gonzalez were the only visiting players to hit water on the fly. Bonds smashed a career-high 49 homers for the season, 25 at home and 24 on the road.

So much for those theories about the new ballpark helping Bonds hit more home runs.

Pacific Bell Park was a smashing success. Going to a game became "an event," the city of San Francisco rediscovered its love for baseball, and it certainly didn't hurt that the Giants — after losing six straight at home to begin the season — compiled a 55-26 record in home games (tied for best in baseball) and won the National League West division.

———————

On opening day of the 2001 season, Barry Bonds had 494 career home runs. Fifty-two of those had come at the expense of the San Diego Padres. The only teams Bonds had hit more against were the Philadelphia Phillies (56) and Montreal Expos (55). It was enough to make Tony Gwynn, the Padres future Hall of Famer, say a few hours before opening day, "he only needs six and he's playing us, so that might happen in three days. He kills us."

In the fifth inning, Bonds turned around a Woody Williams pitch and sent it an estimated 423 feet into the centerfield bleachers: number 495. Bonds also threw out Gwynn at the plate, after catcher Bobby Estalella leaped high into the air to save a high throw and apply the tag and the Giants won, 4-3, opening the season on a bright note.

"I jammed two fingers, that's why they're bleeding," Bonds said. "The ball smacked me straight on my two fingers and I thought it broke the top of my finger. I was just lucky the throw didn't go in the stands because I couldn't feel my fingers. Bobby's the one who made that play. You have to give credit to the catcher because he stayed in there."

Yes, the Bonds media silence was broken after the game. After some prodding with agent Scott Boras a few days before, Bonds was going to do interviews. He laid out the ground rules though: he'll talk after games, not before games; he'll talk about baseball, not contracts.

"I've had a good spring," Bonds said. "I've felt comfortable. Dusty managed me very well in spring training. He didn't overwork me. He allowed me to have a lot of time off and get the work in I needed to get in and conserve my body a little. That's paid off because I feel really strong. I feel flexible and I'm happy right now."

Bonds didn't talk for long. His son Nikolai had a game at 5:30 p.m. and traffic is always a nightmare in San Francisco. Barry grabbed his motorcycle helmet and left.

———

Seven games later, Bonds was still at 495 homers and mired in an 0-for-20 hitless slump that dropped his batting average to .103. He was given a "mental day off" by manager Dusty Baker who said, "you hate to see him struggling like this."

During that week, Bonds went 0-for-13 in three games against the Dodgers in Los Angeles. He also had batteries and other objects thrown at him from the fans in the bleachers, who relentlessly chanted, "Barry sucks." He went 0-for-5 against the Padres on April 10, a night the rest of the Giants had 11 hits in an 11-6 win, and looked lost at the plate.

Baker's advice for the mental day off: "Just hit, hit, hit and not exert too much energy for the game. Then just sit and look at who's hot and who's not. Sometimes you can figure out that way why you're not."

In the Padres clubhouse, Gwynn had an idea of what Bonds was going through. Gwynn reached the historic 3,000-hit club two years earlier, but along the way was made fully aware of the increased attention from the media and fans as he approached the milestone.

"You do get tired of it," Gwynn said. "Everybody wants to know things. How do you hit this guy? I don't think you can honestly go out there and try to hit a home run. But I wouldn't know. That's part of it. That's part of this job. You have to talk about it too. Everybody told me the last 10 (hits) would be the hardest and they were. I think it's because as you get closer, it can happen that day. So people want to be prepared . . . People want to know. They're going to ask you about it, what's it going to mean? How are you going to react. With him, he'll probably give the same answer I gave: 'I don't know.'"

Just looking at Barry Bonds, from his body language, you could sense he was distracted. And he was.

On April 12th, after his "mental day off," Bonds broke out of a slump that had reached 0-for-21 with a fifth-inning, opposite-field homer off Adam Eaton: number 496. Afterward, he unburdened himself to us beat writers.

"I just felt like, you know, you just start thinking about things," Bonds said. "Thinking about how lucky I am to even be in this position in my life." Bonds used the words "star-struck" and "kinda nervous" as he thought about the 500-homer milestone he was approaching.

"I'm trying to block a lot of things out of my mind," Bonds said. "Just get back to basics and just play the game. It's hard to explain the feelings you go through, it's very, very hard to explain. I never dreamt of being in this position to do certain things in your life. You never thought it was possible. Next thing you know, you're knocking on the door.

"You get a little bit nervous. It seems like you're always out there on center stage. You're out there all by yourself, alone. Now I've probably figured out why I don't hit in the playoffs."

Bonds laughed at himself.

"That spotlight," he said, pausing a few moments, "is tough."

The playoffs had always been a sore subject with Bonds. Now he was bringing up the playoffs himself and joking about the slump he broke, which was one away from tying his worst personal streak, in 1991, with the Pirates.

"I was just trying to beat my one in 1991," Bonds joked. "I don't need reminding. They had it posted out there (on the scoreboard). I'm like, 'come on, man, you have to get one hit today. You can't get to 22 and tie the record.'"

Bonds was only 1-for-3 on the day, but looked like his usual self again. He flew to right his first at-bat, homered in the fourth, flew out to deep center in the sixth and walked on five pitches in the eighth inning.

"Much better ABs today," Giants manager Dusty Baker said. "Hopefully, he'll be even better in the series against Milwaukee . . . The thing about the home run was he hit it to left field. That's a great sign that he's staying on the ball."

Added first baseman J.T. Snow: "We know it's just a matter of time. You're not going to keep Barry down very long."

Bonds wasn't about to proclaim himself out of his slump.

"I'm just glad I got a little bit of exercise, dude," Bonds said. "It's just one day. It's early. It's a long distance run. It isn't a sprint."

No, it's not a sprint. But all of a sudden, after breaking his 0-for-20 slump and publicly admitting his emotions, Bonds started sprinting toward the 500-homer club.

The Giants moved onto Milwaukee. Before the sprint, Bonds was in a batting cage at the brand-new Miller Park. He hit and hit. He stopped. He cursed at himself. He hit again. He cursed himself. What the hell was wrong, he wondered? He kept hitting. And hitting. And hitting.

In the first inning that night, Bonds blasted an 0-1 pitch from Brewers starter Jamey Wright 441 feet for a two-run homer: number 497. It was a low-line drive that just kept going and going and going and going.

"That," Baker said, "was a missile."

In the third inning, he flied to left field. Upset at himself for missing a hittable pitch, Bonds raced into the clubhouse, called his dad Bobby on his cell phone and asked him, "What do you see that I'm doing?"

Bobby Bonds was watching the game on satellite at home and offered his son a few pointers. Barry hit a sacrifice fly his next at-bat, doubled in the sixth and drove in more runs (three) than he had coming into the game (two), but didn't call himself out of his slump.

"I have to get over .200 first, then I'll tell you," Bonds said, laughing at his .171 average. "It's not too bad because it's early. If it was July? That would be different. Since it's April, it's OK."

Bonds is historically a little bit of a slow starter. He's hit the fewest homers in April of any month. But that was about to change.

The next day, April 14, produced another homer by Bonds: number 498. It was a three-run shot in the fifth-inning off Jimmy Haynes that traveled an estimated 421 feet. Bonds also doubled and his average climbed to .205 for the season. After looking so hopelessly lost at the plate for six games, Bonds suddenly had three homers and seven RBIs in his last three games — and credited the more consistent at-bats to his conversation with his dad.

"Maybe that's called greatness," Baker said.

April 15 was the finale of a nine-game, three-city road trip for the Giants that started in Southern California and was ending in Milwaukee. Trailing 4-2 in the eighth, Bonds continued what was quickly becoming a pattern: a low-line drive missile over the left-centerfield wall on a 1-1 pitch from David Weathers. The solo homer trimmed the lead to 4-3. It was his fourth consecutive game with a homer. It was number 499.

However, in the bottom of the eighth inning, Bonds dropped a fly ball that allowed three runs to score and proved the difference in the Brewers 7-4 victory. The Giants were off to a 7-5 start, yet maintained a half-game lead in the National League West.

It was safe to say that no player on the verge of 500 home runs ever felt worse than Barry Bonds.

"I straight (messed) it up," Bonds said. "That's the best word I can give . . . I just, wow. That's all I can say. I saw it. I just took my eye off it at the last minute. I took it for granted that I had it and made a beeline to the dugout. That should not have happened."

A reporter from ESPN asked Bonds about reaching 500 homers.

"I don't care about that right now," Bonds said. "If you want to ask me that question, come tomorrow. This ain't a good day to talk about that. I lost a game for my team. I play for this team. I don't care what else happens. My godfather told me if you play this game long enough, strange things will happen. I guess this is one of them."

Brewers manager Davey Lopes, himself a former Dodger, had the best perspective.

"Now he'll get to do it at home," Lopes said. "That's the way it should be. Better yet, they're playing the Dodgers. The stage is set."

CHAPTER FOUR

Welcome to the Club

April 17-18, Home Runs 6 & 7, 500th for career

"Baseball, to me, is history. It's like a classroom. You study each individual, learn something from each one. Babe Ruth. Hank Aaron. Willie Mays. Mickey Mantle. They're the beginning of our history books."

Barry Bonds

NO CLUB IS more exclusive in baseball than the 500-homer club. Not the 300-win club. Not the 3,000-hit club. Every player who has hit 500 homers in his career, and is eligible, is in the Hall of Fame. The only two who aren't, Mark McGwire and Eddie Murray, are considered locks.

When Willie Mays joined the club on September 13, 1965 with a solo homer off Don Nottebart in Houston, he became the fifth member of the club. Membership exploded the next six years, as, in order, Mickey Mantle (May 14, 1967), Eddie Mathews (July 14, 1967), Hank Aaron (July 14, 1968), Ernie Banks (May 12, 1970), Harmon Killebrew (August 10, 1971) and Frank Robinson (Sept. 13, 1971) reached the 500 club.

Willie McCovey was the third Giant, along with Mays and Mel Ott, when he joined the immortal group seven years later in 1978. He was the 12th member. Reggie Jackson made it 13 in 1984 and Mike Schmidt was the 14th in 1987.

It took another nine years before membership expanded. Eddie Murray (at age 40) became the second-oldest player to gain membership. Then in 1999, McGwire reached the club in the shortest at-bats/homer ratio, a staggering 10.63 that was even better than Babe Ruth's 11.76.

As he stood at 499 homers, Barry Bonds had a ratio of a home run every 14.09 at-bats — the third-best rate in 500-club history.

On the eve of immortality, a history lesson is needed: When Bonds hit his 20th homer in 1990, his breakthrough season, teammate and best friend Bobby Bonilla told him, "Look out, 755," a joke about Hank Aaron's all-time career record.

"Forget that," Bonds said. "I just want 300."

Eleven seasons later, he was at 499.

Five hundred general admission tickets are always made available to the public two hours before Giants home games. On April 17, 2000, four hours before that night's game started, the line already stretched about 200 yards down Embarcadero Street toward the players' parking lot. Usually, the line has about 10 people that time of day.

It was a special night and you could feel it. Home runs are different from hits. You never know how long it might take between 499 and 500. It took Jimmy Foxx 20 days to do it, Killebrew 15 days and Mantle 11 days. Robinson did in the grandest of style, hitting 499 in the first game of a doubleheader and 500 in the second game.

With Barry Bonds, however, you just had a feeling. At least, I had a feeling. I just felt Barry would hit one that night.

At least one columnist, if not two or three, came out from every newspaper in the Bay Area. *The San Francisco Chronicle* had eight reporters at the game. All the local television stations sent their sports anchors to the ballpark for a live shot on its evening news. The game was televised on Fox Sports Net. ESPN was planning to cut into its programming whenever Bonds came to the plate.

Dodgers slugger Gary Sheffield, a close friend of Bonds who has always thought of him as an older brother, proved early in the season to be another go-to interview subject for stories about Bonds with quotes like this.

"What he's done, and is still doing, is mind-boggling," Sheffield said. "For a guy to have that kind of speed and that kind of power, and be that kind of athlete? It's hard to say anybody was ever any better than him before his time — or even after his time. We could go on all day about Barry Bonds."

Sheffield, who calls Bobby Bonds his "baseball dad," told me one of his favorite stories about Barry Bonds.

"In '92, I was a younger player, that's when I first got to know him," Sheffield said. "Barry came to the batting cage and said, 'don't pitch to me today. Anything you throw over the plate is going out of the park.' And he lived up to it. He hit two home runs off Andy Benes. And back then, Andy Benes was throwing 96 miles an hour. Barry hit one to straightaway center and another to right field. We walked him the rest of the day."

Then Sheffield talked about Bonds' upbringing and how he was raised.

"When you're raised in a household with Willie Mays and Reggie Jackson and his father Bobby, they're going to put a lot of pressure on you," Sheffield said. "They're going to set the bar real high. He's been able to reach all his goals. He doesn't talk about the pressure. Even if he did, he would never say it. Barry is too proud to do that. He can do anything he believes. That's always special when you have a player like that, especially when he's on your team. He always believes he can win a game all by himself. That takes pressure off everybody else. A lot of people don't realize that to be good, and to be great, you have to say to yourself, 'I can win a baseball game all by myself.' Very few of us can do that."

It's quite common to see Giants legends Willie Mays, Willie McCovey, Orlando Cepeda and Vida Blue — all paid members of the front office — in the Giants clubhouse, chatting with current players or hanging out in equipment manager Mike Murphy's office before games.

That office is where McCovey was sitting about an hour before the April 17th game when I joined a few reporters inside to interview him. I asked McCovey if he was hoping Bonds put the 500th into McCovey Cove.

"I'm hoping he does," McCovey said, a big smile on his face. "He's hit a lot to straightaway lately. I don't know if they'll pitch him inside tonight."

McCovey is a man of few words. But he shared a few other insights, including his memories of his own 500th homer: "We were on the road. I think we were at the beginning of the road trip. It was probably not until we got home that I was able to appreciate it and share it with my friends . . . It was a relief. Finally got it over with. It was great to see all the guys coming out of the dugout."

All over the ballpark, the talk was Barry Bonds before the game. For the manager, one of his jobs is talking to the media before every game. Usually the crowd is just the beat writers. For home games, there might be some columnists also. Dusty Baker found himself talking about Barry Bonds a lot before games during the 2001 season. And this night, with Bonds at 499, was no different.

"As you get older, you lose some of the physical and you lose some of the desire," Baker said. "You have to have a genuine love for the game in order to stay motivated. When you're not motivated, you don't work as hard in the winter.

You don't have the same competitive nature. You have to love the game and love competition to keep working the way you do — or to keep accepting the pain. When you play a long enough time, you have pain somewhere. You can count on it. There's nobody who plays for any period of time and hasn't left something on the field: an elbow, a knee, a neck, a back or something."

Baker then laid out another possible motivating factor that was driving Bonds: "When you've been the best player for a long time, you want to remain the best player. You know some day, somebody else will eventually be the best player. But while you're there, you want to keep that title . . . What's more remarkable than the home runs are the home runs *and* stolen bases. That is where Barry separates himself from anybody."

Indeed, no other player in baseball history had amassed 400 homers and 400 steals in a career before Bonds did it. And now he was closing in on 500-500.

The best setting for Bonds' 500th?

"It would be tonight, a game-winning home run in the ninth inning," Baker said. "I'm pulling for a game-winner homer in the ninth inning. Then we would all be extremely happy."

You don't see this very often. But it's so cool when it happens. The final out of an inning is made and nobody in the stands moves. This was such a night. Not one person moved. At the top of the first inning's conclusion, no rational-thinking fan was going for a bathroom break or food run between innings.

Not when Barry was due up third and sitting at 499.

Darren Dreifort was the Los Angeles Dodgers starting pitcher. Marvin Benard started the inning with a single. Rich Aurilia stroked a hit-and-run single that moved Benard to third base.

Public address announcer Renel Brooks-Moon introduced his name, the instrumental version of Dr. Dre's "The Next Episode" played and 41,059 fans (the Giants squeezed in another 129 seats during the last road trip) rose to their feet as Barry Bonds walked toward home plate. Flashbulbs lit up the dusky sky with each pitch to the plate. On a 1-2 pitch, Bonds took a mighty swing and struck out, eliciting a collective moan from the crowd.

The scene continued in each of Bonds' at-bats that night. If he was due up in the next inning, nobody took a bathroom break.

* Third inning, two outs, nobody on base, the count ran to 2-2 and Bonds sent a towering drive to left-center. Gary Sheffield raced back, to the warning track, to the wall, reached up and caught the ball directly at the 382-foot sign.

* Sixth inning, Dreifort still pitching, Bonds led off the inning. On the first pitch, he grounded softly to first base. It was beginning to appear like history would wait another day.

* Top of the eighth inning, the Dodgers clinging to 2-1 lead, Giants reliever Felix Rodriguez struck out Paul Lo Duca and Jeff Reboulet to end the inning and again send the crowd to its feet in anticipation. Nobody left their seats. Barry was due up second.

I turned to my *Oakland Tribune* colleague, columnist Art Spander, and told him, "In the Cove. This inning."

Aurilia swung at the first pitch, slicing a line drive into the right-center field corner and raced around to third base for a triple.

Baker, it turns out, was about to be one inning off. Barry was coming up in the eighth inning. The Dodgers pitcher was now Terry Adams, a journeyman middle reliever who took over for Dreifort the inning before. Rookie Dodgers manager Jim Tracy had the left-handed Jesse Orosco in his bullpen, but wasn't even warming him up at this point.

Adams' first pitch to Bonds was a ball. The second pitch was a ball. It was looking like the Dodgers were not going to let Barry Bonds beat them in this game, history be damned.

Then Adams made a mistake. He threw a 2-0 slider down and inside. Bonds connected at 9:55 p.m. PT.

"Swung on . . . there it goes . . . high into the San Francisco night . . . and it's . . . into the Cove . . . Barry Bonds has done it!" — *Ted Robinson on KNBR-AM*

Bonds skipped a couple times into the air approaching first base. Immediately, his mom, dad, brothers, Willie Mays and Willie McCovey were ushered onto the field. Bonds circled the bases and jumped high onto home plate as fireworks blasted overhead and water shot up from fountains in right field. The trot lasted 20 seconds. At home plate, the first person to greet him was batgirl Alexis Busch, the daughter of a Giants front office executive.

Aurilia, who scored the tying run, was the next person. He gave Bonds a giant hug at the plate and returned to the dugout. The rest of Bonds' teammates stayed at the top step of the dugout. Gary Sheffield clapped his hands from left field. Tears were in Bonds' eyes already. He waved to his wife and kids in the stands. The game was delayed nine minutes in the eighth inning of a one-run game, causing the Dodgers to fume in anger.

As if the Giants cared.

The ball was fished from the water by the net of Joseph Figone, the same boater who plucked out the first "Splash Hit" nearly a year prior. Robb Nen made it interesting in the ninth, allowing the tying run to reach base and advance to third, but struck out Sheffield to save the 3-2 victory.

Mays and McCovey went into a conference room near the Giants clubhouse. I rushed downstairs and into the room. Bonds' wife Liz entered the room and sat next to me. She was still visibly shaking with excitement. She had a Kleenex in her hand from wiping away the tears of joy. It was very cute and I had a smile on my face when we made eye contact. Still wearing his uniform, Barry took a seat between the Willie's.

"It couldn't be a better dream come true," Bonds said. "I always wanted to be in the major leagues and play alongside my father and Willie. I just didn't know about the age difference. It's an honor. I play left field. My godfather played center field. My father played right field. I get to play with those ghosts. I can't describe what it feels like."

Willie Mays gave Bonds at big hug at the plate.

"When I touched him, he was still shaking," Mays said. "That shows me he realizes what history is all about. You couldn't have a better script."

Willie McCovey wasn't surprised the least bit: "Like Willie, Barry has a flair for the dramatic. I thought he might hit it tonight. And he did. He didn't let us down."

Between furious note taking, I looked at Liz a couple times and saw her wiping away tears of joy.

"I couldn't believe I hit it," Barry said. "Everything was in slow motion. When I hit it, it looked like the ball stopped in mid-air. Then I was, 'wow, I really did it.' . . . I owe Robb Nen a big thank you. He made the night perfect."

Replied Nen: "He doesn't owe me anything. The game owes him."

Outside the interview room, the crowd was chanting the same thing they did before each at-bat and during his curtain call: "Bar-ry, Bar-ry."

"All these people in San Francisco are a part of this," Bonds said. "I felt it, big time. I hit it. But it was like we all did it. It was like the whole town did it. It's overwhelming."

McCovey, knowing firsthand that Mays wasn't initially loved or appreciated when he arrived in San Francisco, felt a changing of attitudes on the night.

"Barry was sort of like Mays when he came to San Francisco," McCovey said. "He was not universally accepted. But it turned around. Barry was the same way. I hope this home run tonight erases all that and he's accepted in San Francisco the way he should be."

In the Dodgers clubhouse, there wasn't much excitement.

"I know it's history, but it was kind of inappropriate at the time," Adams told Dodgers beat writers. "If it was a big margin, like we were way ahead or they were way ahead, maybe. It was just bad timing. It kind of rubbed some people the wrong way. They kind of acted like the game was over. I had to get my focus back and get three outs."

Barry Bonds arrived at 24 Willie Mays Plaza the next day and his first thought was, "what injury could I come up with and not play? But I know Dusty. He's not going to go for it. I'm not the kind of person who's hurt that often."

At least, that's what he told the media when he held court — in a rare instance before the game — in the Giants dugout during batting practice. With 500 homers now done, the talk centered around the next milestones.

* 600 homers? "It depends on my health, really. But it's realistic. A hundred more. Stay on pace and hit 30, 40 a year. That's realistic."

* 500 steals? "A lot depends on your ballclub and it makes a difference that I've got Jeff Kent hitting behind me. He gets a little gun-shy when you try to steal with two strikes on him, so I'll have to pick my spots. But just 28 more between now and the time I'm done. I can fall down five times a year and end up doing that."

*The World Series? "Willie (Mays) always told me, if you play long enough, good things will happen to you personally, but you may never have a chance to win a World Series. So I'd take that over 500 home runs any day."

Bonds also dropped a minor bombshell about the Hall of Fame: "The last uniform I wear is the one I will wear into the Hall of Fame. I'm hoping it's this one."

Bonds described the atmosphere at Pacific Bell Park as, "like a playoff atmosphere. But I did better this time."

It was the second time in a week he'd ripped himself for his postseason failures, a sign that he was a lot more relaxed and not as defensive with the media. He was mentally exhausted though from all the emotions and needing a day off. But he couldn't think of an excuse and Baker wouldn't have allowed it anyways.

So Bonds played again.

And Bonds homered again.

Into McCovey Cove again.

Late in the game again.

Providing the winning run again.

How's that for an encore?

It was now six consecutive games with a homer and now another record was within his grasp, the record of eight games in a row.

"What record are you talking about?" Bonds told reporters after the game. "I don't care about that. I don't need another thing to think about in my life right now."

In the *Chronicle* the next day, columnist Bruce Jenkins wrote: "It's pretty simple now: Barry homers daily. That's six games and counting, and No. 501 was another monster blast in the drink. For all of his career accomplishments, Bonds is on a new mission now, and the possibilities stagger the imagination."

In the *Times*, columnist Neil Hayes wrote: "Say what you want about Bonds, but he doesn't cheat teammates or fans once the first pitch is thrown like so many of his contemporaries. It's easy to loathe the man, no question about it, but it's hard not to love the player. It's almost enough to make you overlook some of the obnoxious things he does, such as when he's crass to reporters before one of the most memorable nights of his career only to address them afterward by saying, 'maybe now you'll write something nice about me.' It was a vintage display, both on the field and off. It was so . . . well, so very Barry. It was the best and worst of Barry Bonds on display, but in 20 years we'll remember his feat more than his customary petulance. It was a memorable night for even his harshest critics."

In the days that followed No. 500 and No. 501, many in the media, especially outside the Bay Area, started to focus more and more on the reaction by Bonds' teammates — or their inaction.

It turned into another memorable moment in the career of Bonds and provided more fodder for Bonds' critics. On the most joyous night of his career, the only people to greet him at home plate were the batgirl and Rich Aurilia — who was at third base.

"Personally, I was disappointed to think that he has alienated enough people in that clubhouse for that to have happened," Hall of Famer Joe Morgan, a Bonds family friend, told *Philadelphia Inquirer* columnist Claire Smith. "But you have to understand that Barry creates a lot of this himself . . . Dusty once told me he never saw anyone work as hard at making people dislike him as Barry does."

The truth, as it always is with Barry, isn't black or white. It's gray and imprecise. Many players honestly didn't know whether they were allowed or supposed to come to home plate — or whether they should stay in the dugout. They knew that a brief ceremony was planned for behind home plate and it would involve both Willie's and the Bonds family.

Yes, there were some teammates who probably figured it was a convenient way to not show their unconditional love for him. But heck no, it wasn't a conspiracy by the entire team to show Bonds up. After all, the home run won the game.

"A lot of people misconstrued that," Baker said. "People were letting Barry have his moment with his family and the Willie's."

Baker knows from experience. When Aaron hit No. 715, he was in the on-deck circle. He raised his hand in excitement, but didn't go running toward home plate. Baker stayed in the on-deck circle.

"I was the Jeff Kent of 715," Baker told me. "If I was on base, I might have done what Richie did, waiting at home plate and giving him a hug. But I stayed back. I didn't want to get in the way of the celebration shot."

Months later, Jeff Kent put it this way, "I was criticized for not high-fiving him after his 500th. But I was allowing him to have his time."

CHAPTER FIVE

Nice Throw

April 19-May 16, Home Runs 8-14

"Who was blamed for it? Me. I didn't throw the pitch.
But you guys blamed me."

Barry Bonds

THE NEWEST BALLPARK treasure is PNC Park in Pittsburgh. Just like in San Francisco, it isn't much of a stretch to say the ballpark was badly needed and saved the franchise.

The Pirates were on the verge of extinction on two occasions. The first came in the mid-1980s. The icon Willie Stargell had retired. The team's glory days — capped by the "We Are Family" 1979 World Series championship team — were long history. The city was still reeling from the drug scandal of the mid-1980s involving former players Dave Parker and Dale Berra, and the Pirates mascot.

In 1984, the Pirates finished in last place and drew just 773,500 fans. In 1985, the year Barry Bonds was drafted, they lost 104 games and there was serious concern the team would leave Pittsburgh as attendance dropped to 735,900.

A group of private and public investors agreed to purchase the team and keep it in town. The next year, with Syd Thrift, the new general manager, Jim Leyland, the new skipper, and Bonds making his major-league debut on May 30, the Bucs still lost 98 games, finished 44 games out of first place and barely went over one million in attendance.

Thrift made a couple shrewd trades, bringing back third baseman Bobby Bonilla (who had been unwisely traded away), outfielder Andy Van Slyke, catcher Mike LaValliere and pitcher Mike Dunne. The team started to gel, competing for the division in 1988 and then starting its three-year run of division titles in 1990.

In the lean years and even during the team's success, it was difficult to draw fans at Three Rivers Stadium. Built in 1970, the facility was part of a period in

American sports when cities were building circular, multi-purpose stadiums that could be used for football and baseball. One of the many problems with these stadiums was the upper-deck seats were terrible for baseball and the lower-deck seats were terrible for football.

Three Rivers was exactly the same as Veterans Stadium in Philadelphia, Riverfront Stadium in Cincinnati and Busch Stadium in St. Louis — no character, artificial turf, symmetrical dimensions, plus layers and layers of concrete.

Predictably, young stars like Bonds and Bonilla became eligible for free agency and the Pirates couldn't afford them — even after drawing over 2 million fans in 1990 and 1991. Bonilla signed with the New York Mets before the 1992 season and Bonds went home to San Francisco for the 1993 season.

The Pirates regressed again. By 1995, attendance was back down to 905,517 because of lingering effects of the players strike and the team finished in fifth place, 27 games out of first place — and, once again, the Pirates were in jeopardy of being moved.

In fact, when Kevin McClatchy bought the team on Feb. 14, 1996, many feared he was going to move the Pirates to his hometown of Sacramento, Calif. Aided by his new friendship with Stargell, McClatchy fell in love with the city and successfully worked with city and state officials to secure funding for a new ballpark.

On April 9, 2001, PNC Park made its bittersweet debut. The beloved Stargell died the same day. The new ballpark had a statue of Stargell down the left-field line, one of many features that drew rave reviews for PNC Park. The ballpark offered breathtaking views from behind home plate of the Pittsburgh skyline and the Roberto Clemente Bridge and offered an intimacy missing in Three Rivers.

The Giants first glimpse at PNC Park came on May 1, 2001. They started the second month of the season with a 12-12 record and were 2.5 games out of first place. Barry Bonds finished April with 11 home runs, five doubles and just two singles.

"Strange man," Bonds said. "Everything is strange right now."

In his ever-continuing good guy moments with the media, Bonds sat at his locker and talked for 20 minutes with beat writers and the eager Pittsburgh media before the first game of the series. Bonds' arrival in the Steel City is always big news and this was no different.

Myself and a couple other beat writers used the off day before the Pirates series to write about another possible "Splash Hit" — an Allegheny River Splashdown.

A Pirates beat writer told me nobody had even hit the water on the fly in batting practice, but only nine games had been played at PNC to that point and batting practice was canceled three times because of weather.

"It would take a bomb," said Reds first baseman Sean Casey, when I talked with him during the previous homestand. The Reds were one of the few teams to play at PNC so far.

The distance to the water, on the fly, is 480 feet — but depends on how you measure it.

The right-field foul pole is 320 feet down the line. Upon clearing the fence, the challenge is just beginning. The batter must also clear the 21-foot out-of-town scoreboard, the 38-foot grandstands, then clear another 80 feet across the concrete concourse and still 50 more feet to reach the river's edge.

It's 443 measured. Taking into account the height necessary to clear everything, the estimates are about 480 feet.

Comparatively speaking, Pac Bell is much easier.

The distance is 307 feet down the right-field line and approximately 352 feet to the water. However, the pier juts out so quickly that unless the ball is barely fair, a player really has to hit the ball about 380-400 feet to hit the water. A ball to right-center must travel between 400-430 feet to get wet.

The *Pittsburgh Post-Gazette* contacted John G. Fetkovich, a physics professor emeritus from Carnegie Mellon University, about the probability of an Allegheny Splashdown. Fetkovich once used statistical data to study the mathematical probabilities of the "Immaculate Reception," the catch by Franco Harris on the final play of a championship game to beat the Oakland Raiders.

His semi-educated guess? "Probably one or two would go into the water on the fly (per year)."

The fan in me had to see how close Bonds would come to reaching water. So during the first day of batting practice, I went to the top row of the grandstands with my notebook. Bonds bunted the first pitch. He took a half swing on the second pitch.

He put the third pitch into the water.

On the fly.

I raised my hands like a football official signaling the field goal was good. Bonds put another one into the water. And another. The crowd was buzzing and cheering and gave him a standing ovation when it was over. In all, Bonds blasted six into the water. Five were on the fly, one bounced in. One barely made it to the water. The other four made it with plenty to spare. And none were hit down the line. They were to right and right-center.

I raced back down to the dugout. Bonds was talking with former manager Jim Leyland. A little out of breath, I told Bonds, "dude, you put six in the water. Five on the fly."

"Yeah, dude, but that's just BP," replied Bonds, who still broke into a big smile.

Bonds didn't have much of a chance to hit water during the first game. He walked each of his first four at-bats, then struck out in his final at-bat. The reaction of the Pirates fans would be typical of what Bonds would see later in this season.

He was mostly booed coming to the plate, although a few cheers were mixed in. Each time it was apparent he was going to be walked, however, most of the crowd booed its own hometown pitcher. When Bonds struck out in the seventh inning, the crowd rose to its feet, cheered wildly and most of them went home with the Giants leading 11-3. The Giants won it 11-6.

During the lengthy Q&A with the media, Bonds told us he'd recently started ranking the rags he got from opposing fans.

"A couple are really good," Bonds said. "Chicago is always good. New York is kinda weak. Sometimes they get some good ones. They say the same things over and over. They bring up your playoff stuff. That's old, dude. Try something new. That's a two."

The heckles that are eights or nine or tens?

"I can't mention those," Bonds said. "Sometimes you laugh. But I just focus on the game. I don't care what they say . . . I say, 'Thanks for coming.' You paid your money. Say whatever you want. It don't bother me."

Bonds had very fond and funny memories of Lloyd McClendon, the new

Pirates manager and his former teammate in Pittsburgh. Bonds told one story about the Pirates going into San Diego on a losing streak.

"Lloyd came into the clubhouse and said, 'everybody get on my back, I'm taking us to the promise land,'" Bonds said. "Then he struck out like twice with the bases loaded. After that, we were like, 'don't call us, dude. We'll call you.' But he won a lot of games for us, too. He did a great job. He's always been a good friend of mine . . . He was always a big inspiration guy, he'd come in with phony articles. If you were hitting like 1-something against a certain guy, he'd bring in some article that said, 'you suck and this guy's great and he's going to blow it past you and stuff.' He'd pin it on your locker. He was always like that. If we went into a slump, he would pump up the team."

The next night, May 2nd, the Giants trailed 4-1 in the fifth inning. Bonds hit a two-run homer off Todd Ritchie, his 12th of the season, to dead center (giving it no chance to land in the river). The blast sparked a Giants rally for a 7-6 victory. The game would most be remembered, however, for an airplane that flew over PNC Park with a banner that read: "Barry — Nice Throw — Sid."

With the sixth overall pick of the 1985 draft, the Pittsburgh Pirates selected Barry Lamar Bonds. At first, Bonds was disappointed. Then his father explained it was a blessing. The Pirates would be rebuilding and Barry could get to the majors quicker on a team without a lot of veterans.

Bonds quickly signed for $125,000 and reported to Woodbridge, Va., home of the Prince William Cannons of the Carolina League, a high-A classification comprised mostly of second-and third-year minor leaguers. It was there he met Bobby Bonilla, who would become his best friend in baseball.

In his first professional at-bat, Bonds tripled. Not too long after, Bonds asked manager Ed Ott, a former Pirate, the quickest way to move up the organizational ladder and reach the majors.

"Swing it," Ott told him.

In 71 games, Bonds swung it to the tune of a .299 batting average, 13 homers, 37 RBIs, 15 stolen bases, 16 doubles and four triples.

Bonds spent the offseason tearing up the Venezuelan winter ball league.

He started the 1986 season in Triple-A Hawaii, one step from the majors. One of his teammates in Hawaii was an infielder named Ron Wotus. Fifteen years later, Bonds had over 500 homers and still counting. Wotus was the Giants bench coach.

"He was a talent from day one," Wotus said. "I'd been in the Pirates organization a little and I'd been in the big leagues a little before that year. I remember Barry coming in as a top pick out of ASU. We knew who he was. We heard all the talk about him. When he got there, he lived up to the billing you heard about him.

"He wasn't considered a home-run hitter," Wotus continued. "He was considered a good hitter, tremendous bat speed. He could hit the ball out of the ballpark, but you wouldn't classify him as a prototypical home-run hitter. As long as he's played, the older he gets, the conditioning and the weights, and the way he works in the offseason, he started hitting more home runs. When Bonds came in, he had a slender build. He could run. He could hit. He could hit it out of the ballpark. But you wouldn't classify him as a home-run hitter."

Forty-four games into the 1986 season, Bonds was batting .311 with seven homers, 37 RBIs and 16 stolen bases. As legend now has it, Bonds was taking batting practice one day in Phoenix and then-Pirates general manager Syd Thrift was watching. Bonds pulled 5-6 balls over the fence in right field.

"I told him any good hitter can do that," Thrift told *Sports Illustrated*, in a famous 1993 article. "But I'd like to see him hit a few over the left field fence. He hit five in a row and said, 'is that good enough for you?' I said it was fine. I had the manager take him out of the game in the fifth inning and I took him back to Pittsburgh that night."

Bonds' first major-league home run came June 4, 1986 off Craig McMurty at Atlanta's Fulton-County Stadium — the same place Hank Aaron broke Babe Ruth's all-time homer record. Thrift smiled when he saw where the ball landed — over the left-field fence.

For those who believe Bonds is on a collision course with Aaron, take note that Bonds' first landed in just about the exact same location, and in the same ballpark, as Aaron's record-breaking 715th.

Bonds might have been a baseball prodigy, but was slow to make his impact in the majors. He batted leadoff, wore Mays' No. 24 and played center. In the final 113 games of the 1986 season, Bonds batted just .223 and struck out 102 times. He endured long slumps that made him question whether he would last in the majors. He cried during the slumps and doubted his abilities.

Truth be told, Bonds was probably overmatched. In most organizations, he would still be in the minors. But he was the best the Pirates had and the team felt they might as well give the kid a chance to show what he could do.

From 1987-89, Bonds put up good numbers. But never great numbers, certainly not the type of a future first ballot Hall of Famer. And not even as good as his father Bobby posted in his first three full seasons.

Bobby Bonds

Year	AVG	2B	3B	HR	RB	SB	BB	SO
1969	.254	25	6	9	35	16	81	187
1970	.259	36	10	32	90	45	77	189
1971	.302	32	4	26	78	48	62	137
Totals	.276	93	20	67	203	109	220	513

Barry Bonds

Year	AVG	2B	3B	HR	RBI	SB	BB	SO
1987	.261	26	3	25	59	32	54	88
1988	.283	30	5	24	58	17	72	82
1989	.248	34	6	19	58	32	93	93
Totals	.258	90	14	68	175	81	219	263

In 1990, something changed. Bonds was bitter about the offseason, when the Pirates didn't negotiate a multi-year contract and went to arbitration instead. Bonds wanted $1.6 million. The Pirates offered $850,000. Arbitrator Roy Goetz chose the Pirates offer, based on their argument that compared Bonds' statistics to players who hit in the middle of the order. It was the second straight season that Bonds lost in arbitration.

Bonds figured if he was going to be compared to middle of the order hitters, like Bo Jackson and Jose Canseco, get him out of the leadoff position. He went to spring training with the mission of requesting it. But manager Jim Leyland had already decided himself to move Bonds from leadoff to fifth in the batting order, so Bonds never had to plead his case.

Bonds, Bonilla and Van Slyke formed the best outfield in baseball. Doug

Drabek and John Smiley were the pitchers who led the resurgence in Pittsburgh. The Pirates won the National League East division and Bonds enjoyed a breakthrough season. Bonds batted .301, slugged a league-high .565, blasted 33 homers, drove in 114 runs and stole 52 bases to become just the second player in history with 30 homers and 50 steals. He also tied for the league lead with 14 outfield assists, won his first Gold Glove and was named the Most Valuable Player.

In the NL championship series, the Pirates lost to the Reds in six games. Bonds had just three hits in 18 at-bats, a paltry .167 batting average. He had no extra-base hits and one RBI. Most people remember this. Few remember that most of those outs came with nobody on base. The Reds walked Bonds five times in his final 14 at-bats in the series, including three times in the decisive game six.

In 1991, Bonds had an MVP-caliber season, finishing second to Atlanta's Terry Pendleton, despite better offensive statistics in nearly every category. There's little doubt Bonds' relationship with the writers had an impact on the voting. How much is up for debate. Pendleton, a more inviting interview subject, benefited from being the best hitter who led a remarkable worst-to-first turnaround for the Braves. The NL West went down to the final weekend that season and it was Pendleton's veteran presence and production that kept the young Braves in contention all season.

The Pirates won the NL East again and did it fairly easily. With little drama the final weeks of the season, Bonds didn't have an opportunity to sway MVP voters with a fantastic finish — like Pendleton did. During the playoffs, Bonds' struggles continued. He had four hits (one double, no homers, no RBIs) in 27 at-bats for a .148 average in the '91 NL Championship Series. The Braves beat the Pirates in a thrilling seven-game series.

Trouble was lurking as the Bucs looked to save money.

In 1992, Bonilla had left as a free agent for the riches in New York. John Smiley, a 20-game winner, was traded away. The saves leader was released in spring training. All these were cost-cutting moves. It was so bad the Pirates saved $20,000 by dumping the old company that made their pants for a company that agreed to do it for free (but couldn't get anybody's pants to fit).

Still, somehow, Bonds carried the Pirates back to the postseason for a third straight time. He went to his second all-star game, earned his third straight Gold

Glove and second MVP in three years — despite having a guy batting .230 behind him in the lineup. How he ever posted such incredible numbers with no lineup protection is still a mystery.

But the playoffs, for a third straight year, were a nightmare. Bonds homered once and actually batted .261 (6-for-23) in the seven games, but the Braves won again — in a dramatic ending that was the cause for the "Nice Throw" banner.

The Pirates took a 2-0 lead into the ninth inning of game seven of those 1992 playoffs, and were riding the arm of ace Doug Drabek. But the Braves mounted a rally, starting with a double by Pendleton. David Justice reached first base on an error by second baseman Jose Lind to put runners at the corners. Sid Bream was walked on four pitches, and at 129 pitches, Drabek was removed for closer Stan Belinda.

Ron Gant hit a sacrifice fly to score one run. The ball was deep and Bonds didn't try throwing the runner out at home, instead keeping the tying run at second. Damon Berryhill then walked to reload the bases and put the tying run at third and the winning run at second. Brian Hunter hit a popup into shallow center that was caught by Lind for the second out.

The Pirates were one out from the World Series. Francisco Cabrera, who had just 10 at-bats in the regular season, represented the final chance for the Braves. The count reached two strikes on Cabrera, putting the Pirates one strike away.

Bonds was playing Cabrera deep and down the line, expecting him to pull the ball. Cabrera hit a single between third base and shortstop. Justice scored the tying run easily, and all that stood in the way of the Braves winning the game was the arm of Barry Bonds and the wobbly legs of Sid Bream, who had five knee operations.

Bonds sprinted to his left and charged the ball. His throw was off-line a couple of feet toward the first-base line. Catcher Mike LaValliere tried a decoy by standing there as if he had no chance. At the last moment possible, LaValliere snatched the ball and quickly reached back to apply the tag.

Bream was safe by inches. The Braves dogpiled on top of Bream. Bonds sat in left field with a look of disbelief on his face. The CBS cameras zoomed on Bonds' face and he shook his head, unable to believe the Braves had won again.

"When Cabrera was up, he hit two line drives that went foul out of the ballpark," Bonds told a group of reporters at the all-star game. "People forget about that. We were all playing shallow at that time. After he hit two rockets, we took two steps backward. We were like, 'wait a minute.' We tried to come in and take away the base hit. But we had to respect his power. Now we're in a tough situation. So we move back. Then what happens? He hits that ground ball through the infield and the runs scores.

"Who was blamed for it? Me. I didn't throw the pitch. But you guys blamed me."

Evidently, the Pittsburgh fans haven't forgotten. They probably will never forget. Bonds was asked about the plane and the banner after the May 2nd game. He shook his head and replied quietly, "waste of money."

His words gave the impression that he didn't care. But reading his body language, looking into his eyes and the expression on his face, you could see that Bonds was hurt.

"Bonds' crimes against Pittsburgh are two," wrote *Pittsburgh Post-Gazette* columnist Bob Smizik. "He never performed well in the postseason and he left us as a free agent to join the San Francisco Giants. There's no defense of the first. He batted .191 with one home run and three RBIs in 20 games as the Pirates lost three consecutive league championship series from 1990-92.

"But to judge Bonds on 20 postseason games, as opposed to the 860 regular-season games he played for the Pirates is, to stay the least, unfair."

The next night, May 3, the final game of the series in Pittsburgh, Bonds displayed his greatness once again to the Pirates crowd. He launched a two-run homer in the first inning off lefty Jimmy Anderson, walked in the third, singled in the fifth, singled in the seventh and was semi-intentionally walked to load the bases in the ninth inning — with the tying and go-ahead runs on base. Jeff Kent, the next batter, struck out to end the game.

"It's frustrating to lose a game, period," Kent said, not answering directly questions about the walk to Bonds. "That's the nature of the game. Sometimes, you have a good day. Sometimes, you don't."

Shawon Dunston and Eric Davis know something about trying to live up to lofty expectations.

Dunston was the overall first pick of the 1982 draft by the Chicago Cubs after batting .790 and going 37-for-37 in steal attempts at Thomas Jefferson High in Brooklyn. Three years later, he was the Cubs starting shortstop.

Outside the ballpark in Chicago, one of the best-selling T-shirts has always been "The Top Ten Lies Told Annually At Wrigley Field." The list changes a little each year. In the late 1980s, one of the "lies" was "Dunston Just Needs A Few Years To Develop."

Dunston played 11 productive seasons with the Cubs and made two all-star games as a shortstop, but never became the superstar expected of overall first picks. He's moved around a lot since then, from the Giants (in '96), back to the Cubs (in '97) before a trade to the Pirates for the stretch drive, to the Cleveland Indians (in '98) before a trade back to the Giants for the stretch drive, to the St. Louis Cardinals (in '99) before a trade to the New York Mets for the stretch drive, and back to the Cardinals in 2000.

Dunston signed with the Giants before the 2001 season for his third stint with the organization. It was manager Dusty Baker, in 1998, who thought that Dunston could make the switch from shortstop to center field, just like Milwaukee's Robin Yount did in the 1980s. Dunston grudgingly accepted a reserve role in 1998 and his greatest value to the Giants was his leadership — both vocally and the example he sets with his effort.

Some players, including Barry Bonds, will only run out groundballs if there is a chance they can reach base. Bonds once told me he would rather strike out than give an infielder the satisfaction of throwing him out at full speed.

Dunston is different. He sprints as fast as he can every time he makes contact. He even sprints in spring training. A soft-spoken man around reporters, Dunston has a big mouth on the field with teammates and is never shy about giving compliments or constructive criticism when time warrants.

Eric Davis was an eighth-round pick in 1980 by the Cincinnati Reds, but when he reached the majors and became a star in 1987, he was burdened with the same tag that was placed on Bobby Bonds two decades earlier — "the next Willie Mays."

He stole 50 bases and hit 37 homers one year, made two all-star game appearances and played a key role in the Reds beating Bonds' Pirates in the 1990 National League Championship Series and, finally, the Oakland A's in the World Series.

It was inevitable that Davis would break down though. He only knew one way to play the game, attacking the outfield walls while going after the baseball and sacrificing his body to make a play. The hard artificial turf and walls in Cincinnati pounded on his body and took a heavy toll on him. Davis wasn't in the lineup enough to continue posting big numbers.

After an injury-plagued and unproductive 1994 season, Davis retired from baseball. He was retired for just one season, returned to Cincinnati in 1996 and was named the Comeback Player of the Year.

The next season is what he's remember for most. Davis was diagnosed with colon cancer on May 27. He underwent surgery on June 13 that removed one-third of his colon, began chemotherapy treatments at the UCLA medical center on July 16, started working out with his Baltimore Orioles teammates on August 22 and made his inspirational return on September 15 to the game. A day after receiving chemotherapy treatments, Davis went 4-for-5 with a home run on September 27 at Milwaukee.

The most memorable homer of Davis' career was a pinch-hit shot in Game Five of the AL championship series against the Cleveland Indians, the day after getting another round of chemotherapy treatments.

Davis and Dunston, inspirational leaders in so many ways and a couple of players who symbolize all that is right with the game of baseball, became teammates for the Cardinals in 2000 — and both signed with the Giants for the 2001 season.

Little did they know the role they would play in Barry Bonds' season.

———————

The next stop in the 2001 season for the Giants was Philadelphia and Barry Bonds didn't slow down his frantic early home-run pace. Trailing 2-0 in the sixth, Bonds hammered a 1-1 pitch off lefty Bruce Chen over the right-field wall to tie the game. The Giants won it, 4-2, improving to 15-13 for the season.

The homer was Bonds' 26th career at Veteran Stadium, tying him with Gary Carter for the most by a visiting player.

Bonds was 5-for-10 with seven walks, three homers and six RBIs on this trip. He'd homered in 13 of his last 19 games, including three straight games, and was tied with Arizona's Luis Gonzalez for the major league lead.

"I don't think he's hot," said Davis, who delivered the go-ahead sacrifice fly. "A lot of games he's hit home runs in, that's his only hit. He'll tell you that. His trajectory is just outstanding. He's getting the ball in the air. As powerful as he is, when you get the ball in the air, you have a legitimate chance to hit a home run every night."

Nine of Bonds' 14 homers had tied or put the Giants ahead.

"You really can't categorize the things he's done," Davis said. "He's getting us back in the game or getting us the lead or tying the game up."

Added Dunston: "That's why (Bonds) is the best player in baseball. He gave him one, and he missed it. Then he gave him another. You can't do that."

Davis and Dunston were being quoted for two reasons: One, they both played crucial roles in the outcome of the game; and two, Bonds wasn't in the mood to say very much.

It was on that night that we beat writers realized what we had suspected: When Bonds didn't feel like talking or wasn't saying much when he talked — and you never knew how often this would be — Dunston and Davis were going to be the "go-to" players for quotes on Bonds in 2001.

It was quite a sight, seeing the three late-30s outfielders all in the starting lineup on the field that night and talking about it, with each other and reporters, in the clubhouse afterward. There was a combined 47 years of major-league experience and 11 Gold Gloves between the three players. Bonds was the kid in the outfield at age 36.

"It's nice to play with experienced players, superstars with Gold Gloves," Dunston said. "They move me around every pitch. They talk to me every pitch. They look after me like a little brother. I just run as hard as I can. I try to be the best outfielder I can."

Dunston wasn't kidding about the "moving around" on every pitch.

"Man, Shawon be wearing me out," Davis said. "I'm emotionally drained after playing with him."

From what?

"That's from telling him where to go," Davis said. "That's my job. I tell him where to go: in, back, forward, left, right, this way, that way. Then I be talking to him and I'm out of position."

All three made great catches in the outfield in this game. Bonds ended the game by sprinting in from left field to steal a potential game-tying hit away from pinch-hitter Kevin Jordan.

"Nothing new," Dunston said. "That's why (Bonds) is a Gold Glover . . . I was on the other end a lot. It's not fun. He can play, man. He can really play."

CHAPTER SIX

Making A Bet

May 11-23, Home Runs 15-24

"Ask God. There's some things I can't understand right now. The balls that used to line off the wall just go out (of the park). I can't answer that question. It's like women. Do you understand why they do some things?"

Barry Bonds

BEFORE THE GREATEST home run stretch in baseball history, the concern of the San Francisco Giants medical staff was the left shin. Back on April 27, a cold Friday night in San Francisco, Bonds was hit by a Kerry Wood 98 mph fastball and three weeks later, the injury was still bothering him and resurfaced during a cross-country flight from San Francisco to Miami. Bonds was favoring the leg and had some tightness in his calf. But he was still playing and still producing.

When the Giants opened a three-city, nine-game road trip in Miami on May 15, Bonds was batting .271, slugging .766 and had added his 15th homer on May 11 against Steve Trachsel and the New York Mets — a solo homer in the fourth inning that gave the Giants a 2-1 lead.

Fifteen homers in 37 games was quite a start — a pace of 66 homers — but still offered little hint of the stretch that Bonds was about to embark.

It started May 17, the third game of the trip. Leading 1-0, Bonds hit a two-run homer off the Marlins' Chuck Smith to give the Giants a 3-0 lead in a game they'd lose 8-3.

Barry homered. The Giants lost. It would become a trend that had the baseball world shaking its collective head in awe, the Giants frustrated by their inability to capitalize on their star's hot streak and Bonds wrestling with his emotions on how he should feel.

* Friday, May 18 in Atlanta: Bonds was intentionally walked, flied out, struck out and then hammered his 17th home run of the season off Mike Remlinger in the eighth inning to give the Giants a 5-4 lead. In the ninth, the usually reliable Robb Nen blew the lead and the Braves won 6-5.

* Saturday, May 19: The start of the game was delayed 76 minutes by rain.

Bonds doubled in the first off Odalis Perez. He hit a solo homer in the third (No.18) to give the Giants a 2-1 lead. He struck out in the fifth. Then the game was delayed by 95 minutes by more rain. When the game resumed, Javy Lopez broke a 2-2 tie with a solo homer. Bonds answered with another solo homer, this one off Jose Cabrera to tie the game 3-all. Then he homered again, his third solo shot, at 38 minutes past midnight, in the eighth off Jason Marquis to extend a 4-3 lead to 5-3.

"If there was any doubt who the best player in the game has been, or is right now, it was answered tonight," Braves all-star third baseman Chipper Jones said. "Barry just confirmed something we already knew. You can't throw him anything over the plate. He just mashes it . . . I've never seen anything even remotely like it."

* Sunday, May 20: Another solo homer in the first inning, a laser beam into the right-center bleachers, this one off John Burkett. Bonds returned to the dugout and simply laughed.

"It was like he was playing whiffle ball in the back yard with a bunch of teen-agers," Giants first baseman J.T. Snow said. "He was sitting next to me on the bench, and he said he didn't know how he was doing it. He was shocked himself."

The next two times Bonds was batting, runners were on base, and the Braves walked him. In the seventh, Atlanta leading 7-3 and nobody on base, Mike Remlinger pitched to him and Bonds blasted a high blast to dead center, 436 feet, for yet another solo homer.

The Atlanta fans gave Bonds a standing ovation.

"It's wild," manager Dusty Baker said. "If I've seen it before, I don't remember it. He's hitting right-handers, left-handers, it doesn't matter. I just wish we could have gotten another victory to maximize the fact he was so hot."

The weekend totals: 10 at-bats, 6 homers (all solo), a combined 3,518 feet traveled, three walks, one double, one Giants victory and 25 awed Atlanta Braves players.

Braves pitcher John Burkett: "Unbelievable. I played with Barry Bonds for two years and I've seen him do a lot of things. But the things he did in this series, that was amazing. For us to get two wins when the guy hit six home runs was amazing."

Braves outfielder Brian Jordan: "That's the first time I've ever seen an individual performance like that. It just shows how great he is. It shows why he's a Hall of Fame player."

Another quote by Chipper Jones was a wakeup call on Bonds' greatness, the first mention in the season of a chilling number in baseball history: 755.

"I think if he really wanted it bad enough, and wants to stick around, he can definitely put a scare in Hank Aaron's (all-time home run) record," Jones said. "He's as good as he's ever been right now. He's not even 37 (years old) yet. He's going to hit 50 this year and he's never done that before. A couple of years at or near 50 and he's right in the thick of things. He hasn't shown any signs of slowing down. In fact, since I've been in the league (1993), I think he's actually gotten better."

Meanwhile, in the visitors clubhouse, Bonds was sitting on a couch and watching TV, eating an ice cream cone and not talking to reporters. Eric Davis noticed the group of reporters waiting for Bonds and called them over to his locker and put the weekend in perspective.

"There are no certain words to describe a thing like that," Davis said. "You don't try to explain it. You just enjoy it. When you get special moments in the game with special people, don't try to figure it out. Just enjoy it. Watch it. Write about it. Don't try to break it down, analyze it or wonder what's happening. Just enjoy it.

"For him to get a standing ovation on the road, I've seen one other person get that — and that was me. It was in Philadelphia. I hit three in one game. Had six in three days. That's something special when you do that, especially when you get a standing ovation on the road."

Before the Giants bus left, when most of the reporters had given up getting quotes from Bonds, he finally spoke to beat writers — in barely over a whisper — about a weekend like none other in his life.

"I've never done a lot of things in life," Bonds said. "I've never traveled the world. Dude, we're trying to win baseball games. I'm tired of being on the losing end against that team. That's all. It's been like this the last 10 years. It's amazing what the Braves do over there."

Jeff Bradley, a reporter from *ESPN The Magazine*, was in Cincinnati working on a story about Luis Gonzalez. The Arizona outfielder was the surprise home run leader with 13 homers after April and had 20 when Barry Bonds went on his Sherman-like march through Atlanta to take over the lead with 22.

"Gonzo" was a mediocre outfielder who spent seven seasons with Houston and Chicago from 1991-97. He averaged 12 homers, batted .243 one year and his highest average was .300. Upon a trade to Detroit in 1998, Gonzalez learned to pull the ball more to take advantage of the short porch in right field at Tigers Stadium. Despite hitting a career-high 23 homers, the Tigers thought so little of Gonzalez, then 30 years old, they sent him to Arizona for infielder Karim Garcia — and gave the D'backs $500,000 to sweeten the deal.

Gonzalez thrived in the desert, hitting a career-high 26 homers and leading the NL with 206 hits in 1999. He followed that with 31 more homers, 114 RBIs and a .311 average while playing all 162 games in 2000. So far in 2001, he'd simply exploded.

Of course, this recent power surge had fans around the country wondering if the reasons weren't legitimate. Whether in the outfield or the on-deck circle, Gonzalez heard people accuse him of using steroids — and they weren't just whispers.

"I'll come up to bat and hear stuff from fans," Gonzalez was quoted in a strong column by highly respected *Arizona Republic* columnist Pedro Gomez, who shot down the rumors as ludicrous. "In a way, it bothers me. But it's the nature of the society we live in. Everybody's assuming there must be something I'm doing. I take it as that's how people are these days. Mostly I try to brush it off because I know the truth. Anyone can come in and test me, my bat, whatever they want, any time. I'm open for whatever anyone wants to test on me."

Gonzalez was invited to join the group of American all-stars in a series of exhibition games against Japan after the 2000 season. It was here that Gonzalez and Bonds met each other and developed a friendship.

"I just played with Barry (in Japan) every day and saw how he does it," Gonzalez said. "He's got a great approach. There's a reason why he hits 400-plus home runs and steals 400-plus bases. He's just a talented player." Countered

Bonds: "I like him a lot. He's a good contact hitter. Right now, the contact he's making is out of the ballpark."

Bradley was preparing to put the finishing touches on the Gonzalez story with a trip to Phoenix to meet his family. But from his New Jersey home, Bradley saw the highlights of Bonds' performance in Atlanta, realized he was going to be in the same city as Bonds and wondered if his assignment was going to change.

Bonds' mood was a little better on Monday, May 21. Maybe it was the warmth of the Arizona sun, or the change in scenery, but Bonds sat at this locker in the visitors clubhouse at Bank One Ballpark and talked to us beat writers for about 15-20 minutes before the start of the series against the Diamondbacks.

Sure, it was only May 21. Still, Bonds had 22 homers in 43 games, an absurd pace of 83 over a 162-game season.

"To talk about it on May 21st is ridiculous," Bonds said. "I could get hit by a truck tomorrow. Then what? 'He was on his way, but damn, he got hit by a car.'"

Bonds was especially amused by his critics in the media who were now showering him with praise. He revealed that his wife keeps a list at home of which writers have written good things about him over the years and which writers have ripped him.

He could laugh and joke about that. But Bonds had no explanation for why this was happening, why he was hitting so many homers with the frequency of nobody else in the enormously rich history of baseball.

"Ask God. There's some things I can't understand right now," Bonds said. "The balls that used to line off the wall just go out (of the park). I can't answer that question. It's like women. Do you understand why they do some things?"

We all shook our heads and laughed.

"I can't understand either," Bonds said. "I tried to figure it out and I can't."

Bonds was in vintage form. Charming and laughing one minute. Confrontational and guarded another minute.

He downplayed his accomplishments and implored the media to just let things happen, instead of "spoiling" it by talking about it before it happens. As an example, he pointed out the media spent so much time talking about Ichiro Suzuki's hitting streak and then it ended.

"Atlanta surprised me," Bonds said. "You don't hit that many balls off that team. Who cares? What's the big deal? They're solo shots. If we were winning, it would be different. Most of those games, we were losing. If it's close, they may not pitch to me. It's different."

Bonds figured that even with this torrid stretch, his final numbers would be the same as always — between 40-49 homers — at the end of the year.

"Todd Helton is going to hit his normal 30-40 homers," Bonds said. "Larry Walker will hit his normal homers. Sammy Sosa will hit his normal. I've had fast starts and still hit my normal homers. It doesn't matter. I'm going to enjoy the ride as long as I can. But it's still going to end up like it always has."

Bonds, ever the party-pooper, also declared himself out of the home-run hitting contest at the all-star game.

"Even in the offseason derby, I lost to Todd Helton," Bonds said, referring to a one-weekend, made-for-TV show that is edited into a month-long challenge on ESPN. "C'mon dude. I'm done. No more home-run derbies for me ever again."

Yes, Barry, but you won the derby at the 1996 all-star game.

"That was luck," Bonds replied. "Mark McGwire got tired. It's too long, too many ABs. I couldn't stay up that long. I don't know how Sammy did it in Atlanta (when he won the 2000 derby). You know how long that home run hitting contest? Ten outs. Three rounds. That's too long."

Bonds was at 516 career homers as he spoke, five away from the National League record for a left-handed batter. What about that record?

"It's a big deal to my dad," Bonds said. "He told me about it."

Well, what about 755 homers, the number Chipper Jones threw out?

"Hell no," Bonds said. "I promise you, with all my heart, I won't be around. I will not be in a baseball uniform that long."

Dusty Baker, the former teammate of Aaron, wasn't ruling anything out.

"He does have a chance," Baker said. "It depends how long he plays. Right now, he's not slowing down any. Those last couple 100 are always the toughest . . . If he keeps hitting them like this, he has a heck of a chance. But he's still a ways away."

True to his word, Bonds hadn't discussed his contract or impending free-agent status at the end of the season. We reporters had miraculously never asked him about it — although, of course, it was a constant topic in print. However, when the notebooks were closed and the tape recorders shut off, somebody mentioned to Bonds how much money this homer streak was going to end up costing owner Peter Magowan.

"I think he has a noose in his bedroom right now," Bonds said, laughing and walking away.

Bonds walked to the field and stretched with his teammates. As usual, he wasn't too far away from Shawon Dunston. Now in his 16th year, Dunston has played for six teams in his career — and now in his third stint with the Giants. He's been a teammate of Sammy Sosa, Mark McGwire and Bonds. So he knows something about watching home run hitters.

Having witnessed this ridiculous week of homers, Dunston told Bonds, "you're going to break Big Mac's record this year." Bonds laughed. Just as he told the media, Bonds thought the idea of him hitting 71 homers was absurd.

To emphasize the point, Bonds looked at Dunston and told him, "If I do it, I'll buy you a new Mercedes."

The crack of the bat was the loudest I've ever heard in my life. I think the ball left the yard in about 1.8 seconds. I think it left a vapor trail. I still can't believe what I witnessed. I'm just glad I didn't blink. I'd have missed it. I've watched replays of it, over and over, and still can't believe it. I shook my head. I'm still in awe.

The use of war-like reference and exaggerated adjectives in baseball writing is something we're all guilty of doing. But this one was worthy. You simply couldn't use a word like "hit" or "smacked" or "drilled" with this home run. Something more was needed. It was a "rocket" and a "missile" and a "laserbeam" — if not a "scud missile."

I settled on "line-drive missile" for my game story, choosing to save the hyperbole for later in the season. This was the night I realized the biggest challenge of this season would be finding new and creative ways to describe the home runs that Bonds was hitting. To this day, I'm still trying to find words to describe this home run with the proper justice. All I know is the ball was still rising when it cleared the 20-plus-foot wall just to the right of dead center at the spacious Bank One Ballpark and went down a tunnel. The estimated distance was an embarrassingly low 442 feet. No way. That ball was still rising when it reached the 442-foot mark.

That was Bonds' sixth homer in the last three games, seventh in the last four and 22nd in the last 34 games. It came on a 2-0 pitch off Curt Schilling in the fourth inning.

Four batters later, J.T. Snow hit a slicing fly ball down the left-field line that he thought was a homer. Third-base umpire Charlie Reliford called it foul. Snow was irate, ended up striking out, flung his bat and helmet, was ejected and charged after Reliford in anger.

It was Bonds who held back Snow, doing his best sumo wrestler impersonation to prevent his teammate from attacking the umpire. Then Baker took up the argument, lost his temper, was also ejected, and Bonds needed all his considerable strength to keep his manager and first baseman a safe distance from the umpire.

In the sixth inning, Bonds just missed another homer, sending a towering fly ball to center that was caught. Then in the eighth, with Arizona continuing a ridiculous shift that placed second baseman Jay Bell in shallow right field, Bonds absolutely crushed a line drive that went right into Bell's glove.

In my scorebook, I wrote the following: L-10.

Schilling went the distance, Arizona won 4-2 and the Giants were 2-5 on the road trip.

"When things aren't going your way, they aren't going your way," said Bonds, in complete disbelief. "The man was in the right place. Just a tough loss, dude."

———

When he woke up Tuesday, May 22, Jeff Bradley had a message waiting for him from his magazine. He wasn't exactly shocked. The planned Luis Gonzalez story was on the backburner. Now he was writing the Bonds story. Bradley, who sat next to me in the BOB press box for the series, wasn't thrilled because he didn't have much time to do the story — but saw this assignment coming and was excited.

Gonzalez had offered his cell phone number to Bradley and told him, "call me if you need anything else."

Bradley approached Bonds about an interview for the story and was told, "you just can't show up and get an interview, dude."

Bradley was told to go through Bonds' personal publicist, Steve Hoskins. Here's the funny part about Bonds though: After telling Bradley he wouldn't do the interview, they ended up B.S.ing a good 10 minutes for three consecutive days about when and where they would do the interview. That's all the time Bradley needed, truth be told.

Bonds, on a kick about the media suddenly loving him after years of hating him, asked Bradley why *ESPN The Magazine* had never done a story on him before now.

"We did one on you last year," Bradley replied.

"Oh yeah," said Bonds, who was on the cover.

The Arizona press was still buzzing, and players and coaches were still talking about Bonds' homer off Schilling and the liner to Jay Bell in shallow right the night before.

"The shift has almost become a common practice," said Bob Brenly, the affable Arizona rookie manager, former Giants player and coach, and former Arizona announcer. "Every team has access to the same charts as we do, which say Barry hits the ball to right. He's not a ground-ball hitter to begin with. When he does hit it on the ground, he hits it to the right side. Even when I coached with the Giants, we used to say, 'if Barry would just bunt once in awhile, it would force the defense back into a more legitimate alignment and he might get some more base hits. But Barry isn't too concerned with bunting for base hits. He should be familiar with that shift by now. It doesn't really bother him. They did it to Ted Williams and it didn't bother him either. Barry hits the ball over the shift most of the time. He's evolved to a point in his career, where, if he gets a pitch he's looking for, whether it's inside or outside, he's going to hit it in the air — and he's going to hit it a long way."

This was the moment in the season when it officially became stupid to pitch to Bonds. Why bother? The walk-Bonds strategy wasn't new, but the "will they pitch to Bonds?" hype — which most of the public wouldn't realize until late September — actually began here in Arizona.

Keep in mind, Bonds entered the season with 400 more walks than strikeouts. He walked over 100 times in a season eight times, including a personal high 151 times during the last place 1996 season when Bonds had no protection whatsoever and still hit 42 homers. Bonds entered the season with 320 intentional walks, the most in baseball history. It's a record he set in 1999, passing the 293 by Hank Aaron. So it's not like walking Bonds was a new concept.

Arizona was the fitting team to be playing the Giants when this debate heated up. It was in 1998, Arizona's first year of existence, when then-manager Buck Showalter walked Bonds with *the bases loaded* and two outs in the ninth inning. The strategy worked. The walk forced in a run to trim Arizona's lead to 8-7, but Brent Mayne lined out to end the game. The strategy worked.

Brenly told reporters before the game he would consider walking Bonds with the bases loaded in the right situation. "He's definitely locked in," Brenly said. "There's been guys throughout this game, when they're locked in, they get called 'the most feared hitter in baseball.' Right now, that's Barry Bonds. No question about it. There is no easy way to get him out."

As for Bonds' missile off Schilling, Brenly, who has seen almost every game in the BOB's three-plus years, added, "In this ballpark, that's the hardest I've ever seen. Of course, I wasn't in Atlanta the last couple of days."

Brenly's strategy of pitching to Bonds would become evident immediately. In the first inning, two outs, nobody on base, left-hander Brian Anderson pitched Bonds ultra carefully and walked him on six pitches. The crowd booed. In the third, a runner at second, first base open, Brenly intentionally walked Bonds to get to Kent, the reigning MVP, and the 32,323 fans at the BOB booed their own manager even louder — and this was in May!

In the fifth inning, Arizona leading 3-1, a runner at first and two outs, Bonds did something that again had the reporters shaking their heads — he singled. It was just his eighth single of the season. Leading off the seventh, Arizona now leading 8-4, Byung-Hyun Kim pitched to Bonds and he flew to left.

In the ninth, Arizona comfortably ahead 12-5, Russ Springer went after Bonds with a fastball — and Bonds crushed another to dead center for his 24th homer. But once again, Bonds' homer came in a Giants loss. The team was 11-13 in games Bonds had homered.

"It's very frustrating," Bonds said. "It would be a lot more gratifying if we were winning. It's not even worth talking about when you're not winning . . . Just thank God it's only May. It would be nice if it was helping our team win games. It's not doing much . . . We're a better team than how we're playing now. We've got to find ways to win games. We're not playing defense well and things we've done well in the past, we're not doing. We're out of sync."

Well, Bonds wasn't out of sync. He'd homered in six consecutive games for the second time this season. The nine homers in six straight games set a NL record.

Back in San Francisco, *Chronicle* columnist Ray Ratto wrote, "Barry is having exactly the kind of walk year every player dreams of having; the kind where every at-bat makes a cash register stand up and ring. He was going good when the Giants struggled, he was going good when the Giants won, and he is going good again now that they are back in stumble-and-fall mode."

On the final game of the road trip, Bonds and Kent were flip-flopped in the order. It was Bonds' idea. Baker was thinking about it for a couple days and decided to try it, an attempt to get the slumping Kent some better pitches to hit.

Kent had a first-inning sacrifice fly and walked twice. Bonds saw his six-game homer streak end, but his hitting streak reached 12 games with two singles — a run-scoring liner after Kent walked and another that would have been a routine 4-3 out if it weren't for the ultra-exaggerated Bonds shift.

The Giants won the game, 5-1, defeating Randy Johnson and ending the horrendous 3-6 trip on a positive note — Bonds' nine homers notwithstanding.

"We just won, that's all that matters," Bonds said. "Sometimes you have to mix things up to get things going . . . If I don't hit any home runs and we win, then I won't hit any more."

CHAPTER SEVEN

It's No Stretch

May 24-June 11, Home Runs 25-32

*"This one was really hard because (McCovey) was
sitting in the first row. I'm like, 'Go home, you're
making me nervous' . . . It's great to hit 500 and 521
in McCovey's Cove. I really wanted to jump over the
fence and give him a hug and say, 'I hit it into your
Cove.' And the other neat thing is I got to do it in
Willie Mays' yard."*

Barry Bonds

BASEBALL MOVED WEST in 1958. The Giants moved to San Francisco and the Dodgers settled in Los Angeles. Willie Mays was already a full-fledged star. He'd already made "The Catch" — long before Joe Montana-to-Dwight Clark — in the 1954 World Series at the Polo Grounds to take away extra bases from Vic Wertz.

Mays already had four all-star appearances and one MVP trophy when he arrived in San Francisco with the Giants. The feeling among many locals, however, was that no matter how great Mays was, he still belonged to New York — and always would.

Willie McCovey was different. McCovey made his major-league debut in 1959 in San Francisco. He was the city's first baseball star and beloved from day one. His nickname was "Stretch" because of his mammoth size and ability to stretch for throws from infielders at first base. McCovey actually started as a left fielder, stationed next to Mays in center, as Giants managers went back and forth deciding who should play first base and who should play left field between McCovey and Orlando Cepeda, both future Hall of Famers.

The 1968 season was so dominated by pitchers, the rules were changed. The size of the mound was dropped from 15 inches to 10 inches high. The highest batting average was Carl Yastrzemski's .301 mark. Bob Gibson had a 1.12 ERA. Denny McClain won 31 games. Don Drysdale threw 59 2/3 consecutive scoreless innings. And even in this year, Willie McCovey hit 36 homers and drove in 105 runs — the best in the league in both categories.

McCovey followed that season by leading the league again with 45 homers and 126 RBIs in 1969, the first year Bobby Bonds was a starter and five-year-old Barry Bonds was a regular in the Giants clubhouse. McCovey was the Most Valuable Player that year.

Mother Pat Bonds would drop off Barry and younger brothers Rickey (one year younger) and Bobby, Jr. (six years younger) at the clubhouse on game days. Barry was immediately drawn to Willie Mays. He spent hours hanging out in his locker, playing catch with him in the outfield and shagging flyballs during batting practice.

When Barry roamed the Giants clubhouse, he didn't spend as much time with McCovey as he did with Mays. McCovey was big and intimidating. He didn't have the outgoing personality and engaging laugh as Mays. McCovey was a much quieter man. Young Barry wouldn't dare interrupt his preparation for games. But he idolized McCovey and daydreamed of the future.

McCovey played 22 seasons in the National League and finished with 521 home runs, six all-star game appearances, 18 career grand slams (second-most career to Lou Gehrig) and the most homers (231) at Candlestick Point history.

As the San Francisco Giants flew home from Arizona in the wee hours of May 23, Barry Bonds was three home runs from tying McCovey for career home runs — in his 15th season, seven fewer seasons than Stretch. McCovey wasn't upset that he was about to be passed on the all-time home run list, though.

"Once you've hung them up, that's all you can do," McCovey told the *Times*' Joe Roderick. "There's a lot of guys who were already ahead of me. There's a lot of guys who are not going to approach my record. Records are out there to be broken and eventually they're all going to be broken. I'd rather see him do it as a Giant than someone else. I held the record for 22 years."

The record is a little obscure. Not a lot of people paid it a lot of attention. McCovey is the owner of the homer record for left-handers in the National League — and remains very proud of it. Like everyone else, McCovey was in awe of what Bonds was accomplishing.

"Nobody has ever done what he's done," Stretch said. "We're watching history. Nobody has reached that total that quick."

In his first game back at 24 Willie Mays Plaza, it took Bonds three innings and two at-bats to give the home crowd a glimpse of what he'd been doing on the road the past week in Miami, Atlanta and Phoenix. Back in the lineup's third slot, his 25th homer came May 24 against Colorado's John Thomson.

And, what do you know, the Giants even won a game that Bonds homered.

"It's a show and we get to see it for free," Giants right fielder Armando Rios said. "I don't think he's ever been in better shape than he is right now. You just hope it's contagious and everybody else starts picking it up here and there."

The pitcher that night was Shawn Estes, a media darling because of quotes like this: "I probably would have been slighted if he didn't hit one tonight. It's almost like you expect him to hit a home run, and you're disappointed when he doesn't."

Bonds wasn't in much of a mood to relive his road trip with the columnists who watched the show from their television sets and now wanted to chime in their opinions now that the Giants were back home. And, of course, Barry got ripped for it.

Mark Purdy of the *San Jose Mercury News* wrote, "Such fun. Such swell fun. To see a performer at his peak, breathing the ether of near-perfection, making it happen appearance after appearance . . . Trouble is, in Bonds' case, it's also so sad. Because there's no way Barry Bonds will let you go along for the ride with him. No way. No how."

Purdy was hoping that Bonds would open up talk a little more about his homer streak. But just like most baseball players, Bonds didn't want to talk about his personal achievements when the team wasn't winning. That didn't make him all that unique. But he was getting ripped for it.

So, again, it was left to the manager to make the press happy. They were looking for an explanation of how Bonds continues to hit homers when pitchers don't want to get beat by him. And, again, Baker went back to his years with Hank Aaron to explain it in a way the press could understand.

Baker said, "I used to always ask Hank, 'how come I don't get the pitches you're getting?'"

The answer, Baker continued, is the worst thing for a hitter is a relaxed pitcher. And no pitcher in his right mind is relaxed when Hank Aaron or Barry Bonds is at the plate.

"So maybe a guy would try to throw a monster curve and it just spins up there," Baker said. "Or maybe he'd try to throw a 97 mph fastball when he can only throw 91 and there's no sink or movement on his pitch. All I know is, when I got up there (after Aaron hit), the ball was diving, darting, everything."

———————

The *ESPN The Magazine* story hit the Internet on May 29 for the issue dated June 11. Bonds had ended up sitting down and doing a 30-minute interview with reporter Jeff Bradley and was cooperative in the photo shoot. Bonds had a big smile on his face for the cover photo, under the headline: "Is Barry Bonds ready to be loved?"

Noting the standing ovation in Atlanta and the boos in Arizona when he was walked, Bradley wrote, "so it appears America may have room in its heart for Barry Bonds after all. Now, the question is, does Barry Bonds have room in his heart for America? Is he ready to be loved?"

Scouts aren't allowed to have their names used in stories because it's considered a form of tampering. But they are wonderfully opinionated and make for great copy. An NL advance scout who witnessed Bonds' destruction in Atlanta had the best quote in Bradley's story: "It wasn't even like watching big league games. It was like watching the six-foot kid in Little League, knowing if he put the bat on the ball, it was gone."

It wasn't just the media who had begun talking about 70 homers. All the scouts did that weekend in Atlanta also.

"Everyone knows it's his contract year, that he's hired Scott Boras for a reason, and that Barry motivates Barry," the scout told Bradley. "He's capable of hitting 75 out of spite, because he believes he hasn't gotten his due. That selfishness could help him. But you do wonder if he's capable of embracing the whole thing the way Mark and Sammy did in '98, accepting that he has to talk about it with the press. Mark had a little trial-and-error, but became a master of taking care of a story that was all about him in a way that didn't offend his teammates. Same with Sammy. Maybe Barry can learn from them, or maybe

Barry can do it his own way. But I think an injury is the only thing that will keep him from giving it a run."

Bradley asked Bonds if the standing ovation he received in Atlanta was the first of his career. In typical Bonds fashion, he replied that he's been playing the game for 15 years and can't remember. Perhaps it got Bonds thinking, though.

A month later, when Roy Firestone did an *Up Close* special on ESPN, Bonds glowingly talked about how much it meant to him that the Atlanta fans gave him the standing ovation — and how it was the first time any fans had ever done that.

As a sidebar, it's common for the author of the ESPN magazine's cover story to write something from a personal standpoint on the subject, which is called The Pulse.

Bradley wrote it would be easy for Bonds to change his bad guy persona by "managing the press" in the phony/unreal manner that Tiger Woods and Alex Rodriguez have learned to do — saying something politically correct and effective, while really saying nothing substantial. Bonds could do it and become more popular overnight.

"But personally," Bradley wrote, "I'd rather he just keep doing what he's been doing for the last 15 years. That is, hit home runs and be a prima donna. Make reporters jump through hoops to get 15 minutes of his time. Hit a ball 500 feet off Curt Schilling and tell the press, as he recently told me, 'even if I could explain how I did things like that, you still wouldn't understand because it's not something you can do.' I have no problem with that type of response, because it's honest . . .

"Put me on the list of people who wants to see Barry eclipse Mark McGwire's record 70," Bradley concluded, "as well as on the list of people who want him to remain true to himself."

———◆———

Ever the trooper, Willie McCovey patiently sat in the first row at Pacific Bell Park next to the Giants on-deck circle for all 18 innings of the Giants-Diamondbacks 1-0 game on May 29 — so he could be there in case Bonds passed him and Ted Williams on the all-time homer list.

Bonds' 26th for the season, and 520th in his career, came two days earlier, Sunday, May 27 against Denny Neagle. The homer put the Giants up 3-0, they won it 5-4 and were back to two games over .500 for the year. It was also the 12,000th home run in Giants franchise history.

The numerologists will have some fun with this info: The first home run in Giants history was hit by a guy named Monte Ward back in 1883. Ward hit 26 homers in his career. He was also a pitcher and gave up 26 homers in his career. And the 12,000th homer was Bonds' 26th of the season. Pretty cool, huh?

Bobby Bonds hit the 8,000th homer in Giants franchise history.

Barry also hit the 11,000th in franchise history.

Nikolai Bonds will probably hit the 14,000th.

McCovey usually sits in a luxury box because he doesn't get around very well these days and the elevators make it easier for him. But on the night he was so close to home plate it seemed his shadow covered the batters' box, the 18-inning game lasted five hours and 53 minutes, didn't end until 1:10 a.m. and the D'backs prevailed 1-0 in a game that rekindled memories of the legendary Juan Marichal-Warren Spahn duel in 1965.

Both pitchers went the distance that night and Willie Mays ended it with a solo homer to leadoff the 15th inning. Bonds had chances to match his godfather for ending a classic scoreless game, but was intentionally walked three times and went 0-for-5 — including a double-play grounder that was scored 6-5-3, the third baseman making the pivot at second base because of the exaggerated Bonds Shift.

The 18-inning game was on the heels of a 12-inning game the day before and Giants catcher Benito Santiago had caught all 30 innings. Santiago achieved legendary status when he told trainers and reporters at nearly 2 a.m., "I feel fine. I don't need no treatment. Hey man, I can go another 13 innings."

(Santiago's durability really doesn't have anything to do with this book about Bonds, but it was so cool it deserves mentioning.)

Our topic was Willie McCovey and "Stretch" was back in the same seat the next night, waiting for Bonds to knock him down a notch on the all-time list. Bonds walked into the clubhouse that night, passed me and a couple people and said to nobody in particular, "I'm still dying" as he walked over to his lockers.

McCovey didn't have to wait very long this night.

Back to batting cleanup again, as Baker was flip-flopping Bonds and Kent almost daily in the lineup, Bonds hit the first pitch of the second inning off Robert Ellis into — where else? — McCovey Cove and pointed to "Stretch" after crossing home plate. Four innings later, Bonds hit a 3-1 pitch to straightaway center off Ellis for a two-run homer that moved him into sole possession of 12th on the all-time list.

Bonds' homers accounted for the only three Giants runs in a 4-3 loss, completing an Arizona sweep, dropping the Giants back below .500 for the year and continuing a bittersweet stretch of homers for Bonds. The Giants were now 11-13 in games he'd homered.

"It's a great honor to have that accomplishment," Bonds said, in a press conference room, sitting next to McCovey. "But we're in the business of trying to get back to the postseason. It's really hard to really enjoy it. I know Willie would understand. It's really hard when you're not winning games."

Bonds reached over the railing and shook McCovey's hand after the second homer of the night.

"This one was really hard because (McCovey) was sitting in the first row," Bonds said. "I'm like, 'go home, you're making me nervous' . . . It's great to hit 500 and 521 in McCovey's Cove. I really wanted to jump over the fence and give him a hug and say, 'I hit it into your Cove.' And the other neat thing is I got to do it in Willie Mays' yard."

Bonds called it a, "dream come true" — his favorite phrases when the topic is Mays or McCovey.

"Ever since I was a little kid, my biggest dream was to play with these guys," Bonds said. "I just couldn't let you know how that feels as a child, wishing you could be on a certain team, wishing that you played with a certain player. To be able to do it in the same uniform as the men that you looked up to all your life is a blessing. I truly believe that the players I grew up around had something to do with this."

McCovey passed the torch to another Giant with pride.

"That's the thing I'm most proud of, he was able do it as a Giant and not as a Pirate," McCovey said. "I wouldn't be pulling for him if he was still with the Pirates. This stays in the family. I'm glad he did it here . . . I'm glad he was able to do it at home, while I was able to see it in person. Like he said, the main thing here is winning. I'm glad he got it over with, so now he can concentrate on winning."

McCovey wasn't the only famous left-handed slugger that Bonds passed on that evening. He also put Ted Williams in his rear-view mirror. In many ways, Bonds and Williams are similar.

Both had reputations for being surly with the media. Williams is the last player to bat over .400 in a season, hitting .406 in 1941 — but he lost the MVP that year in balloting by the baseball writers to Joe DiMaggio, who set a record that still stands for hitting in a remarkable 56 consecutive games that season.

Williams was the first player to see teams employ a "shift" against him. Opposing teams put three infielders on the first-base side because Williams was such a dead-pull hitter. And, like Bonds decades later, Williams refused to change his swing and try to dribble a single through the opposite way. Williams defied the shift by hitting through it or over it.

Many consider Williams the greatest hitter who ever played the game. DiMaggio, before his death, said it himself. Others will say Williams was the greatest fisherman, as well.

The point about their personalities is significant. Williams refused to tip his cap to the Fenway Park crowd upon hitting a home run in the final game of his career. He hated the writers and the feeling was mutual. But as Williams has aged over the years, you don't hear much about his personality. Only about his greatness as a hitter.

You can't help wonder if time will be as kind to Barry Bonds.

———

Coors Field has been called many things since opening its gate in 1995. "Coors Light" and "Hitters Paradise" are the two most popular. The ball carries at least 10 percent more in the thin altitude. Breaking pitches don't break as much. When free-agent pitchers Denny Neagle and Mike Hampton signed lucrative long-term contracts with the Rockies in the offseason, many believed they were committing career suicide.

To compensate for the ball traveling so far, the ballpark's designers pushed the fences back and made the outfield the most spacious in baseball. But all that has done is lend itself to more bloop hits, more gappers and more baserunners easily taking an extra base — leading to even more offense.

The possibilities of Bonds and his 28 homers-in-two-months hitting at Coors Field was titillating for fans and the media. But history was not on Bonds' side. For all the ballpark and altitude does to help hitters, Bonds has never quite warmed up to Coors Field. When he and the Giants arrived on June 1, Bonds' career average was .276 at Coors and he had "only" eight homers and 22 RBIs in 123 at-bats. However, Bonds does have his lone all-star game homer, in 24 at-bats, at Coors Field in 1998 off Cleveland's Bartolo Colon.

In the 2000 season, Bonds was just 4-for-31 (.129) against the Rockies and suffered a frightening back injury at Coors Field that was so painful, Bonds dropped to the ground as if he'd been shot after taking a swing. He laid motionless for nearly five minutes before he finally got up and was helped off the field. It was so serious all of us beat writers devoted our entire game stories to Bonds' condition and the consequences to the Giants. Bonds ended up missing four games, then returned to the lineup and promptly homered in his first game back.

The man does have a flair for the dramatic you can't deny.

The weekend in Coors was pretty uneventful from Bonds' standpoint. He did homer once, his 29th of the year, in the first game off Shawn Chacon, giving the Giants a 2-1 lead in a game they'd win 11-7 to start the series. But he was quiet the rest of the weekend, closer Robb Nen blew one game, the Giants lost another game and Jeff Kent summed up the state of the now 27-29 Giants this way: "we suck."

Thank goodness for the Padres. They were coming back into San Francisco for the second of three trips, their old friend Bobby J. Jones — who ended their playoff run the previous season with a one-hit, complete-game shutout — was the starting pitcher for the opener of a four-game series. That was good news for everybody in a Giants uniform, especially Bonds and Shawn Estes.

Bonds just missed a homer to dead center in his first at-bat, settling for a sacrifice fly that Mark Kotsay caught at the warning track. Bonds hit a ball in his next at-bat to just about the exact same place, only five feet deeper for a homer — his 14th in the last 18 games and 30th for the season. He was walked intentionally in the fifth and singled to right in the seventh. Estes pitched eight shutout innings, improbably took over the lead in the ERA department and the slumping Robb Nen had an adventurous ninth for the save.

How ridiculous was it getting? Well, Bonds was now on pace for 87 homers in the season and he was just getting warmed up.

The next night, June 5, Bonds singled on the first pitch he saw from Wascar Serrano in the second and came around to score. Jeff Kent walked in the third inning in front of Bonds' 31st homer that I described as a "scorching missile" in my game story. Why on earth the Padres were pitching to Bonds was beyond my grasp. Then they got smart. He was walked on four pitches in the fourth and sixth innings — and the crowd was unmerciful in their booing.

The ageless Benito Santiago, who was batting .318 at the time, turned the boos into cheers with a much-needed single that scored the go-ahead run and Armando Rios singled home an insurance run that was needed because Nen allowed a run in the ninth before getting the final out for the save.

"I can't remember the last time we've won two games in a row," Bonds said, after the June 5 win. The answer was May 23-24.

"We're all gonna hit," Bonds said. "Benito has been hitting all year. We just have to put it together at the right time."

Speaking of timing, ESPN wasn't too thrilled with Baker's decision to give Bonds the next day off. The self-proclaimed world wide leader in sports was unabashedly on the Bonds Bandwagon and the Giants were being shown to the nation just about every time ESPN had the opportunity.

When the media gathered around Baker in the Giants dugout on June 6, I joked that once ESPN saw the lineup card, they were going to televise a different game. I don't think Baker realized it was a joke.

"I already heard about it," said Baker, who made the lineup decision a few days earlier. "They don't tell me how to make out my lineup."

Baker's average was giving Bonds a day of rest about once every 10 days this season.

"He's at the age where you have to give him a day off every once in awhile, or you run the threat of losing him later," Baker said. "When a guy gets hurt, most of the time it's when he's fatigued."

Bonds wasn't needed on this night. The Giants scored two runs in each of the first three innings and that held up as they improved to 8-1 on the year against the Padres.

Meanwhile, in St. Louis, reporters were obviously figuring it was about time to get Mark McGwire's feelings on his three-year-old record getting challenged. This was McGwire's first printed statement:

"First of all, there's no reason to talk about it until someone hits 60 homers by September," McGwire said. "I always said to hit 61, you've got to hit 50 by September. And now, to break 70, you need 60 (by September). Before, people talked about how hard it was to hit 60, 61. Now they're talking about hitting 70 — like it was easier to hit 70."

Baker, as usual, looked like a prophet when Bonds returned to the lineup on June 7 — after his day of rest — and homered yet again, his 32nd of the season. Bonds was back in the third spot in the order, where he would remain for three months. He walked (on five pitches), doubled, lined out to first and hit a towering drive from reliever Brian Lawrence to dead center for a ball estimated to be 451 feet — the longest in Pac Bell's two-year history.

In the series, Bonds was 6-for-9 with four walks, three homers, a double, five runs and six RBIs. The Padres won the series finale, 10-7, and it was closer Trevor Hoffman striking out Bonds on a nasty changeup to end the game. As always, the post-game focus was still on Bonds. He was now at 32 homers after 60 games, a staggering pace of 86.

"I've never seen anything like this," Bonds said. "But I don't know what to say. I'm just trying not to separate things from the team. We played good for three days. You can't win every game . . . We won three in a row and I can't remember the last time we did that. We just need to put some more wins together."

Equally staggering, at least to me, was the number of homers he was hitting to straightaway center. His last three, four of his last five, and 13 overall, were to center. I asked Bonds why he's hitting so many to center this season.

"I have no idea what's going on," Bonds said. "I've never seen anything like this."

That goes for everybody.

CHAPTER EIGHT

Like Father, Like Son

June 12-21, Home Runs 33-38

*"Everywhere I go, people ask me, 'did you see what
Barry did today? They tell me the latest on what he's
doing. I hear that a lot more than I used to hear . . .
The whole country is watching him."*

Bobby Bonds

BOBBY BONDS was signed by the San Francisco Giants in 1964, the same year his son Barry was born in Riverside. Bobby reached the majors at age 22 in 1968, the year Bob Gibson had a 1.12 ERA and Olympic track stars Tommie Smith and John Carlos put a black glove on their hands and raised their arms above their heads on the medal stand as the national anthem played in a showing of "black power."

The San Francisco Giants opening day outfield in 1968 was Jim Ray Hart in left, Willie Mays in center and Jesus Alou in right. Willie McCovey played first base. Juan Marichal was the star pitcher. Gaylord Perry, one of four future Hall of Famers, was also on the staff.

These were the men who taught Barry Bonds the game of baseball.

Bobby hit a grand slam in his first game and quickly became one of baseball's brightest young stars. He was an everyday player by the end of the season and spent seven years with the Giants, making the all-star team in 1971 and getting named the Most Valuable Player of the 1973 midsummer classic. With his combination of power and speed, Bobby Bonds was labeled "the next Willie Mays."

The '73 season was the best of Bobby's career. He came in third in the Most Valuable Player voting with a .283 average, 39 homers, 96 RBIs and 43 stolen bases. One homer was taken away because of a rain out, costing him the distinction of becoming the first 40-40 player (of course, nobody considered this a big deal at the time).

Bobby won his fourth Gold Glove in 1974 and recorded his sixth consecutive season with at least 20 homers and 20 stolen bases, but it was his final season in San Francisco. If there was one pattern of the Giants in the early

1970s, it was signing talented young African-American outfielders and then trading them.

Bobby Bonds, George Foster, Garry Maddox and Gary Matthews were all traded away. The Giants never had anything good to show for them and all four had productive careers. Foster starred for the Big Red Machine in Cincinnati that won World Series in 1975 and 1976. Maddox was on the Phillies 1980 World Series team. Matthews led the Cubs to the division title in 1984.

Bobby Bonds' departure from San Francisco started a nomadic existence that would see him play for eight teams in the next eight years. The impact on Barry is difficult to determine. In some interviews, Barry said his dad moving around was cool because it allowed him to see a different part of the country every summer and take batting practice in different ballparks. In other interviews, Barry said he would sit at home and ask, "why isn't Dad home?"

Even when Bobby was home, Barry didn't understand his Dad was tired from traveling, tired from night games, and not always in the mood to take his kids to the arcade and batting cages as often as he did in the offseason.

Mother Pat was a fixture at all of Barry's youth games. Father Bobby was also at most of the games, but Barry never saw him. For fearing of stealing the crowd's attention, Bobby parked his car by trees in the outfield and watched games from there.

The baseball odyssey took Bobby Bonds to the New York Yankees in 1975, the California Angels for two seasons, a split between the Texas Rangers and Chicago White Sox in 1978, and the Cleveland Indians for his final productive season in 1979 (.275 average, 25 homers, 85 RBIs, 34 stolen bases).

Age and injuries were cruel to the elder Bonds. They started taking their toll in 1980 with the St. Louis Cardinals, limiting him to 86 games and contributing to a .203 average, five homers and 24 RBIs. Bonds played just 45 games with the Chicago Cubs in 1981, batted .215 with six homers, five steals and 19 RBIs. He was 35 years old. It was his final season in the major leagues.

Bobby Bonds finished his career with a lifetime .268 batting average, 332 homers, 1,024 RBIs and 461 stolen bases. And remember, he batted leadoff just about his entire career. He holds the single-season record for most homers (11) as a leadoff batter in a game. He was part of the 30-30 club five different times.

Bobby bristles at the suggestion he didn't live up to his "potential," a word that haunts the talented Bonds family.

"I was compared to Willie Mays, I was the next Willie Mays right from the beginning," Bobby said in an interview on the eve of the 1990 playoffs, after his son started living up to his so-called potential. "Anything I did that wasn't what Willie did meant I never lived up to my potential. I hit 30 home runs six or seven times and I didn't live up to my potential?

"I never compare myself with Barry. I told Barry right from the start, 'you are not the next Bobby Bonds, the next Willie Mays, the next Willie Stargell, the next Roberto Clemente; don't ever get caught with me and you.' I never met anyone from NBC, CBS or ESPN walking around with a Pulitzer Prize, so I guess they didn't live up to their potential.

"I think I had an outstanding career," Bobby continued. "I invented power from the leadoff spot. I drove in 100 runs leading off, yet I heard people say I didn't live up to my potential."

Barry has made bitter statements that history hasn't looked upon his father more favorably.

"You hear all this talk about Ken Griffey Jr. and his father, and the Ripkens," Barry said, also on the eve of the '90 playoffs. "But they haven't done anything compared to us. It's crazy, it's almost like my father is finally getting recognition now because of my accomplishments, and that hurts me.

"My dad is regarded as one of the greatest players in the game. He should be in the Hall of Fame. What Ken Griffey's done, what Cal Ripken's done, that's nothing. We're in the history books, man, for the first father-son to crack 30-30 . . . They never did my dad right. They never gave him the respect he deserves. Why should I believe things will be any different for me?"

———

Bobby Bonds was the Cleveland Indians hitting instructor and first-base coach between 1984-87. Then he was out of baseball for five years, nobody can exactly say why, until longtime family friend Dusty Baker hired him to be his hitting coach in 1993, Baker's rookie year as manager and Barry's first year with the Giants.

Besides the genes, Bobby taught his son how to think on the playing field and pick up a lot of little things most players never see.

"I played with Bobby in Chicago at the end of his career and I marveled at the little stuff I learned from him," Giants broadcaster Mike Krukow told *Santa Rose Press Democrat* beat writer Jeff Fletcher during the season. "He knew about pitchers tipping what's coming, middle infielders tipping. Middle infielders tip pitches more than anybody. Those guys (Bonds and his son) understand that stuff. They see the game in a different way."

In 1997, Bobby was replaced as batting coach and reassigned in the Giants organization, a decision that left his son bitter. Since then, Bobby has been a special assistant for the Giants minor league system. He travels around the country instructing and teaching minor leaguers, which was allowing him to catch about 85 percent of the Giants games in person or on his satellite dish.

Even when he missed a game in 2001, it wasn't taking Bobby long to find out what his son did — in airports, hotels or taxi cabs.

"Everywhere I go, people ask me, 'did you see what Barry did today?' "Bobby told me, in an interview on Fathers' Day. "They tell me the latest on what he's doing. I hear that a lot more than I used to hear . . . The whole country is watching him."

Even as a former hitting coach, Bobby was like the rest of the country in not having a definitive answer on why Barry was demolishing so many pitches over the fence this season.

"You don't try to figure it out," he said. "You have to remember, he came into this season with almost 500 home runs, not five. The capability is there. It's not surprising. But it's amazing. There's a difference between surprising and amazing. Take Mark McGwire. When he hit 70, was it surprising? No. Was it amazing? Yes. Same with Sammy Sosa. It's amazing because it doesn't happen all the time."

Bobby passed along a naturally weary eye toward his son when it comes to dealing with the media. For example, Bobby wouldn't let me use a tape recorder in the interview. My note taking is decent enough, but I'm unconvinced any reporter can get every word somebody says — especially somebody who talks as fast as Bobby Bonds — with shorthand or furious scribbling. I tried to explain this to Bobby, but he only agreed to this interview if I put the tape recorder away.

"I'm just as happy as any other father," Bobby said. "My son is doing something to make me very proud. But any father that is able to see his son do something he always wanted, you're proud. You don't have to be Barry's dad to be proud of your son. I'm sure your father is proud of you being a journalist, doing something you always wanted."

Bobby also talked to the *Times'* Joe Roderick on Father's Day and told him, "He doesn't think about it and I don't think about it. This is June. It's too early to talk about those things. It's not something he's even considered. People have to understand that the Giants are going to be playing almost all division games in September. Do you think they're going to pitch to him then? They're not pitching to him now. There are a lot of things you have to consider — injuries, the standings, his swing. There are lot of things that could prevent him from doing it."

If you noticed, Bobby never said "the record." It was always "*it*" — a pattern that a lot of superstitious baseball types were now using with Barry Bonds.

Over 150,000 fans turned out for the Giants-A's series at the now-corporately named Network Associates Coliseum the weekend of June 8-9-10. The A's won two of three games in the meeting of Bay Area rivals. The Giants only victory came with the aid of a passed ball in the ninth inning and a Barry Bonds intentional walk that set the stage for a game-winning Jeff Kent single in the 11th inning.

Bonds kept hitting the ball hard — three line shots, two in the final game that died at the warning track — but he had just one hit and was held without a homer for the first series since May 7-10 against the Expos, and just the second series all year.

The two Bay Area teams were heading in opposite directions, dramatized by a team meeting called by Shawon Dunston that lasted 48 minutes after the game had ended. The Giants, unable to find itself and now 31-32, wouldn't reveal many details from the closed-door meeting. Bonds blew off the press entirely after the game.

It was left to Kent, ever the team spokesman, to address the media — even though it was unlikely that he said even one word, let alone paid close attention, to whatever words were spoken in the meeting.

"This team, this organization, has always played for the long haul," Kent told a huge crowd of reporters. "It's always played baseball through September. We're not worried about where we are now. We're not worried about what articles are being written about us, who is getting fired, who wants to be traded. We've never worried about that. We're not a 'poor-me' team. We don't play that way. We keep battling. (We're just) making sure our attitude doesn't falter, making sure we maintain a certain respect for the game. We just covered a lot of things. That's what a team meeting is all about."

Manager Dusty Baker used the interleague games in Oakland to make Barry Bonds the designated hitter, giving him what Tony La Russa called "a half-day off" when he managed in the American League. Bonds was the designated hitter in two games, played left field once, then enjoyed the Giants' day off on June 11.

"He should be a lot stronger now," Baker predicted before the June 12 game against the Anaheim Angels. "You'll see the effects this week."

That Baker really is something with his predictions.

On the first pitch Bonds saw, his lightning quick bat turned on an inside fastball from Pat Rapp in the first inning and wrapped it just inside the foul pole for No. 33 on the year. Typical of Bonds' bombs, this one kept rising after it cleared the 20-foot high fence and splashed into McCovey Cove. It was the 15th all-time "Splash Hit" in 1.5 years — and 11th by Bonds.

"I felt really, really good," Bonds said, when asked about the recent rest. "I hope I get to do it again."

Was that a clue the free agent-to-be Bonds could be playing for an American League team next season, whereby he can DH more often?

"We're not at that point," Bonds said, smirking. "Yet."

The Giants beat the Angels 3-2 that night. They won 1-0 behind the pitching of Russ Ortiz and the home run by team-meeting caller Shawon Dunston the next night. And they completed the sweep with a 10-4 victory that was highlighted by Bonds' 34th homer and nearly his 35th.

A two-out walk by Angels starter Ismael Valdes to Bonds in the first inning wasn't smart. It ignited a two-run rally. Bonds doubled in the second inning, just missing a homer with one of those liners that in years past would go off the wall, but were staying up and going over fences this year. Bonds was intentionally walked in the fourth to load the bases and Kent tripled home three runs on a ball that sure-handed centerfielder Darin Erstad inexplicably missed with his glove. Then with the Giants leading 6-3 in the sixth, somebody named Louis Pote decided to go after Bonds, and homer 34 was crushed to the deepest part of Pac Bell.

"That whole team is not Barry Bonds," a slightly irritated Angels manager Mike Scioscia said. "He's a huge part of it. But a guy like Kent has 50 RBIs. They have (J.T.) Snow back and (Rich) Aurilia is killing the ball. If you make the decision to not give Barry anything to hit, which is the way to go, you have to take care of the rest of the lineup. We didn't get that done today."

Long before the Giants swept three games from the Angels, general manager Brian Sabean was keeping himself busy with ways to retool his ballclub. Disappointing catcher Bobby Estalella was designated for assignment and sent to Triple-A Fresno. Reliever Alan Embree was dumped in a trade to the White Sox. And now Russ Davis, a quiet third baseman liked by his teammates and the media, was designated for assignment before the Giants-A's rematch at Pac Bell.

Sabean was just getting warmed up, doing some house cleaning that was setting the stage for his wheeling and dealing the next month.

Barry Bonds didn't take long to add the A's to his victim list when the teams met again across the bay the following weekend at Pacific Bell Park.

Mark Mulder fell behind 3-1 in the first inning and threw a fastball on the outside corner. Bonds hit it over the left-centerfield fence for his 35th homer of the season. Bonds singled in the third and then Mulder tried to go inside on Bonds with a 1-1 pitch in the sixth. Bonds pulled it down the line for his 36th homer. Two solo homers for Bonds and the Giants were 3-1 winners.

"It wasn't like I was throwing cookies out there," Mulder said. "The first (Bonds homer) was a 3-1 fastball away, a pretty good pitch. I was going after him to try to make him hit a home run away, and he did it. The second one was a mistake, a slider that just didn't move. It was down, but it was out over the middle of the plate."

How on earth do you pitch to Bonds at a time like this?

"Just walk him," Giants starter Shawn Estes said, laughing. Estes went on to say something about mixing pitches inside and outside and I interrupted him.

"That's exactly what Mulder did tonight," I told Estes. "He pitched him away and Barry hit it out to left. He pitched him inside and Barry pulled it down the line. What can you do?"

"I'd probably throw him changeups, get him ahead on his front foot," Estes said, "and I'd cross my fingers."

Estes kept talking and the crowd of reporters mobbed Bonds as he came out of the shower. But I continued talking with Estes because he's always honest and insightful. Estes explained Bonds' zone to me like this:

"I'll make probably 10 mistakes a game," Estes said. "Maybe one or two will get hit for a base hit, maybe one will get hit out of the park. If I make 10 mistakes to Barry Bonds, he'll hit nine home runs right now."

It was officially impossible to pitch to Barry Bonds. Or so was my theory.

And proving my theory, A's pitchers held Bonds hitless the next two games of the series, walking him twice. The Giants won two more games without their star doing anything, sweeping the series and running their winning streak to six games as they headed back to San Diego.

Back in St. Louis, McGwire was already showing signs of impatience as reporters asked him about Bonds' amazing pace — now at 85 after the weekend series against the A's.

"That's all it is, a pace," McGwire said. "It's virtually impossible to keep up with what he's doing. I find it very hard to believe managers are going to give him pitches to hit. Personally, I wish him the best of luck. I know how difficult it's going to be. Until he or somebody has 60 by September . . . I can't emphasize that enough. Do you realize, once he gets to 40, how difficult those next 31 are going to be? That's what people don't understand."

Something about home run "pace" needs to be clarified because the media talked a lot about Bonds' pace during the season and you'll hear a lot more about pace in this book. Proper credit goes to Mike Klis of the *Denver Post* who reminded me, and many others, something about McGwire's season.

Almost every newspaper was starting to run daily graphic boxes by mid-June that showed how many homers Bonds had hit through the Giants number of games, then compared that to how many homers McGwire had after the same number of games in 1998.

That method is flawed because McGwire played in 163 games in 1998. One game that season was postponed because of rain with the score tied after five innings and never completed. Since the score was tied, the entire game is replayed. The stats from the rained-out game and the makeup game are both used, which is how a 163rd game is possible.

Mac had 65 homers through 160 games in 1998. He hit one in game No. 161, two in game No. 162 and two more in game 163 to finish with 70.

Barring a rainout or one-game playoff, Bonds was only going to play in 162 games. So judging him from McGwire's 1998 pace — for instance, "Bonds is two games ahead of McGwire's pace" — wasn't practical. It was more accurate to project how many Bonds would hit if he continued hitting homers at the same frequency the rest of the season, even though just about everybody believed it was humanly impossible to maintain that same consistency all season.

OK, with the pace stuff clear, now back to McGwire.

He wasn't doubting Bonds' chances. He was just criticizing the media for making such a big deal about it — just as he'd done from April through August of his record-breaking 1998 season.

"You can't say yes, you can't say no," McGwire said. "If somebody gets lucky enough to have 60 home runs by September, they have a legitimate shot. Until then, they don't. I find it quite hilarious that for 37 years, people treated 61 like nobody will ever get to it. And I was lucky enough to reach 70 and now they're talking about 70 like it's a piece of cake."

———————

Barry Bonds was making home runs look like a piece of cake and the whole country was now officially watching him. On June 19, the Giants were in San Diego to play the Padres. Yet after a Dodgers game against Arizona, the callers on the Dodgers post-game show only wanted to talk about Bonds — not their own team.

Was Bonds worthy of breaking McGwire's record? Does Bonds' pursuit cheapen or taint McGwire's record? Is Bonds a jerk? Does Bonds' personality make it difficult for fans to love him and support him the way they unequivocally cheered for McGwire and Sammy Sosa in 1998?

These were the questions that were debated on North American airwaves, inside bars and barber shops, throughout the stands and even clubhouses of ballparks.

It was also the debate I had with my friend, Ferris Shahrestani, as we drove to San Diego during a brief break in my season to visit our friends from college. Ferris is a life-long A's fan, reveled in the Bash Brother years of the A's in the late 1980s and was swept up in the emotion of the McGwire-Sosa chase in 1998. Ferris felt so strongly that he didn't want Bonds to break the record, he told me was making a voodoo doll to stop Bonds — and still believes to this day that it worked.

A Canadian radio station called my cell phone that day and asked me to come on the air and talk about Bonds. I was in the parking lot of Qualcomm Stadium and getting heckled with a few "beauty, ehh?" lines from my friends. Most of the questions were about Bonds' personality, how he was "handling" all the extra media attention and whether he was "worthy" of holding such a presitigous record.

If I remember correctly, I chickened out and responded something like, "well, that's a question for the fans to answer and I think we're going to find out before the end of the season."

A night later, I thought I'd get a break from the "All Barry, All the Time" existence I was living. I went inside a club in downtown San Diego with newlywed friends Greg and Rachel Block. It was the type of club that is about dancing and techno music and cosmopolitan drinks for women in short black skirts; the type of club that has no pretense of being a place for sports fans to mingle. So imagine my surprise when I overheard two women and a male standing next to the dance floor and talking about whether Bonds would break the record — and whether they wanted to see him do it.

The debate wasn't going away unless Bonds stopped hitting homers. And Bonds still wasn't slowing down. His 37th came June 19 in San Diego, a shot down the right field line that had Tony Gwynn and the Padres amazed at how

Bonds was able to keep the inside fastball by Adam Eaton fair. The Giants lost that game, 4-3, in 15 innings, another difficult extra-inning loss.

During batting practice the next day, Rickey Henderson, the best stolen-base thief of all time, went into the Giants dugout, stole all the Bonds bats he could find and took them away. The thief waved the bats toward Bonds' way and taunted him near the cage, before Bonds came over and wrestled the bats away from Henderson.

"I need to disinfect these," Bonds said aloud. "If I don't get a hit tonight, I'm going to . . ."

Realizing he had a big audience of players and media, Bonds didn't finish the sentence, but started blowing on the bats and wiping away Henderson's .215 batting average germs.

Disinfecting wasn't needed. Bonds hit his 38th that night off Rodney Myers, a two-run homer in the eighth to extend a 5-3 lead and the Giants won. Bonds also broke up a heated disagreement that nearly turned into a fight in the dugout between Armando Rios and Rich Aurilia. Rios, who keeps track of his numbers pretty closely, thought Aurilia should have tried to score from second on a single. Aurilia was held by third-base coach Sonny Jackson.

Bonds doesn't normally break up fights. He's the biggest on the team, so it's a good idea for him to get between the two teammates though. Even though he broke up the fight, it's pretty doubtful that Bonds helped mediate the talks between the two players, who smoothed things over a day later.

Bonds was rested before the finale of the series, which the Giants won, a smart idea by Baker, considering the attention that was awaiting him in St. Louis.

"They probably will boo me because Mark McGwire is their guy," Bonds said, predicting the scene. "Why wouldn't they boo me? He's their man. That record belongs in St. Louis. He broke it in that uniform. If I were in St. Louis, I'd boo anyone who threatened my guy's record. But they don't have to worry."

They don't have to worry, Bonds kept insisting, because he's not chasing McGwire and he has "not a chance" of breaking McGwire's record.

"The gut feeling in my heart, I don't think so," Bonds said. "I'm not Mark McGwire. I'm just not that powerful a hitter. Mark is so much stronger than I am. The difference is, even when Mark is tired, the ball goes 520 feet. When I'm tired, or a normal guy is tired, it goes 230 feet. Mark hits the ball out of the park and we hit it to the shortstop. If someone was as big and strong as he was, I'd probably say that person has a chance. Mark can miss a ball and hit a home run. We can't miss a ball and hit a home run.

"I do have a good chance to get 50 for the first time," Bonds added with a laugh.

Barry wasn't sure what he'd say to McGwire when they saw each other. But Dusty Baker knew he wanted to pick the mind of Tony La Russa, his manager when his playing career ended with the Oakland A's in 1986, about how to handle the media circus the home-run chase brings.

"I was there for Hank Aaron," Baker said. "But that was different because I was a player, not a manager, and there weren't 82 newspapers. There wasn't CNN, ESPN, Fox Sports, Fox Northwest, Fox Southeast, Fox Northeast, Fox Central, Fox South."

Everybody laughed and Baker, not missing a cue, replied, "That's the truth."

CHAPTER NINE

Big Mac's Land

June 22-28, Home Run 39

"My godfather (Willie Mays) won't talk to me, my dad won't talk to me, Willie McCovey won't talk to me. It's the loneliest thing I've ever gone through in my entire life. Nobody returns my phone calls. The only people who talk to me are my kids. My daughter gives me home-run tips from her seat. She tells me to keep my hands high."

Barry Bonds

MARK McGWIRE WAS inching closer and closer to 61 homers. As a rookie in 1987, McGwire burst onto the scene by bashing 33 homers at the all-star break. He tailed off in the second half, still finishing with an impressive 49 for the year — a rookie record that still stands.

From 1988-92, McGwire averaged 34 home runs a season on Oakland A's teams that won four division titles, three AL pennants and one World Series championship. The next two seasons were painful. Heel and back injuries kept McGwire on the disabled list for all but a combined 74 games. He just hit nine homers each season. It was during this time he contemplated retirement. It was also during this time that McGwire studied the game and learned patience and set the stage for a career renaissance.

Finally healthy in 1996, McGwire hit 52 homers for the last-place Oakland A's. At the all-star game that season in Philadelphia, he put on one of the most impressive home-run shows in history, for both frequency and distance, and reached the finals. Worn out from the early rounds, however, McGwire hit just one in the final round, Barry Bonds hit two on two swings to win the contest — and McGwire gave him an enormous bear hug that, we're only half-kidding here, might be the root of Bonds' back problems to this day.

In 1997, McGwire was again healthy and again bashing homers at a frequency that had fans and media bringing up the name Roger Maris and his record of 61 homers. The media's speculation wasn't just focused on how many homers McGwire would hit. It was also which uniform McGwire would be wearing when it happened. A free agent when the season ended, it was widely assumed, and known, the A's would not be able to re-sign McGwire. They were in a rebuilding phase with young players and McGwire wanted to win immediately.

On July 31, the waiver-wire trading deadline, then-A's general manager Sandy Alderson shipped McGwire to St. Louis, where he was reunited with his former skipper in Oakland, Tony La Russa, for pitchers T.J. Mathews, Blake Stein and Eric Ludwick. At the time, McGwire had 34 homers in 105 games. Between the intense speculation on where he would be traded, then learning new pitchers in a new league after the subsequent trade, McGwire went 71 at-bats without a homer and fell off the Maris pace.

Switching leagues was something McGwire wanted to avoid. Earlier in the season, he'd ruled out a trade to any NL team — and as a player with 10 years in the league (the last five with the same team) he had the power to veto any trade. The presence of La Russa, not to mention many other former coaches, players and even the trainer from Oakland, convinced McGwire to accept the trade to St. Louis.

It wasn't just the new pitchers McGwire had to learn. He was adjusting to a new city, a Midwest style of life greatly different for the man who spent his entire life in California. But the crowd support at Busch Stadium, and everywhere around the baseball-crazed city of St. Louis, quickly won over McGwire's heart. He signed a four-year, $36-million contract extension on September 16 and celebrated with a 517-foot homer against Los Angeles.

Mac found his long ball swing and finished with 24 homers in St. Louis, giving him 58 for the season. If it weren't for the two-week slump that coincided with the trade, perhaps McGwire would have set the record. Or perhaps he'd have never gotten that close without the enormous support in St. Louis, a drastic difference from the small crowds in Oakland.

Nonetheless, from day one of the 1998 season, all eyes were focused on McGwire.

He started quickly, hitting a grand slam on Opening Day and four homers in four games to start the year. McGwire had 27 homers on June 1, 37 on July 1, and 45 on August 1.

As the attention intensified, however, McGwire withdrew in his comments and enthusiasm. He was uncomfortable being the sole focus of the media. He didn't want to distract from the team. As word spread of his incredible batting-practice shows and fans began turning out in record numbers two hours before the game, McGwire said he felt like "a caged animal" in the batting cage.

When the media kept asking him about Roger Maris and 61 homers, McGwire constantly replied that it was only about the team — and there was no story until somebody reached 50 homers by September 1.

Well, by September 1, McGwire had 55 homers. And McGwire had company in the pursuit of Roger Maris. Twelve days earlier, the Chicago Cubs' Sammy Sosa took over the home run lead with his 48th homer in the fifth inning of a game against Mac's Cardinals. McGwire tied Sosa in the eighth inning of the same game and hit a game-winning homer in the 10th to reclaim the lead. The two continued a frenzied pace that electrified the nation.

Big Mac launched his 56th and 57th homers on September 1 in Florida, then 58th and 59th on September 2. Five days later, McGwire tied Maris' record in St. Louis off Mike Morgan. The next day, August 8 at 8:18 p.m. CDT, McGwire broke Maris' record with a line drive that barely cleared the wall off Steve Trachsel of the Cubs.

The delay in the game, it should be noted to the Dodgers and Terry Adams, was 11 minutes. McGwire went into the stands and hugged the Maris boys, who were in attendance. As part of the celebration, Sosa spontaneously sprinted in from right field and gave McGwire a hug. It was an amazing moment in baseball history.

Sosa's involvement in the great home run chase was a welcome surprise. Originally signed as a 17-year-old kid in the Dominican Republic by the Texas Rangers, Sosa never put up these types of power numbers in the minors. He was traded to the Chicago White Sox in 1989 and across town to the Cubs in 1992. From 1993-1997, Sosa developed into a bona fide power hitter, averaging 34 homers with a high of 40.

Still, his slow start offered no clue of his eventual total. Sosa had just 13 homers on June 1. Then he hit a record 20 homers in the month of June, and nine more in July gave him 42.

Sosa's personality was far different than McGwire's. He was willing to do interviews before games, after games and it didn't matter for how long. He smiled, he laughed, he joked, he told the media, "baseball been very very good to me."

Repeatedly, Sosa would call McGwire, "the man."

In essence, Sosa had fun with it. McGwire was left with no choice. He was forced to have fun with it. So he did. And the final two months provided a classic duel between two sluggers.

"We were mad if they didn't have it on the JumboTron during games because we were all excited about it," Barry Bonds said. "It was something that you never thought would happen and you've got two guys doing it at the same time. That was incredible and they kept switching positions. One goes ahead of the other, and the other comes back and hits two homers. It was almost like a Muhammad Ali boxing match."

Sosa, once again, briefly overtook McGwire for the lead with his 66th in Houston on September 25, the third-to-last game of the season. Forty-five minutes later, McGwire tied Sosa with his 66th off Montreal's Shayne Bennett in St. Louis. Expos manager Felipe Alou instructed his young pitchers to challenge McGwire the entire series. McGwire hit two on Saturday to reclaim the lead and two more on Sunday to finish with a whopping 70 — a finish of 23 in his final 40 games.

Out of respect to the New York Mets and Giants, who were competing with the Cubs for a wild-card berth, the soon-to-be NL Central champion Houston Astros had to play games to win that final weekend — and that meant pitching much more conservatively to Sosa and he went homerless the final two games of the season to finish with 66 homers.

———•——•———

Reporters from all over the country descended on St. Louis on June 22, 2001 for the much-anticipated McGwire-Bonds show. Five hours before first pitch, the line outside the media entrance at Busch Stadium was already forming. It was 15 minutes before a Bonds press conference was supposed to start and the gates still weren't open. One angry local cameraman tried convincing others to join him through another door and exclaimed, "They can't stop us if we all go at once!"

As it turned out, there would be order. Bonds was brought to an interview room by the Cardinal clubhouse, and journalists were there from newspapers ranging from Indianapolis to New York, plus ESPN and the local television stations.

Agent Scott Boras was there. Bonds was charming, humorous, self-deprecating and emotive during the first of what Giants media relations officials had planned as periodic question-and-answer sessions before the game — so Bonds could answer all the questions once and avoid having wave after wave of reporters coming by his locker asking the same questions before each game.

The same thing was done for McGwire three years earlier. If similar things were done for Roger Maris back in 1961, it would have made a big difference.

Like a politician, Bonds stuck to his stump speech on McGwire's 3-year-old record: "I don't want his record. I want his (World Series) ring. Well, I don't want his ring. I want my own."

The most fascinating revelation by Bonds might explain his new-found friendliness with the media.

"You are the only guys who talk to me," Bonds said, laughing. "My godfather (Willie Mays) won't talk to me, my dad won't talk to me, Willie McCovey won't talk to me. It's the loneliest thing I've ever gone through in my entire life. Nobody returns my phone calls. The only people who talk to me are my kids. My daughter gives me home-run tips from her seat. She tells me to keep my hands high."

McGwire did an informal round of interviews with the media inside the Cardinals clubhouse. Mac wasn't very happy to be doing the interviews. For one thing, he was injured again and not playing well. For another, he continued to admonish reporters for making such a big deal about it so soon.

In handicapping Bonds' chances of breaking his record, McGwire did say that Bonds has an "excellent chance," but continued to criticize the media for hopping on the story's bandwagon so soon.

"You have Rich Aurilia having an outstanding year over there and he's not getting talked about," McGwire said. "Their team is coming around right now and they're going to be fighting for the West. It is sort of disturbing. This is a team sport."

Aurilia was getting talked about plenty — at least in the Bay Area. His blistering start, combined with a friendliness that earned him the "good guy award" by Giants beat writers the year before, was just about the only other positive with the Giants up-and-down season to date worth writing about.

Aurilia, 29, had a lifetime .270 batting average, but was hitting .354 at the time and was the leading vote-getter for shortstops in the National League.

McGwire called Bonds' first three months, a "fantastic, outstanding year so far, remarkable. You can't put it into words. What he's doing right now is unbelievable. What he's done is just incredible. At this point right now he's surpassed anything I've done. It's remarkable watching him from the other side . . . He's got an excellent chance of doing it. He's got two things going for him. He's very healthy and he's getting really good pitches to hit. That's what it takes.

"You call them records for a reason, right?" Big Mac continued. "They're meant to be broken. Ever since I saw the movie '61*' the most disturbing thing I saw was how the New York media treated Roger Maris and how the commissioner put an asterisk next to the record. If somebody is lucky enough to break it, there's nothing I can do. Right now, it's pure speculation. The second half of the year is the toughest time in baseball. If you're in the pennant race, and he's the main guy on that team, if you're the manager on the other team you don't let him win the game."

Put another way, the Giants wouldn't be playing the Expos the final week of the season with Felipe Alou instructing his pitchers to go after Bonds because neither team was trying to make the playoffs.

"Everything has to be so right," McGwire said. "From what I'm seeing and what I'm reading, for 37 years you guys were writing about how difficult it was to hit 62 homers. And now you guys are writing that hitting 70 is like hitting 62. I find it quite hilarious."

———•◦•◦•———

Barry Bonds and Bobby Bonilla first met at Class-A Prince William of the Carolina League in 1985. Despite their different backgrounds, they hit it off immediately and became close friends.

Bonds was the California kid who grew up in an upper-middle class white neighborhood and spent his days at Candlestick Park hanging around Willie Mays. Bonilla was from a tough neighborhood in the Bronx and he spent his days simply dreaming of how to escape the life he knew.

Bonilla was traded from the Pittsburgh Pirates organization to the Chicago White Sox, then wisely reacquired by then-GM Syd Thrift midway through his 1986 rookie season, the same year Bonds made his major-league debut.

"We're real tight," Bonilla said in a 1988 interview. "When we're in San Francisco, I stay at Barry's place with his folks and he does the same when we're in New York. We've just hit it off well since we first met. We've been friends right from the start."

Bonilla was a media darling from the beginning, the happy-go-lucky kid from the Bronx who figured the worst day in the majors was still 10 times better than a bad day in the Bronx. As Bonds came into his own in 1990, many reporters found themselves getting turned away by Bonds for an interview, or not getting much out of the interview, then heading over to Bonilla and having him save the story.

It was Bonilla who made the quicker impact in the majors. The switch-hitting Bonilla was an all-star in 1988 at age 25 and finished the season with a .280 average, 32 homers and 120 RBIs.

Bonds came into his own in 1990 batting behind Bonilla, and the MVP race came down to the close friends. But this wasn't like the 2000 MVP race between Bonds and Jeff Kent. Bonilla told reporters that Bonds was the MVP, because while their offensive numbers were similar, Bonds had 52 steals and played Gold Glove defense.

Bonds finished first. Bonilla was second. The duo took immense pride in being the best No. 4-5 hitters of a lineup in baseball. They also took great pride in finding ways to motivate each other.

Quite often, as Bonilla started walking to home plate in the first inning, Bonds would say to him, "are you going to get on base this game or should I just put my helmet and bat away right now?"

Eager to shut up his good friend, Bonilla would inevitably get three or four hits in the game. Bonds would smile because that meant more RBI chances for him.

Like his friend, Bonilla also struggled in playoff losses to the Cincinnati Reds and Atlanta Braves, hitting a combined .250 (11-for-44) with no homers and two RBIs in 13 games.

Bonilla was the first to defect Pittsburgh, cashing in on free agency after the

1991 season to sign a five-year contract with the New York Mets. Going home wasn't what Bonilla expected.

The aggressive and larger New York media was much different than the media in Pittsburgh, and that ever-persistent smile was sometimes wiped off his face. In the worst moment, television cameras rolled as Bonilla approached a reporter and asked him to take a swing at him. The Mets, in those years, were a mess. All the hitting stars from their 1980s playoff teams were gone. Only Sid Fernandez and Dwight Gooden remained on the pitching staff and neither was the pitcher they once were.

Bonilla was expected to make up for the loss of Darryl Strawberry, who signed with his hometown Los Angeles Dodgers as a free agent in 1991, but he struggled in his first year, batting .249 with 19 homers and 70 RBIs. Like he did with people who criticized his dad, Bonds defended his friend's season by telling reporters that players like Howard Johnson had much worse sub-par seasons than Bonilla.

One problem, that has continued to this day, is Bonilla doesn't have an ideal position. He was tried at third base, right field, left field and first base over the years. His best position is probably the outfield, but he isn't great at any of them.

Bonilla rebounded with all-star seasons in 1993 and 1995, the fifth and sixth all-star game appearances of his career, and was traded to the Baltimore Orioles at the trading deadline in 1995. He remained productive, driving in 116 runs in 1996 and was a member of a team that lost in the playoffs to the Yankees.

Bonilla signed with the Florida Marlins in 1997, an expansion team in just its sixth year of existence. It reunited him with former Pirates manager Jim Leyland and proved the wisest decision of his baseball life.

Owner Wayne Huizenga went on a major spending spree before the '97 season, adding Bonilla, pitcher Kevin Brown, outfielders Moises Alou and Gary Sheffield, plus veterans Darren Daulton and Jim Eisenreich, and signing Cuban defector Livan Hernandez for the pitching staff.

The Marlins won the wild card, Bonilla batted .333 and hit a homer to help sweep Barry Bonds and the Giants in the division series. The Marlins upset the Braves in the championship series and defeated the Cleveland Indians in seven games of one of baseball's best World Series ever.

It proved to be the last productive season of Bonilla's career.

Huizenga tore apart the franchise in that offseason, forcing general manager David Dombrowski to trade away all the high-priced players so the team would be easier to sell. Bonilla was among those traded, getting shipped to the Los Angeles Dodgers in the season.

Bonilla has since played for the Mets again (1999), the Atlanta Braves (2000) and signed with the St. Louis Cardinals in 2001. Injuries and age have turned Bonilla into a part-time player who has averaged seven homers and 30 RBIs from 1998-2000.

Through the years, Bonds and Bonilla have remained best friends. When they were young players in the league, they stayed at each other's parents' houses on the road. Now they are both millionaires many times over and still often stay at each other's houses.

Bonilla used to show off his World Series ring to Bonds, but he doesn't anymore. He knows how much his friend craves one and how it depresses him to not have one.

———

For the big Bonds-McGwire showdown at Busch Stadium, a fan held up a sign for the opener of the three-game series on June 22 that read: "70 is Magnificent. 39 is Junk Bonds."

The local hero McGwire gave a reminder he was still the home-run king, blasting another 500-plus-foot blast off Livan Hernandez in the eighth inning. Bonds was held hitless (he was walked three times, once intentional), but the Giants still won easily, 10-5, in the opener of the series.

As he left the ballpark, Bonds talked to Bob Nightengale of *USA Today Baseball Weekly*, in town to do a cover story, and admitted to the scribe he wasn't sure how he's supposed to act with so much new attention.

"Do you think I should change?" Bonds asked Nightengale. "Should I change? I mean, if I changed and started acting nicer to people, what will people think of me?"

Nightengale told him that people will think he is phony and it's insincere.

"I just wish people would accept me for who I am," Bonds said. "Why should I change? Why should I stop being honest? Look, I'm not going to be somebody I'm not. I just won't do it. I don't care what people say or what the media portrays me to be, I'm proud of who I am. The Bible says you don't have to be nice, or not nice. Just speak the truth. Jesus always spoke the truth. Not everybody liked him, either."

Later that night, Bonds and Bobby Bonilla, his former Pirates teammate and best friend, went to a club in St. Louis.

"I've never received that much attention at one time," Bonds said. "You get it here or there. But nothing like I saw in St. Louis. And the people there were really nice. It seemed like everybody in the entire club said hello and congratulated me. Some said they hope I break it. Some said they hope I don't break it. But they all congratulated me anyway. They were all nice. It was different."

Indeed, life was very different for Barry Bonds. The next day, he hit yet another homer, his 39th, off former all-star Darryl Kile, a solo homer in the first inning. That continued the ongoing record for most homers by the all-star break.

The Cardinals scored three runs in the eighth off the usually reliable Felix Rodriguez to take a 5-4 lead, the Giants tied the game in the top of the ninth and the Cardinals won it, 6-5, with a run in the ninth off Robb Nen.

ESPN, continuing to televise Barry whenever possible, picked the Cardinals-Giants game for its Sunday national game. Barry and Big Mac both went 0-for-4, the Cardinals won, the Giants headed back home to play the Dodgers, and Bonds opened the series with . . . yet another press conference.

"The San Francisco Giants organization suggested it," Bonds said. "They suggested it would be a lot easier to accommodate everyone at one time. I agree with them because I think it's fair for (me) as an individual and as a player to prepare (myself) for each and every game. And it's also fair to give the media their opportunity to write their stories. I just feel at this time . . . it's a little bit safer and instead of giving individual interviews you get everyone together and if you write a different story then you must deal with your peers."

Among the highlights from that afternoon: Bonds reiterated he'd still prefer to not participate in the home-run hitting contest, but realized that baseball officials have a way of convincing a player to do it anyway; Bonds understood the attention he was getting, but reminded people they are missing out on Luis Gonzalez's season and he's the MVP right now; Bonds wasn't hurt by the organization not offering him a contract in spring training; and Bonds just wanted to hit 50 homers to get godfather Willie Mays off his back and stop nagging him.

The previous weekend, Bonds only talked to McGwire about family, not home runs. But he was curious about something that he might ask the big redhead that upcoming weekend when McGwire and the Cardinals came to San Francisco.

"How do you enjoy something when everyone else isn't?" Bonds said. "That would be the one question I ask him. I can handle things on my own a little bit, my own way. But handling certain things when everyone else around you isn't handling things well. How do you do that? How do you not separate yourself from the team? And how do you not allow the media to separate you from the team? And how do you talk with the organization and how would they want to handle the situation as well?"

Actually, that was five questions, not one, but most journalists weren't sticking to one question either. So Barry could be excused.

Neil Hayes, a columnist from the *Times* who has been critical of Bonds throughout his career, asked Bonds if he felt this is a second chance to show the world who the real Barry Bonds is.

"No," Bonds replied. "Ants kinda walk their way toward food and whatever's going good, they kind of cling onto it. I would say you guys (in the media) have to look in the mirror for yourself to see why are you doing it all of a sudden? Why are you changing? I don't believe that I have changed at any time. I feel I'm the same person. I feel that I'm handling certain things a little better than I have in the past. But I don't feel that I'm any different."

Perhaps this was just Bonds being stubborn. He'd absolutely changed. He'd admitted many times that he'd changed, particularly in the past 18 months. The change was gradual over time, but if you had to pick a time when it started, the 2000 spring training would be the best place. Bonds realized it was easier to just smile and give people a few minutes, then it was to blow people off. Plus, he said, he was getting too old to fight with the media. He'd rather save that energy for games.

Nonetheless, by comparing the media to ants in this lengthy pre-game news conference, Bonds let it be known that he'll give his time — but he isn't about to apologize for the past 36 years of his life and ask the media to forgive him.

The more Bonds talked, the more he sounded like Mark McGwire in 1998 — and it wasn't coincidence.

"My wife is tired of seeing me on TV," Bonds said. "So am I. We don't even turn on the television anymore. It's strange. When you don't have (media attention) and then you make a great play or hit a game-winning home run, I think you really go to look at it to stroke your ego a little bit. But when it's on every single day, it gets annoying after awhile. You're like, 'this is too much.' Especially when there's so much else with the game going on, and the main focus is on this one person, when there's so many other teams and so many other players that are doing other things as well. I think it takes away the whole perspective of the game of baseball."

If Bonds was tired of seeing himself on the television, he couldn't resist watching himself once more. As he finished the news conference, Bonds left that room and returned to his "corner" of the clubhouse.

When Pacific Bell Park opened, equipment manager Mike Murphy assigned Bonds the entire side of the smallest wall of the clubhouse: four lockers in an area that included a famous $3,000 vibrating leather chair and a 27-inch television that can only be seen by Bonds.

The Bonds corner of the clubhouse is a shock to most first-time visitors and lends itself to Bonds' prima donna image. The truth, as always, is a little different.

Murphy suggested Bonds get the vibrating chair to help his chronic back pains. Bonds paid for the chair himself. Bonds never requested, or demanded, an entire wall in the clubhouse. Murphy just did it, figuring that if he put another player next to Bonds, they would constantly have waves of reporters in their locker. Most superstars get an area of a clubhouse with the most room.

Bonds uses two of the four lockers on that wall. There are 55 total lockers. Most of the other veteran players also have two lockers. Bonds' son Nikolai uses the third locker. The fourth was empty, until the superstitious Marvin Benard moved into it early in the 2001 season to try and change his fortune. Nikolai isn't the only player's son with his own locker, too. Most of the kids who are regulars at the ballpark, including Shawon Dunston's and J.T. Snow's, also have their own lockers, complete with a nameplate that says "Lil Shawon" or "Snowflake."

Bonds sat down in the reclining chair in front of his lockers, turned on the vibrators for his back, flicked on the big-screen television and switched the channel to ESPN — where an *Up Close Prime Time Special with Roy Firestone* was on the television.

As it started, I realized that I was the only writer in the clubhouse. This doesn't happen often and I debated what my strategy would be. I decided this was one of those moments when the best thing a beat writer could do is simply blend into the clubhouse as much as possible, not say a word to attract attention his direction and simply observe the scene.

The Giants home clubhouse is enormous. It's 2,788 square feet and probably 40 yards from one end (where Bonds' lockers are) to the other end. It's one of the longest in the National League. There are leather couches and chairs at both ends, plus seven television sets. The veterans of the team usually own the remote controls.

What I observed was Bonds watching himself. I observed a couple players watching Bonds, curious about what he had to say. I observed a couple players watching Bonds, yet pretending they were watching something else on another television, because they didn't want their teammates to think they were watching Barry or cared. I observed one veteran player make a wise crack at another player for watching it. I observed some players going out of their way to not watch it.

And I observed three teammates whispering to each other, "is he really watching himself down there?"

———

By now, the Barry Bonds Homer Story had three parts: one, did he hit another?; two, did they pitch around him?; and three, if they pitched around him, did Jeff Kent and the hitters behind Bonds make them pay for it?

The first night against the Dodgers, June 25, the hitters behind Bonds made them pay. Bonds walked with two outs in the first. Kent singled. Armando Rios doubled them both home. In the eighth, Bonds walked with runners at first and second to load the bases. Kent doubled home two runs. Kent had also homered and that's how all the Giants runs scored in a 5-2 victory. The Dodgers were 38-37 at this time. Eric Karros was injured. Adrian Beltre still wasn't 100 percent. Andy Ashby was out for the year. They'd just lost Darren Dreifort for the year. And Kevin Brown had just returned, but clearly wasn't 100 percent. It was a time when most people rolled their eyes and figured the Dodgers were about to do their usual collapsing act.

Indeed, the Dodgers led the next night, 5-2, and Kevin Brown, who had always tortured the Giants even more than most teams, was on the mound to start the sixth inning. Brown gave up three consecutive hits, was taken out of the game and the Giants scored six runs in the inning — including an RBI single by Kent after Bonds was walked.

However, in the next inning, Paul Lo Duca hit a three-run double, scored from second on a bang-bang play at the plate, pumped his fist exuberantly and the Dodgers retook the lead. Lo Duca added a three-run homer in the ninth, called the victory "the biggest of the year" for the Dodgers — and Giants general manager Brian Sabean would later say, "that was the game when I knew the Dodgers weren't going away all year."

Before that game, the *Chronicle's* Henry Schulman talked to Terry Adams — the pitcher who gave up Bonds' 500th homer two months earlier and stewed during the nine-minute game delay — about his feelings two months later. As a result of the injuries to Ashby and Dreifort, Adams had been converted from a middle reliever and was starting the next night. Adams' feelings hadn't changed much.

"I was more upset at that point and the home run was part of the loss," Adams said. "I was part of that stuff with Mark McGwire and Sammy Sosa in '98. I was pitching for the Cubs and obviously I was there when McGwire hit his 62nd off Steve Trachsel. They didn't stop the game and have all those people come onto the field and cars come onto the field. That came after the game. I think the Giants handled it the wrong way. There was nobody out and we fell behind late in the game. It was inappropriate to stop the game at that point."

Adams' memory wasn't very good. The nine-minute halt after Bonds' 500th homer was two minutes *shorter* than the delay after McGwire broke Maris' record. But, again, the facts never seem to matter when the subject is Barry Bonds — or when you're talking about Giants-Dodgers bad blood.

On June 27, Adams started and the Giants game-day operations crew made sure they reminded Adams he gave up Bonds' 500th throughout the game. The trivia question, as Adams warmed up before one inning, asked which Dodgers pitcher gave up the 500th homer. The replay of the 500th leaving the bat and landing in the bay — and the home run call of Jon Miller — was played over and over.

Adams got a measure of revenge, going after Bonds in each at-bat instead of pitching around him, holding him to a 1-for-4 night, allowing just three runs in seven innings, and the Dodgers won 7-3 to take the series.

"I was feeling for Terry," Kent said afterward. "I felt for him when they stopped the ballgame when Barry (hit the homer). That's a phenomenal record, but there's not a need for disrespecting anybody in this game. I'm not saying what they did today was disrespecting him, but that was kind of turning the knife when they didn't need to turn the knife."

CHAPTER 10

All Talk

June 29-July 8, Zero Home Runs

"I'm learning the more I talk, the worse I'm doing"

Barry Bonds, July 2.

THE MOST NECESSARY requirement for a legendary homer is the lack of video evidence. The facts can be distorted so much easier if there isn't video to reveal the truth. Take Babe Ruth's "called shot" in the 1932 World Series. In the legend, Ruth pointed to center field with two strikes and called his shot to the Cubs, who were heckling him from their dugout. No video exists to dispel the myth; and, let's face it, it makes for a great story and adds to the legend.

The most legendary homer in Barry Bonds' career came at Junipero Serra High School, an all-boys private school of 700 in San Mateo, California, which is located along the San Francisco peninsula.

Having produced 10 major-league players, Serra has the distinction of producing the most major-league players of any U.S. high school.

No video exists to ruin the story of how far the ball traveled, but my *Oakland Tribune* colleague Joe Nolan got some great responses on the legend for a story he did late in the season.

The popular version is the ball soared over the right-field wall, over the trees that define the backdrop, carried eight lanes of El Camino Real traffic and hit off the third story of a building across the street.

"I've heard it went through the street and it hit the building," Joe Kmak, a sophomore at Serra that year, told my colleague. "I've heard it hit cars. I've heard windows. I've heard people. But it is just a perfect park for a myth like that. It's just one of those great Paul Bunyan stories."

Keep in mind, Bonds was a *freshman* at the time.

"He hit it at least across the street," varsity coach Dave Stevens said. "It did clear El Camino. It's been done, but by seniors. Never by a freshman."

As a high school junior, opposing coaches were already instructing their pitchers to not give Bonds anything to hit.

"(A) coach told his pitchers not to pitch to him," said Tim Walsh, who was Bonds' freshman baseball coach and now the Portland State football coach. "But the kid made a mistake and Barry hit it on the football field. The coach charged out to the mound to yank the pitcher, but it was probably a good pitch. Barry was just that good."

Scouts, as you might figure, were heavily following the talents and accomplishments of Bobby Bonds' son at this high school. Barry had already signed a national letter-of-intent to attend Arizona State University, where his cousin, Reggie Jackson, starred in the 1960s. The collegiate scouts were long gone, but the pro scouts believed Bonds would reject college for the instant cash and turn pro.

As another legend goes, the pro scouts knew what Bonds could do with an aluminum bat. So they asked him to use a wood bat in a game.

"So he used one the next game, at West Sunset Park against St. Ignatius," Stevens said. "Barry's first time up, wham, he hit the ball 30 to 50 feet into the sand dunes over the right-field fence. I looked up and all the scouts were gone. They'd seen what they came to see."

The same perception of Barry Bonds' personality that would follow him for the next 20 years was already visible at Serra High. If you knew him and were part of his inner circle of friends, he was cool, a good friend and somebody who loved to giggle. If you weren't part of his group, he could be perceived — fairly or unfairly — as aloof, indifferent or even cold.

Barry was already famous. On top of being Bobby's son, he was a three-sport star athlete. He was a point guard who could dunk as a freshman and loved to take over a game in the final two minutes. He was a wide receiver, kick returner, punt returner and free safety in football, blessed with the speed to outrun anybody. And he was a center fielder with a lightning quick bat. And he was already struggling to figure out how to handle that fame.

Stevens and basketball coach Kevin Donahue gave their young star Bonds plenty of extra attention. They would talk about jealousy, the way the other students treated Bonds, and the way Bonds treated other students.

If somebody was friendly, Bonds didn't know if it was because they were just being friendly, if they were friendly because of his father or if they were friendly because he was the best prep talent in California. If they weren't friendly, was it because of jealousy?

And, don't forget, Bonds was a black kid living in a predominantly white neighborhood and going to a rich private school that had very few minorities. Many believe jealousy is what left Bonds off one of California's most prestigious prep all-star teams, despite hitting .467 as a senior. The tryouts for the northern California squad were held the morning after Bonds' senior prom. Bonds fell asleep during the workout and the coach — perhaps jealous of Bonds, perhaps feeling sympathy toward the other players, or perhaps being the type who likes to make statements to players who fall asleep during workouts — left Barry off the team.

It didn't matter to the San Francisco Giants that Bonds wasn't on the all-star team. They took him with their second selection in the 1982 amateur draft. Bonds initially asked for a $100,000 signing bonus. Bonds came down and was willing to sign for $75,000. The Giants final offer was a $70,000 bonus. They refused to offer anything higher. When the Giants refused the extra $5,000, Bonds elected to attend Arizona State.

At least, that's the popular version of the story and it has been reported for almost two decades to the point where it's assumed to be true. For whatever it's worth, though, back in 1983, then-Giants general manager Tom Haller told The *Oakland Tribune* the two sides were more than $5,000 apart and the team offered Bonds more than $75,000.

———

Barry Bonds got down on his knees, leaned down, put his hands into thick gray cement and said, "I feel like a kid."

It was the morning before the game on Sunday, July 1. The Giants were honoring Bonds for his entry into the 500-homer club and part of that ceremony was having Bonds' handprints and signature on a bronze plaque that now appears on the walkway next to McCovey Cove, beyond the right-field wall at Pacific Bell Park.

Forty-four days had passed since Bonds reached 500 and now he had 533 career homers. In that time, Bonds had passed Eddie Murray, Mel Ott, Eddie

Mathews, Ernie Banks, Ted Williams and Willie McCovey — five Hall of Famers, and Murray would appear a lock once he becomes eligible in 2003. Serra High's Dave Stevens was there. Former Pirates manager Jim Leyland was there. It was the final game of a weekend series against the Cardinals, so Mark McGwire was there.

"The ceremony for 500 home runs is for an accomplishment, one that not many guys have reached," Bonds said. "But the chase that everybody is talking about (70 homers), that's a separate thing. I don't want to separate myself from my teammates. This is difficult for me, trying to explain it day in, day out. I can't explain it. I don't know what's going on. I'm doing something I can't explain."

McGwire doesn't like talking about his 1998 season. He swears the only time he ever thinks about it is when a reporter brings it up to him. When he's retired in the future, McGwire says he will reflect on it. But McGwire was being forced to think about his 70-homer season once again, because he was back in the Bay Area, and too many writers were interested in his thoughts.

"He's got a hell of a chance to do it," Big Mac said. "How would I feel about it? I definitely would know what he went through to do it. It's not going to be easy. He's got a great, great start for it, but he's got a long ways to go. You think about it. Four guys in the history of baseball have hit 60 home runs. Two of them have done it twice. Now you're talking about somebody breaking 70 when he hasn't even hit 50? That's why I say if he's lucky enough to get to 60 in September, you guys can go all-out with your pens and paper, because then it's legitimate."

McGwire felt the problem was too much obsessing with the record itself and not enough appreciating what Bonds is doing here and now. Mac's example was hitting "only" 65 homers the year after.

"A lot of people don't even know that I hit 65 the next year," McGwire said. "The media builds something up so great, that if somebody doesn't get to it, yeah, they might think that he sort of failed at it, which is wrong."

Bonds and McGwire are not friends. They didn't play in the same league until 1997 and only really talk when Bonds is at first base. But when asked if he would embrace Bonds if he were to eclipse his mark, McGwire nodded in the affirmative.

"I would embrace him as much as anybody would," Mac answered. "But I can't repeat this enough — there isn't anybody on this Earth who knows exactly what goes on except for me. And don't forget, we're talking about breaking 70. Back then, we were talking about breaking 61. You're going to have to go 10 more to do it.

"There are so many things that can go wrong."

On July 2, it was back to Los Angeles. And yet another news conference for Bonds.

"I'm learning the more I talk, the worse I'm doing," Bonds said. "I think I've only hit one since these press conferences started. I'm just happy we're doing well as a team. There's other things to discuss other than what I'm doing. We have Calvin Murray running around like he's 'Say Hey' Willie Mays out there. He's saved a lot of games for us."

The Giants came into the series with a 44-37 record, six games behind Arizona in the NL West. Bonds was in a 2-for-17 slump. He'd walked 10 times during the six-game stretch, just the second time this year he'd gone six games without a homer. Bonds maintained the interviews haven't been a distraction and he's not physically tired.

But manager Dusty Baker wasn't very happy.

"I wish (the media) would leave him alone some," Baker said. "He hasn't been as hot lately. I hope (the interviews) are not taking his energy away. Leave him alone and let him play. But that's the way of the world. There's nothing you can do about it."

If anything was bothering Bonds, it was the right wrist that he slammed into the top of the fence on June 29, while taking away a home run from Albert Pujols. That certainly wasn't the type of play that somebody who only cares about hitting 71 homers in a season would make.

Bonds put his body in jeopardy going after the ball. He crumpled to the ground immediately after saving the game with the catch. He missed the final two innings, but hadn't missed a game because of the injury. The Giants quickly added padding to the top of the fence for future instances when Bonds scales the wall to take away a homer.

Results from fan balloting for all-star game starters were also announced

July 2, and Bonds was the National League's top vote-getter for the third time in his career. He was elected to start for the eighth time and was going to make his 10th appearance. Jeff Kent and Rich Aurilia, the Giants double-play tandem, were also named starters.

"It's amazing to have three starters off the same team," Bonds said. "That's very impressive. That's something the San Francisco fans have a lot to be proud of. It's very rare to get three."

That night, Bonds threw out a runner at third base in the first inning and reached over two feet above the wall to take away a homer from Paul Lo Duca — a catch certainly in the all-time top five of Bonds' career, if not his best ever. It was the third time this season, and second time in four days, that Bonds had taken away a homer.

Many fans in the left-field bleachers — who chanted "Bar-ry sucks" and booed him the rest of the night — responded with a standing ovation and the "we're not worthy" bow made famous by the *Wayne's World* skits on *Saturday Night Live*.

"I don't care about a catch right now," Bonds said after the game.

Bonds was 0-for-4 on the night, now 4-for-39 against the Dodgers for the season and the Dodgers rallied from a 6-5 deficit to win 8-6 and the victory went to Terry Adams for the second time in six days.

"When a team has your calling card, they have your calling card," Bonds said. "(The Dodgers) are charging it up big time. They've got mine all year. I have to cancel that son of a bitch. I can't afford it they're running my bill up so high."

Nikolai Bonds, a second baseman and outfielder, called his dad in Los Angeles and told him about his team's second consecutive Little League championship.

"That's great, I love you," said Barry, a hint of sarcasm in his voice because he's never won a championship. "Dad will get there sooner or later. Glad somebody in our family is winning. He was like, 'you can do it, Dad. Just try. Try real hard.'"

On July 3, it was more frustration for Bonds and the Giants. Bonds' bid for his 40th homer in the seventh inning died at the warning track and inside the glove of close friend Gary Sheffield. The Giants led 3-1 in the eighth, the Dodgers tied the game on Lo Duca's homer and took the lead on a Marquis

Grissom double. Bonds was 0-for-3 with two walks, including an intentional walk in the ninth by closer Jeff Shaw with two runners on base and two outs.

Jeff Kent looked for a slider, got a slider on the first pitch, but popped it shallow right, where Eric Karros made the catch to end the game.

"They walk Barry all the time," said Kent, talking about the subject he hates talking about more than anything. "Would you rather face a left-hander who's leading the league in home runs or a right-hander hitter — when Shaw is a heck of a lot better against right-handers? It's almost a no-brainer. I'm not too worried about them taking a backstep to get to me. It's no big deal. I've burned them before. I'll burn them some other time. It's the nature of the game: You can't (come through) all the time."

That night, wife Liz threw Bonds a surprise early birthday party at the Belly Lounge in Los Angeles (Bonds didn't turn 37 for a couple more weeks). Sheffield told his friend they were going out after the game and lured him to the event.

"Gary drove me all around Los Angeles," Bonds told me. "I told him, 'why did we drive all around the freeway, when we could have just taken (Interstate) 10 to this spot?' I saw a couple players on my team coming in. I was like, 'wait a minute. I don't ever go to the same places as my teammates do.' I didn't put two and two together. My wife got me good."

The guest list was approximately 150, including actress Farrah Fawcett and actor Paul Walker. Even family friend Bill Cosby phoned him. Manager Dusty Baker, trainer Stan Conte and most of Bonds' teammates were at the party, except for those who live in Southern California like Robb Nen and J.T. Snow. Jeff Kent was not there.

The next night, before 54,636 on hand for Fourth of July fireworks, Shaw did pitch to Bonds in the ninth inning. The Giants had scored three runs in the top of the eighth to tie the game, only to see the Dodgers take the lead on Sheffield's 17th homer in the bottom of the eighth.

With one out and nobody on base, Shaw went after Bonds and won the battle, retiring him on a fly ball to center. Kent followed with a two-out single one night too late and Armando Rios grounded out to end the game. The Giants had lost their fifth straight game to the Dodgers in nine days and their record was 44-40 for the season.

In the finale of the four-game series in LA, Bonds was 1-for-3 with a hit by pitch and walk. The entire Giants lineup was in a funk except for Rich Aurilia.

This game was the start of a two-month stretch when the gritty shortstop put the Giants on his shoulders and delivered more clutch hits than anybody in baseball. Down 2-1 in the eighth, Aurilia hit a sacrifice fly off Chan Ho Park to tie the game, then singled home Eric Davis with the go-ahead run in the ninth. Robb Nen recorded the final three outs and the Giants salvaged the final game of the series.

Back in San Francisco the next night, Bonds had two doubles and a walk in five plate appearances against four different Milwaukee Brewers pitchers. Bonds' menacing shadow was in the on-deck circle in the 11th inning, when Aurilia ended the game with a single to left to score Felipe Crespo.

"I've seen Barry go through this every year," Baker said. "He goes two or three weeks before he gets his power stroke back."

Bonds decided he would participate in the home-run hitting derby after all. He didn't make a big deal about it, informing a Giants official and major league baseball. Bonds was bringing Giants bullpen coach Juan Lopez to pitch to him in the derby and also invited Lopez's family to join him in the private plane they were taking to Seattle.

One of Baker's annual trademark speeches to his team comes before the final 10 games leading into the all-star break. Baker refuses to let his team go into vacation mode early and places a big emphasis on finishing strong. With two games left, the Giants were 5-3 so far on the final 10 games.

The Brewers (40-43 when they arrived in town) provided an opponent the Giants were capable of sweeping (especially at home), which would give the Giants a four-game winning streak heading into the break, and lots of momentum.

The opposite happened. The Brewers blew out the Giants 13-3 on July 7, then beat them 6-4 in 13 innings on the final game of the first half — an extra painful loss for the Giants considering they loaded the bases in the 10th, 11th and 12th innings and failed to score.

The Giants ended the first half with a record of 46-42 and were 5.5 games behind Arizona in the NL West.

Bonds didn't homer in the final two games, concluding a stretch of 14 games without a homer to end the first half. He still had a record 39 at the break. He was still on a pace for 72.

And he was still going to Seattle for the all-star game as the biggest story in baseball.

CHAPTER 11

Going Gonzo for Bonds

July 9-11, All-Star Break

"I've never had this much attention before . . . I've seen more positive articles about me this year than I ever have my entire life. You're thankful for that. But I just want to see what it's like when it's over, when I'm not hitting 39 home runs. Will you revert me back to something else?"

Barry Bonds

THE REIGNING CHAMPION in the family, 8-year-old Nikolai Bonds, sat there in disbelief, his mouth wide open, his eyes gazing at the wave after wave of reporters who were surrounding him and his father inside the ballroom of the Sheraton Hotel in downtown Seattle.

Nikolai wasn't worried because . . . well, his father was smiling and relaxed, cordial, charming, cracking jokes, telling stories and bantering with the media. At times, Nikolai was in awe. At other times, he was bored and ready for something new.

This is how it works on the first day at the all-star game. Rather than unleashing hundreds of reporters into the clubhouses before the all-star workout, Major League Baseball takes its all stars into a massive ballroom at a swank hotel near the ballpark, puts each player at a table, then opens the doors and stays clear as credentialed media members roam the room and ask whatever questions they want.

The media gets the American League players for 60 minutes, then the National League players for 60 minutes.

From the time the doors opened, until long after security began asking the media to leave, Barry Bonds' table was packed. Reporters from all over the world come to the all-star game and the biggest story was Barry Bonds, the coverboy of that week's *TV Guide* under the heading, "THE BEST OF HIS TIME."

All topics were fair game.

The reporter from *GQ* magazine asked Bonds which suits he prefers wearing.

"I'm not into fashion," Bonds responded. "I wear jeans. And suits when I have to."

The reporter from a Venezuelan TV station asked Bonds what he remembers about playing winter ball there in 1985.

"Oh man, that was a long time ago, dude," Bonds said. "I can't remember. I remember I had a nice apartment. Oh yeah, and their women are beautiful. I think they're the prettiest anywhere. That's the truth . . . but those were my younger days. My wife is the prettiest."

The reporter looked at his cameraman with a wide grin, knowing they had something great to send back to their country.

All the reporters from Japan asked Bonds about Ichiro Suzuki, the best player in Japan who came to America and captured the imagination of Seattle Mariners fans with his speed, athleticism and talent.

"He's finally in the right league," said Bonds, who played against Ichiro years earlier in an exhibition tour of Japan. "He's in the league he needs to be in. He needed to be over here playing. He's at the highest level now . . . Ichiro was in a class by himself. If he didn't make the move, he could have walked away bored. But he wouldn't be fulfilling his whole potential."

Another reporter asked who was next in the Bonds baseball family after Bobby and now Barry. That certainly got Nikolai's attention and he leaned forward, just like the media, to hear the response.

"He doesn't have to do anything. Baseball's been goooooood to Dad, huh?" said Barry, looking at his son and smiling wide. "He can just go to school and be educated. He likes football. He's been in more championships than I have. He's won two. I won one in Babe Ruth. He won two back-to-back. He called me up, 'hey, Dad, I won another championship.' I told him I'll get one someday. He told me, 'just try, dad, you can do it.'"

The reporter from Boston asked Bonds if the stories of him making more of an effort to get along with his teammates this season were true.

"Do you like everybody you work with?" Bonds asked the reporter.

"Absolutely not," the reporter replied.

"Me neither," Bonds said. "And that answers your question."

And it was on to the next topic.

Bonds didn't go into detail about it. But he clearly was making more of an effort to be a better teammate. Since his 500th homer, Bonds seemed more relaxed in general and was talking with teammates more frequently. Some of this is a credit to Shawon Dunston and Eric Davis' presence.

One day, I actually saw Bonds and Kent talking in the clubhouse. Well, Kent was reading a motorcycle magazine (as always), didn't look up from the magazine much to make eye contact with Bonds, and most of his responses were like, "uh huh."

Give Bonds credit for trying. He was sitting in an empty locker next to Kent's, chatting with him and genuinely making an effort. Near the end of their conversation, I actually saw Kent look up, make eye contact and share a laugh with Bonds. The veterans on the beat could never recall Bonds and Kent talking in the clubhouse like that before.

We joked about potential tabloid headlines: "BONDS AND KENT TALK!"

Across the Sheraton ballroom, Luis Gonzalez, a mere four homers behind Bonds, had about 40 fewer reporters around him. When I arrived at his table, the count was three reporters.

"It's kinda weird for me to be in this thing," Gonzalez said. "Right now, I have 35 home runs. But I'm not one of these guys that hit Manny Ramirez or Mark McGwire tape-measure home runs. I hit line drive home runs and I've hit some squeakers that just went over the wall. The bottom line is it going over the fence, so you can trot around the bases."

Gonzalez was then asked what's more difficult: chasing Bonds or chasing his triplets around the house.

"Chasing triplets," he replied, not wasting a moment. "Nobody expects me to be chasing Bonds right now. To me, I'm getting a lot of attention with this home run thing. The record that I would want to get is the total bases (457). That's Babe Ruth. Nobody's come close to it. I'm semi-close to the pace. I don't know if I can continue to do it. Everybody lives for the home runs. I like to be the total package offensively."

Roger Maris had Mickey Mantle.

Mark McGwire had Sammy Sosa.

Now it was appearing Barry Bonds had Luis Gonzalez as his sidekick for the home run race — which Bonds still wasn't interested in, and still didn't think he'd ever accomplish.

"Barry always gives me a hard time," Gonzalez said. "We see each other 150 times with this unbalanced schedule. We go down there (to San Francisco) in a couple weeks. We're good rivals, the Diamondbacks and Giants. But this gives the fans creativity to yell at me when I go into San Francisco, and they'll probably yell at Barry when he comes to our ballpark. That makes it exciting for all of baseball. People always look for some kind of rivalry. We're friends. We went to Japan together and had a lot of fun. He's doing something special.

"I like being that darkhorse, laying in the weeds behind him," Gonzalez continued. "He's getting the brunt of everything. I'm just sitting back, having fun and enjoying our season with our ballclub. He always tells me that I should have called him after he hit a homer or things like that. I don't know if he'll tell you, but I think you need somebody behind you. It pushes you. Like in the winter, a lot of players hire a strength and conditioning coach because you need somebody to push you. Everybody can go to the gym, but does that mean you are getting a good workout? No. You need somebody to push you around to motivate you a little. When you have somebody behind you, it keeps you on your toes."

Not wanting to say in one place very long, I bounced around the room and talked with one all-star after another.

The topic, of course, was Barry Bonds.

My first stop was Colorado first baseman Todd Helton.

"It amazes me that pitchers still think they can get fastballs inside on him," Helton said. "When they do, the ball gets wet. Even with the quickness, he's able to keep the ball fair. It's harder than you think . . . He'll be at a disadvantage because his home park is probably the worst in the majors to hit in, definitely in the National League. It's terrible."

My second stop was San Diego first baseman Ryan Klesko.

"He's the type of guy who can hurt you in all aspects of the game," Klesko said. "That's why he's so good. If you walk him, he can steal a base. If you throw him two pitches that are the same, he recognizes that quicker than most hitters. You can't keep throwing him the same pitch. Some hitters have weaknesses and pitchers keep trying to hammer them on the same spot. Barry adjusts, pitch after pitch. I've seen a guy throws a nasty slider down and away — and he'll miss it. Then he throws it again and Barry hits the ball out to left-center. That's how quick he adjusts and how short and quick his swing is. Defensively, offensively, base running, he does it all."

I was curious if players around the league were following Bonds' season as closely as the fans and media in the Bay Area were doing.

"Oh yeah, you turn on the TV and it's like, 'Barry must have hit another one today.' He hit a few off us," Klesko said. "They weren't just pulling the ball. That one he hit to dead center into the wind was amazing."

My third stop was Cincinnati first baseman Sean Casey.

"We were all following it," Casey said. "We'd always see the pitches he'd hit out. They looked like great pitches to hit. But we probably don't know the count is 3-2 and he's waited all that time to get that pitch. Oh yeah, we're following him. We're players. But we're fans also. We were fans before we were players."

My fourth stop was Colorado outfielder Larry Walker.

"What he's doing this year is nothing short of spectacular," Walker said. "Trust me, we finish a game and we're in the clubhouse and SportsCenter comes on, we're looking at the Bottom Line to see if Bonds hit another home run. You shake your head. 'Is he hitting off a tee or what's he doing?'"

The line around Bonds hadn't diminished much. I couldn't resist. I had to hear what else was being asked.

" . . . I don't think I've ever had a bad relationship," Bonds was in the middle of saying. "Everybody is good when something is good. We'll see how good you are when things are not good. This (slump) is the best thing that's ever happened to me because we'll really really get the true meaning of media. I've never had this much attention before. I've tried to accommodate at times. And there's been times when I've been tired. I've seen more positive articles about me this year than I ever have my entire life. You're thankful for that. But I just want to see what it's like when it's over, when I'm not hitting 39 home runs. Will you revert me back to something else?"

Bonds was asked about Ichiro again.

"With him and Nomo, it almost brings tears to your eyes," Bonds said, coming up with something new, instead of repeating what he said earlier. "This game is for all nationalities. It's wonderful that all these players are here, playing baseball and representing their countries. They're showing what a great country this is to embrace all the nationalities. I think it's the greatest thing. I think everybody should recognize it and grasp it. They are history. Chan Ho (Park) and all these guys are making history. They are not only history for their country, they are history for this game."

Bonds was asked what it feel likes to be so close to the Top 10 all-time home-run list.

"Every time I get to somewhere special, I always hit a dead zone," said Bonds, the 0-for-21 slump in April before the 500th homer the perfect example. "I can't get a hit. It takes me awhile. Once I get there, I'll be able to get to the next phase. I always get stopped. Maybe I have to stop thinking about it. When you're a baby playing baseball, you don't think about being in the top 10 all-time in home runs. Butterflies go through your stomach. It's unreal. There's no way in my lifetime, signing with the Pirates back in 1985, 15-odd years later, somebody saying you're about to enter the top 10 all-time in home runs."

And then he's talking about that vision, that zone that hitters get into.

"If you lose that vision, you just lose it," Bonds said. "It's there and then it's gone. Right now, I don't know where it is. I'm not noticing things. It's all gone. I don't know why I had it for those moments or those spurts. That was a moment of spurts, the things I was doing. I could see everything so fast. And now, I see everything so slow. It's weird. It's the weirdest thing. Like Tony Gwynn said in San Diego, 'Barry is seeing the ball so fast, so early, that he knows what pitch it is as soon as it leaves the pitchers hand.' You can do that. Then when you can't, there's no explanation."

Later in the day was the home-run hitting contest, the marquee event of the all-star workout that precedes the game. The contest starts with eight players. They keep swinging until they make 10 "outs." An out is anything that isn't a home run. The four players who hit the most homers advance to the second round. And they do it again, swinging until they make 10 outs. The scores do not carry over to the next rounds. It's a long process that lasts over an hour, the big reason Bonds told reporters in May he didn't want to participate.

In the first round, with Giants bullpen coach Juan Lopez pitching to him, Bonds got off to a slow start. He then heated up and finished with seven homers in the first round — his longest a 476-foot moonshot. The Oakland Athletics' Jason Giambi stole the show with 14 homers. Luis Gonzalez and Sammy Sosa, quite naturally, rounded out the foursome that went on to the second round.

The foursome were seeded and Gonzalez out-homered Bonds 5-3 to move onto the finals. Sosa out-slugged a fatigued Giambi 8-6 to join him in the finals. Both players were tired in the last round, but Gonzalez hit six to Sosa's two to win the derby.

"You're not laying in the weeds anymore," Bonds told Gonzalez.

Later in the night, Bonds stopped by the set of ESPN's *Baseball Tonight*. He brought son Nikolai and older daughter Shikari on the set with him. At the very end, host Karl Ravech asked Nikolai if he thinks his dad can break McGwire's record.

"Yeah, if he tries," answered Nikolai.

About an hour before for the all-star game started, Barry Bonds was angry. And he couldn't hold it inside anymore. Perennial all-star Tony Gwynn, in his 20th and final season in baseball, was invited to the game as an honorary player. Gwynn was injured most of the first half and didn't want to attend the game at the expense of a deserving player. He agreed to attend, but was not playing.

"Man, it's a damn shame what's going on," Bonds yelled in the National League clubhouse. "We bring this man all this way to honor him, and we're not going to give him an at-bat. Come on, we've got to get this man an 'AB.' We've got to do it."

Mets manager Bobby Valentine was the skipper of the NL squad. In the fifth inning, Valentine called Gwynn over and told him to grab a bat and helmet and go the plate. Sure, he wasn't supposed to hit. But who was going to say something if Gwynn just walked to the plate?

The crowd would surely cheer wildly. Like the commissioner was going to stop the game and tell Gwynn he couldn't bat, right?

Gwynn politely declined the offer. He wasn't feeling well physically. His knee was killing him. And after Cal Ripken, Jr. — who is also retiring at the end of this season — hit a first-pitch homer in his first at-bat, Gwynn wasn't about to make a fool of himself at the plate.

Barry Bonds went hitless in two non-eventful at-bats. He was out of the game when his most memorable moment came in the sixth inning. Tommy Lasorda was coaching third base and in classic-Tommy form, rooting and cheering on the NL squad. Even with a sold-out stadium buzzing, Lasorda could be heard in the press box.

But Lasorda's attention had shifted momentarily away from the action when a bat slipped out of the hands of Vladimir Guerrero and sailed in Lasorda's direction. Lasorda didn't see it until the final second and awkwardly avoided it, falling back and tumbling over. It was scary for a second. Then Lasorda started smiling and yucked it up for the cameras.

Bonds ran onto the field with a chest protector for Lasorda.

"That was one of the most bizarre things I've ever seen on a baseball field," said New York Mets catcher Mike Piazza, the godson of Lasorda. "I was just glad he was OK. You could see the bat flying and you knew he did not see the bat. For him to be alright and laugh about it, gosh, I was just so scared. It was cute, too, that Barry (Bonds) brought out the catcher's equipment."

Added Bonds: "When I got to him I think he was more embarrassed. We all got a kick out of it."

Lasorda, of course, milked the crowd for all it was worth. Then he downplayed it with reporters after the game.

"Nobody was hurt," Lasorda said. "The fans loved it. I'm fine. I can't believe all these people were worried about me."

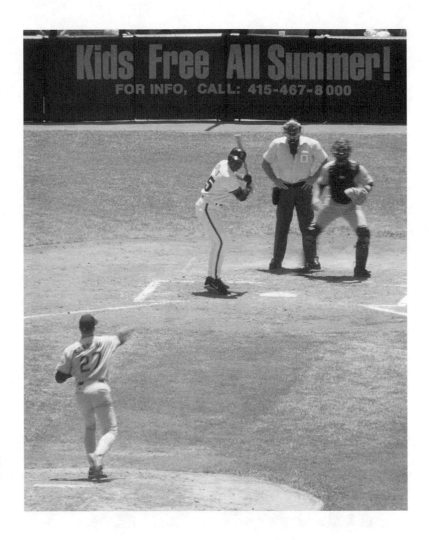

No player has been intentionally walked more in his career than
Bonds, including this free pass in 1995, when the Giants try
luring fans back to the park after the strike with free admission for
kids (1995).

TOP: Fans throughout the country, like these in Seattle at the home-run derby, were captivated whenever Barry Bonds was at the plate (July 9, 2001).

ABOVE: It appears smoke is coming off Barry Bonds' bat during this afternoon game against the Oakland Athletics (June 16, 2001).

On Family Day, the proud father Barry puts daughter Aisha on his shoulders and poses with wife Liz, son Nikolai and daughter Shikari (July 22, 2001).

TOP: Fans outside Pacific Bell Park use any flotation device possible to join the action inside McCovey Cove and await a potential historic home run (October 7, 2001).

ABOVE: The ominous clouds lurking above are nothing for a pitcher compared to the sight of Barry Bonds in the on-deck circle, eyeballing another homer into McCovey Cove (July 20, 2000).

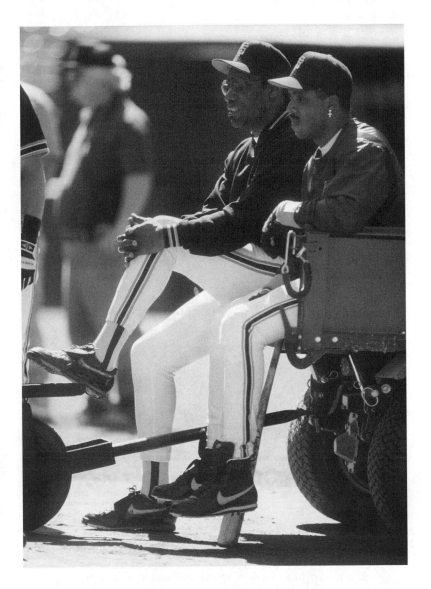

Bobby Bonds, shown here with his son Barry, was the Giants batting coach from 1993-1996. To this day, Barry still considers his dad his most important batting coach and often calls him for advice when slumping (1993).

A common sight after a Bonds home run, his son Nikolai greeting
him at home plate and an embrace (1999).

An eight-time Gold Glove winner adept at taking away home runs from opponents, Bonds was robbed himself by a young fan in the fifth game at Pacific Bell Park (April 2000).

Barry Bonds jumps into the air as he watched home run 73 sail over the fence to establish the new record on the final day of the regular season.

CHAPTER 12

Calm before the Storm

July 12-25, Home Runs 40-42

"You know, I'm not shocked anymore by anything he does. In a way, it was just more funny than anything else. It just really played into the legend of Barry Bonds."

Giants head trainer Stan Conte

THE ALL-STAR GAME was over, but the all-star hype wasn't for Barry Bonds. The San Francisco Giants, conveniently enough, were starting the second half of the season at Seattle's Safeco Field.

So, for a lot of the media already in town, in particular, those on the East Coast who don't venture this far west very often, it made sense to stick around for a few more days, write more stories about Ichiro, the Mariners, Bonds and the Arizona Diamondbacks, who were arriving in Seattle after the Giants left.

Upon winning the home-run hitting contest, *ESPN The Magazine* decided it was time to run the Luis Gonzalez story that was planned for May and canceled when Bonds went on his homer binge. Gonzalez wasn't upset when the author, Jeff Bradley, told him the story was being held.

"Guess I'll have to hit more homers," Gonzalez said a smile.

Bonds started to stay at a hotel different than his teammates — a practice that Cal Ripken, Jr. and his best friend on the Baltimore Orioles, Brady Anderson have been doing since the mid-'90s. Ironically enough, Bonds stayed at the Madison Renaissance, the hotel that served as the media headquarters. I was shocked when I came down in an elevator from my hotel room one night and nearly ran into Bonds as I quickly exited the elevator and he was getting on.

We didn't say much to each other beyond "hello" and "hey, dude." Barry had more of a puzzled look on his face, like, "what's your hurry, dude?"

The hurry, of course, was "last call" was approaching soon and I was meeting two friends from college, Eric Winter and Rick Benitez, in a Seattle bar. Eight months later, Winter would perform the miracle of getting this book published.

For all the attention of his record 39 homers at the break, Bonds was also in a 13-game homerless drought. This statistic was shared with Dusty Baker before the opener of the second half of the season on July 12 and the ever-optimistic manager continued his knack for prophetic pre-game statements.

"That means somebody is in trouble," Baker said. "Home runs and RBIs usually come in bunches. For most guys, 50 percent of their damage is done in 33 percent of the time."

For instance, Bonds hit 19 of his 39 first-half homers (roughly half) in a 31-game stretch (roughly one-third).

Less than two hours later, on the first pitch he saw in the second half, Bonds destroyed a 2-0 fastball low and inside from Paul Abbott. Bonds' 40th homer tied Jimmy Foxx for 10th on the all-time list and gave his team an early 1-0 lead. The pre-break woes continued though. Closer Robb Nen blew a 3-2 lead in the ninth and the Giants lost 4-3 in 11 innings.

The blast added Safeco Field to Bonds' ballpark hit-list. In all 25 ballparks he'd ever played, Bonds had gone deep at least once. Safeco was the last remaining.

Even though he didn't win the home-run hitting contest Monday, Bonds felt he might have re-found his swing — which is the opposite of what usually happens.

"Most of the time, guys that get screwed up in home-run hitting contests are the guys going good already," Baker said, "Not the guys going bad."

One homer didn't snap Bonds out of his hitting funk though. He added an RBI single in the first inning of the second game against Seattle, which the Giants won 5-3 to give the Mariners a rare loss. Overall, Bonds was 3-for-13 in the three-game series, including eight hitless at-bats to end it.

In the series finale, a 3-1 Mariners win, Bonds lined out to deep center off Arthur Rhodes, just missing a two-run homer that would have tied the game. Bonds wasn't walked once in the series as the talented Mariners pitchers went after him successfully.

The last 10 road losses for the Giants now had the following margins of victory: 1, 1, 1, 1, 2, 4, 1, 1, 4, 2.

"It bugs you more how you lost the one-run games, versus just the one-run losses," Kent said. "We've lost a lot of games we were winning in the 7th, 8th, 9th innings. We've allowed teams to come back on us. It's not just our pitching. We can't score enough runs. It's twofold. That's what bugs you."

The Giants were 47-44, unable to put together any type of run, and now had lost four of their last five and seven of their last 10 games.

"The losses are wearing on us now," Aurilia said. "One-run losses hurt, but any loss hurts. When you lose by one run, you can think the game over and say, 'what could we have done differently?' Then we got blown out last weekend at home (13-3) and you say, 'what the hell did we do?' Right now, all the losses are tough."

The next stop was Arlington, Texas, and the interleague games against the Rangers provided Bonds another opportunity to practice being a designated hitter, which Bonds did for two of the three games. Compared to the rest of the season, this series was probably the most uneventful of the year.

Bonds went 0-for-4 in the first game, a 7-6 Giants win saved by Robb Nen despite putting two runners on base in the final inning. The next night, Bonds was 0-for-1, walked three times (the Texas fans booed each time), and after Bonds grounded out in the top of the eighth inning, most of the 32,682 fans exited the Ballpark in Arlington — despite their home team clinging to just a 2-0 lead. The Rangers held on for the victory.

In the Texas finale, Bonds was 1-for-2, walked twice (bringing more boos) and was lifted for a pinch hitter in the ninth inning of a 10-2 lead. Lifting Bonds for the final innings of a lopsided game was a normal move by Baker, but it earned him the wrath of the Texas fans who had waited an extra inning for the single purpose of seeing Bonds get one more at-bat.

For the series, Bonds was 1-for-7, walked six times, scored three times and didn't homer.

He'd now hit just one homer in 19 games.

The seasonal pace was now down to 69, the first time it was below 70 since the media started paying attention to it in late May.

Maybe Bonds and McGwire were right. Maybe hitting 70 homers wasn't as easy as Bonds was making it look months ago. Maybe pitchers weren't going to give him the chance. Maybe the summer heat and the pennant race pressure were going to be too much.

Yeah, right.

The more you watch Bonds, the more you believe in the "calm before the storm" theory to his hot streaks. If he hasn't done anything in awhile, look out. He's about to get hot.

From the 94-degrees in Texas, the Giants returned to San Francisco and a first-pitch temperature of 62 degrees to face the Colorado Rockies on July 18. Mike Hampton, who had never lost to the Giants in the regular season, was on the mound and struck out Bonds on three pitches in the first inning. Hampton appeared on top of his game after three scoreless innings.

Leading off the fourth, Bonds powered out his 41st homer of the season, but winced as he rounded the bases because he felt pain in his back. Trainer Stan Conte wanted to take Bonds out of the game as a precaution, but Bonds refused. It was an important divisional game, Hampton is always tough and Bonds didn't want out.

An inning later, a runner on base, Bonds walked to the plate in noticeable pain. The over-exaggerated shift was on, Bonds laid down a bunt and grimaced the entire way as he labored down the first-base line, only to have the ball roll foul. Concern would be an understatement at this point. I thought for sure Bonds was going to be removed from the game. Why risk it?

"He was bunting because he couldn't really swing," Baker would say later.

Bonds stayed in the game. Hampton threw a fastball away, Bonds barely swung his arms, used no legs and no trunk rotation and tried not to move his back. And he sent the ball over the left-field fence for a home run that I still consider, unquestionably, the most miraculous of the season.

Even Bonds had a look of "how in the world did I just do that?" on his face as he circled the bases and returned to the dugout.

"Hurt or not, he's still a powerful hitter," Hampton said. "Tonight he was better than I was."

The two homers tied and passed Mickey Mantle for ninth on the all-time list. The Giants lead was now extended to 4-0, Bonds agreed to exit the game and the Giants rolled to a 10-0 victory.

"You know, I'm not shocked anymore by anything he does," Conte said. "In a way, it was just more funny than anything else. It just really played into the legend of Barry Bonds."

Added Rich Aurilia: "I've seen Barry for five or six years now, and nothing he does surprises me. . . . I think it kind of eased people's minds when he came back and hit that second homer."

Bonds received treatment in the clubhouse as the game continued. He left the clubhouse before reporters entered. When he arrived the next day, Bonds walked into the clubhouse, went directly to Conte and basically said, "I'm fine. I'm playing."

Of the swing, Bonds told beat writers, "I didn't have a choice. I was going to be late on that ball no matter what."

When the ball left the yard, Bonds was in shock.

"It hurt more when I twisted because the muscle was so tight," Bonds said. "It was like I couldn't breathe. They wanted to take me out of the game, but I was like 'no, no, no.' Hampton has kicked our butts ever since he's been pitching. I didn't want to leave the game and give him any chance to raise his confidence."

And he was going to play that night. "It's nothing like it was last night," Bonds said. "I've played in worse situations than this."

Conte didn't think Bonds would be able to play. But was surprised with how he felt Thursday morning.

"It was surprising only because he was in a fair amount of discomfort," Conte said. "I wasn't too worried about it because in that particular area (of the back), there's not a lot of things bad that can happen . . . I don't think this will be a chronic thing because he's never had this particular problem before. It's a fluke thing — partly because he's never had it before and partly because that's what I want it to be."

Bonds took it easy in batting practice, not rotating his hips with any extra force, while still blasting his usual assortment of pitches over the fences. That night, Shawn Chacon retired him in the first and fourth innings. Bonds was walked on five pitches in the sixth and eighth innings, then intentionally walked to load the bases of a 1-1 game in the ninth. Jeff Kent was then walked on four pitches by Colorado closer Juan Acevedo, bringing home the winning run.

With the exception of the 10-0 victory over Hampton, the Giants offense was still terribly inconsistent and struggling to create runs by any means other than Rich Aurilia and Bonds. The first-place Diamondbacks were next in town Friday, July 20 and the Giants opened the series with a 1-0 victory in yet another classic pitchers duel between these teams.

Bonds was 0-for-2 with two walks against D'backs starter Miguel Batista. Ramon Martinez' solo homer accounted for the only run. Pitcher Livan Hernandez allowed two hits in seven shutout innings and the trio of Felix Rodriguez, Aaron Fultz and Robb Nen recorded the final six outs to preserve the victory.

The next morning, July 21, I found myself in a Westin Saint Francis hotel room in San Francisco and somebody was putting makeup on my face. It could mean only one thing: television.

ESPN's award-winning *SportsCentury* series is one of the best programs on television and the network was working on a piece about Barry Bonds. A few writers and I sat down individually for 30-45 minutes and gave our impressions of Bonds to the ESPN producers.

Afterward, I had a renewed appreciation for what athletes must feel after an interview. It was doubtful ESPN was going to use more than 15-20 seconds of what I said on the air. I was already joking to my friends that whatever sound byte they use, I'm going to claim it was taken out of context.

The Giants offense continued to struggle in that day's game. Old nemesis Curt Schilling was on the hill and took a no-hitter into the seventh inning. It was broken up by a single from Armando Rios, the only hit Schilling allowed in seven innings. The Diamondbacks opened up a 9-0 lead, Schilling came out early because of it and the Giants scored two meaningless runs off reliever Erik Sable in the 9-2 loss.

The annual Father-Son whiffleball game was Sunday, July 22. No player cherishes this day the way Barry Bonds does. Knowing that he was lucky, growing up in the Giants clubhouse every day and playing catch with Willie Mays, Bonds knows exactly what this game means to the children of the players.

Watching him, you got the sense that Bonds realizes the kids look up to him the way he looked up to Willie Mays. And Barry went out of his way to make them feel special.

Barry probably hopes that in the future, one of those kids will chase his records. Barry will probably show up to the ballpark one day in a new suit, tell the kid, "you can't catch all my records" and tell him to stop by the house and pick up one of those suits every time he breaks a record.

Barry pitched to all the kids in the game, including his three. He encouraged them all, basking in their innocence and cheering like any other father when he sees his children make contact with the ball. At one point, he even held up Benito Santiago's six-month-old daughter and ensured she made contact with the ball. Then Barry provided her a personal escort to first base, making sure she arrived safely.

The cute scene of the late morning went away once the real game started.

The D'backs blew out the Giants again, 12-4 this time, and it was former Giant Matt Williams who broke open the game with a double on a 3-0 count with a seven-run lead. The Giants were furious about the so-called breach of baseball etiquette.

Rookie Chad Zerbe threw a fastball behind Williams in his next at-bat and both benches emptied. Williams and Baker had to be physically separated in a sad afternoon that seemed impossible considering their level of friendship. It dates back to Baker's days as the Giants hitting coach when he took the rookie Williams under his wing and taught him about hitting, fishing and life. Williams has called Baker his mentor a million times, teaching him the right and wrong way to play the game.

The Giants headed to Colorado next and their season was starting to slip away. They were in third place and back to 5.5 games out of first place. Even at Coors Field, the hitters paradise, their offense was lifeless. Hampton went the distance in an 8-2 victory on July 23, the only runs scoring on Shawon Dunston's meaningless pinch-hit, two-run homer in the eighth.

Bonds walked in the seventh to go over the century mark on the year — the ninth time in his career he was walked over 100 times. He singled in the ninth to snap an 0-for-13 streak.

His pace was down to 68 for the year. And, believe me, the homer record story was dead. For three months, it had become common practice to mention early in any game story what Bonds had done — because even when he didn't hit a homer, it was news.

But now, a homerless game wasn't even mentioned by any of us five traveling beat writers. Sixty still seemed realistic. But seventy? It seemed impossible.

It didn't get any better on July 24, the day Bonds turned 37 years old. Aurilia hit a two-run homer and Bonds doubled, but the Giants lost 6-4 and their record fell back to 52-49 for the season — a season-high 6.5 games out of first place.

The offense was downright moribund at this point — 12 hits and six runs in two games at Coors Field for goodness sakes — and in major need of a jumpstart. Nobody knew this more than general manager Brian Sabean. As always, he wouldn't be afraid to act quickly and pull the trigger to inject life into the team.

One week earlier in Arlington, a Rangers beat writer asked a San Francisco writer if the Giants might be interested in first baseman Andres Galarraga. The 40-year-old Galarraga was languishing as a platoon player in a new league, unable to adjust to the designated hitter and unusually miserable.

The Bay Area writer made an argument for why the trade was unlikely, but finished the conversation with "anything can happen." The Texas reporter decided to run the story anyway in his paper and it was on ESPN's *Rumor Central* within 24 hours. People who knew how the rumor started enjoyed a good laugh.

A lot changed in the next week. Sabean saw how many left-handed pitchers his team was about to face, knew the offense was in deep trouble and in need of a jolt, first baseman J.T. Snow was still injured and not able to play, so he started working the phones.

Within 24 hours, a trade was made. Sabean sent three minor leaguers, none of whom was considered much of a prospect, to the Rangers and landed . . . none other than Andres Galarraga. Sabean told writers he wasn't done dealing, either.

For the final game in Colorado, with his team's offense in a deep funk and the season in jeopardy of slipping away, Baker decided to rest a slumping Bonds (2-for-17, seven walks in last six games), a gusty move no doubt. But the savvy Baker wasn't panicking. He was looking to the series in Arizona and figuring this division race was going to be decided in late September, not late July.

Galarraga woke up in Dallas at 5 a.m. on July 25, left Texas a couple hours later, landed in Denver about 10 a.m., went directly to the ballpark, met his new teammates, was fitted for a uniform, talked to the media and Baker inserted him into the fifth spot in the lineup.

With the Giants trailing 3-1 in the fourth, Galarraga doubled and scored two batters later. An inning later, he singled home two runs for a 4-3 lead.

Pedro Feliz, Marvin Benard and Calvin Murray all hit solo homers in the sixth inning. Shawon Dunston another a solo shot in the seventh, Galarraga singled home another run for a bonus in the eighth and the Giants won, 9-3, making both Sabean and Baker look like geniuses yet again.

Curt Schilling was the stereotypical pitcher with the million-dollar arm and 10-cent brain. He would show up at the ballpark with his hair dyed orange one day. His hair spiked into a Mohawk another day. He put in different earrings. He stayed out late. He had no concept of how to prepare himself for a start.

His career turned around one afternoon in a Houston weightroom where Roger Clemens was working out, as usual, and he asked a trainer to bring Schilling over for a talk. Schilling had idolized Clemens and was eager to hear what he had to say.

For over an hour, Clemens chewed out Schilling's ass, telling him he was disrespecting the game, not dedicating himself and needed to rededicate himself to the game.

"It's one of those conversations your father has with you when you're going down the wrong path and he wants you to make a right turn," Schilling said. "My career turned around after that. I'm very grateful he took the time to make a point to talk with me . . . It was a lot about respecting the game. I've approached the game differently after that."

In 1992, Schilling had the fourth-lowest ERA (2.35) in the National League, the lowest opponents average (.201), was second in complete games (10) and tied for third in shutouts (four). All this, despite being a reliever until mid-May.

The next year, the Phillies made the playoffs and Schilling relished the role of pitching on the big stage. He was the MVP of the championship series against the Braves, despite not winning a game, because he allowed three earned runs in 16 innings in two starts. In the World Series, he was known for two things: putting a towel around his head when teammate Mitch "Wild Thing" Williams tried to close games; and throwing a five-hit shutout in game five, the day after an offensive slugfest won by Toronto, who won the series in six games on Joe Carter's memorable series-ending homer.

From 1992-99, Schilling won 93 games and had an ERA above 4.00 just twice. He thrived on complete games, taking pride in finishing games at a time when most starters were content with 6-7 innings.

On August 2, 1998, the Giants and Phillies were playing a series in Philadelphia. Tempers were already hot between the two teams when Bonds stole second base with the Giants comfortably ahead by seven runs in the fifth inning — a breach in the unwritten baseball rule book, although the exact inning of when you draw the time depends on who you ask.

The next time Bonds came to the plate, Ricky Bottalico drilled him in the leg with a pitch and Bonds charged the mound for the first time in his career. Many people were actually curious to see if Bonds' teammates would ever run out onto the field to support him in a fight, but indeed they did as both benches emptied on that day.

In the war of words afterward, the Phillies ripped Bonds for only caring about stats. The outspoken and never-camera-shy Schilling said what many in baseball believed, but few had the guts to say on the record: "This guy's a first-ballot Hall of Famer, no doubt. But when you don't play the game right, bad things happen. What he did was bull, and he knows it. There's no excuse for anybody at this level playing the game that way."

Alex Arias, who homered earlier and later was plunked after Bonds was plunked, said, "I've never had any respect for that guy. No doubt he's a great player, but do you want to be great piling up stats when they don't mean anything? I'm sure he stole half his bases that way. He's a stats guy. That's all he worries about."

Bonds was suspended three games for charging the mound. In the Bay Area, Schilling and Arias' comments resonated with Bonds' harshest critics.

"He is not a leader, on or off the field," *Chronicle* columnist C.W. Nevius wrote. "He declines to bother with mandatory team stretching before many games, and he has exasperated generations of old-school baseball fans by refusing to run out routine ground balls because he feels the pointless effort takes too much out of him. Yet he continues to steal bases at times when the only reason can be to pad his stats. The whole fuss in Philadelphia . . . was vintage Bonds. It would be fascinating to know how many of his 437 steals were cheapies like that one."

The Nevius column ended like this: "That's the Barry Bonds that baseball will know. As his skills erode, Bonds says he will play out his contract, which runs through 2000, and fade away. If so, he will be known as a player who was just a notch below the greats — talented but mercurial, an odd guy who often annoyed his teammates and always mystified them. Nice numbers, though."

Bonds was officially labeled a selfish player who only cared about his statistics. His shaky relationship with the media worsened. And he'd never forget what Schilling said about him.

On July 26, 2000, Schilling was traded from Philadelphia to the Arizona Diamondbacks. At the time, the Giants were two games behind the D'backs in the NL West standings and conventional wisdom around baseball was the D'backs would run away with the division title. The Johnson-Schilling combo was compared to Sandy Koufax and Don Drysdale. Baseball pundits concluded the D'backs were the team to beat in the playoffs.

The Giants were in San Diego and we beat writers went to Bonds for his reaction to the Schilling trade. It was one of those moments when Bonds didn't want to be interviewed. But his reaction to the questions were printed anyway because they were so good.

"He doesn't beat us," Bonds said. "What's he done?"

At that time, in 26 career games against the Giants, Schilling was 3-6 with a 3.16 ERA and two saves. Earlier that season, the Giants beat the Phillies 7-3 on Memorial Day, scoring four runs off Schilling in the seventh to erase a 2-0 deficit.

"Frankly, I don't give a (expletive) where he goes," Bonds said. "It's irrelevant. He's not just playing against us. You have to win the whole season. By the time we play Arizona, we might already know what's going on, one way or the other."

Bonds, it turned out, was right. Schilling was a bitter disappointment, going 5-6 with a 3.69 ERA in 13 starts. Randy Johnson, perhaps fatigued from overwork early in the season, didn't pitch well the final two months. Arizona collapsed, the Giants ran away with the division, clinching it and celebrating it at home after defeating the D'backs.

By the time Schilling faced the Giants, the race was over. Still, Schilling got in another jab at Bonds before the night of the clincher.

"Barry Bonds is a first-ballot Hall of Famer," Schilling said, always using that disclaimer first. "I'd vote for him every day of the week and twice on Sundays. But when he retires, he's still going to the biggest (expletive) who ever lived. Ask his teammates. Ask anyone on their team or in their clubhouse. He is who he is."

Bonds took the high road, responding by saying, "That's his opinion. He's never played with me."

The next night, Schilling started and fanned Bonds twice and pitched a complete-game victory — a start he would later say set the groundwork for his 2001 season.

Schilling started quickly in 2001, highly motivated to redeem himself and reach the postseason. He improved to 7-1 on May 21 in the victory over the Giants memorable for the enormous blast Bonds hit against him. He improved to 14-4 after nearly no-hitting the Giants on July 21.

And now, on July 26, it was Schilling against the Giants again, the opener of a crucial four-game series at Bank One Ballpark.

Arizona was in first place, 1.5 games ahead of the Dodgers, 6.5 ahead of the Giants.

At stake? Only the season.

CHAPTER 13

The Race Is Back On

July 26-August 13, Home Runs 43-50

"(Bonds) definitely has a chance for 70. I don't know how many he's going to hit. He's such a great player, a great power hitter. If he's meant to be the man, he'll do it."

Sammy Sosa

"CLASH OF THE TITANS" screamed the headline in the *Arizona Republic* as the home-run race between Luis Gonzalez and Barry Bonds collided with the National League West race. Bonds had 42 homers, but just three homers in his last 28 games and his pace was down to a season-low 66. Gonzalez had three in his previous two games, pulling him within one of Bonds at 41 homers.

Before the game, the scoreboard at BOB showed replays of Arizona hitters rocking the Giants pitchers the previous Sunday, the benches clearing, Williams and Baker needing to be restrained and the Scorpions song, "Rock You Like A Hurricane" was rocking through the sound system.

A few days earlier, Williams still couldn't fathom why his mentor was so upset at him, essentially going stir crazy, unable to sleep, and realized he had to call Baker to talk about what happened. They didn't discuss the details of their conversation to reporters, but both said "sorry" and "I love you" and agreed to forget the incident.

Bonds, meanwhile, was doing his homework on Curt Schilling. He was studying videotape and the statistics. He knew Schilling had become a different pitcher than in years past. He was throwing first-pitch strikes at a remarkably efficient rate, his control was better than at any point in his career and he was pitching deeper into games because his pitch counts were so much lower.

In most instances, the first pitch would be the only hittable pitch a batter was seeing against Schilling. By the end of the season, this statistic was dramatic. If the first pitch was put into play against Schilling, hitters were batting .429. If Schilling got ahead 0-1, batters were hitting .174.

Bonds knew this.

In the top of the first inning, nobody on, two outs, Schilling threw a 75 mph changeup and Bonds smoked a line drive that was caught in medium deep right-center. It was an out. Yet Bonds knew he was onto Schilling this night. In the fourth, Arizona leading 1-0, Rich Aurilia got a rare hit on an 0-1 pitch from Schilling, hitting an opposite-field homer to tie the game 1-1.

The next batter was Bonds. He was looking to be aggressive early in the count. He jumped on the first pitch he saw and hammered it 378 feet to right field for his 43rd homer of the season. An inning later, Arizona had regained the lead 3-2 and the Giants were rallying. Pitcher Livan Hernandez singled, Marvin Benard walked and Aurilia surprised the Diamondbacks with a bunt single to load the bases for Bonds.

Once again, Bonds looked for a first-pitch fastball. Once again, he saw it. And once again, he didn't miss it. Bonds was actually a little late, but he's so strong and Schilling throws so hard, the ball rocketed through the dry desert air — 102 degrees outside BOB, 79 degrees inside — and into the left-center bleachers for a grand slam. The Giants won the game, 11-3, handing Schilling a rare loss.

"That," Baker said, "was a big slam by Barry. That was huge."

The Giants knew, however, that one victory and two Bonds homers does not a weekend make.

"(Arizona's) not under any pressure," said Bonds, now up to 44 homers. "We're the ones under pressure. Every one of their wins is closer to our grave."

Surely, the homers off Schilling were special for Bonds. Schilling is one of the best pitchers in baseball. He'd been critical of Bonds over the years. Bonds had no desire to gloat over this night though.

He had an intensity in his eyes in a post-game news conference. He was in no mood to discuss home-run records. He called the chances of breaking Mac's record, "not realistic. I had my opportunities. But I slumped off a little bit."

And as for Gonzalez, "we're not having a home-run contest. He won that at the all-star game."

The next night, Aurilia gave the Giants a 1-0 lead with a solo homer in the first inning. Three innings later, Bonds hit another rocket, over the famous hot tub and deep into the right-centerfield seats and the game was tied 2-2. Two batters later, Andres Galarraga annihilated a Brian Anderson fastball to dead center for a solo homer.

In the fifth, the Giants scored two runs to break it open. Aurilia had an RBI single, Bonds was walked, Kent made them pay with a two-run double and Galarraga singled home Kent. The Giants won 9-5 and the offense was suddenly on fire, coincidence or not, since the arrival of Galarraga.

The Giants had 29 runs, 42 hits and 12 homers in three games with "The Big Cat." Galarraga was 6-for-14 (.429) with two doubles, a homer, six RBIs and four runs scored in the three games.

"He's gotten off to a great start," said general manager Brian Sabean, who made the trade for Galarraga. "It's obvious he can still hit."

Aurilia compared the Big Cat's personality to teammate Kirk Rueter, who is nicknamed "Woody" because of his facial resemblance to the lead character from the movie, "A Toy Story."

"I'll tell you what's nice to see is Andres is always out there smiling," Aurilia said. "We have another 'Woody' on the team. Woody (Kirk Rueter) always has a smile on his face. And so does Andres. I really think he's having fun here with us, getting a chance to contribute. We appreciate that. And I'm sure he does too, being back in the National League and away from the DH."

Bonds, who has long been friends with Galarraga as opponents over the years, refused to jump on the Andres-is-savior bandwagon. I asked him that night if Galarraga's presence is helping him see better pitches.

"Nobody can protect Barry but Barry," Barry said. "There ain't no other Barry. He'll help Jeff."

But Bonds was happy with the two wins. "These two games show what we're capable of doing," he said. "I guess with our backs are against the wall, we play our best baseball."

Saturday, July 28, was Luis Gonzalez bobblehead night and the line to get inside for the collectors item began at 4 in the morning. Three hours before the game, the parking garage across the street from the ballpark was already half full (usually it only has a handful of cars at that time.) The line stretched down the long block to America West Arena.

All this waiting, mind you, in 105 degree heat.

Only 15,000 of the precious ceramic dolls were given away and with a sellout crowd of over 49,000 attending, it created high demand. There were reports of fights among fans to get the bobblehead.

Gonzalez's popularity has skyrocketed on the road since winning the home-run hitting contest during the all-star game. But he's already a bona fide hero in this market, where he lives year-round with his wife and their triplets.

If the season was over now, Bonds proclaimed Gonzalez the "no-brainer" for Most Valuable Player.

"He's having an amazing year," Bonds said. "He has a chance to win the triple crown. . . . That's a once-in-a-lifetime thing when someone has a chance to win the triple crown. He has a legitimate chance to do it."

Nobody had won the triple crown — leading the league in batting average, home runs and RBIs — since Carl Yastrzemski in 1967. Gonzalez came into the Saturday game fourth in average, second in homers and first in RBIs.

That wasn't the record Gonzales was eyeballing, though.

"The record that I would want to get is the total bases," Gonzalez said. "That's Babe Ruth. Nobody's come close to it. I'm semi-close to the pace. I don't know if I can continue to do it. Everybody lives for the home runs. I like to be the total package offensively."

Ruth had 457 total bases in 1921. Gonzalez had 293 total bases, which put him on pace for 456.

It was Gonzalez's promotional night, but it was Bonds and Aurilia and the Giants weekend. Aurilia was the hero again in the third game of the series, homering in both the fifth and sixth innings, a pair of two-run shots. The Giants shelled newly acquired starter Albie Lopez and won, 11-4, in a series that was looking like a turning point in the season.

If the Giants were to complete a near-improbable sweep, they would have to defeat Randy Johnson.

Bonds doubled home a run in the first inning for a 1-0 lead. Matt Williams' two-run homer in the second gave Arizona the lead, where it remained until the eighth inning. On a 1-2 pitch, Aurilia tied the game with a dramatic homer off Johnson. In the ninth, Marvin Benard hit an opposite-field, two-run homer off Byung-Hyun Kim, barely inside the line, and the Giants won 4-3 to complete an amazing weekend.

Aurilia, who lives in Scottsdale in the offseason and always hits well at BOB, carried the team with a homer in every game and five overall.

Simply put, the Giants were back in the race — four games out.

And Bonds was back in the homer chase — a pace of 69.

General managers don't have nicknames, but I dubbed Brian Sabean "The Sultan of Swap" for his moves the final week of July. I thought the nickname was pretty clever, not to mention accurate, but I haven't seen it anywhere else in print since. So I think the nickname had a shelf life of one day. Oh well.

Sabean knew the Giants needed some help, and the "win-now" mentality of his early years with the Yankees organization has served him well. First, he landed Galarraga in time to ignite the offense. Next, he added Philadelphia reliever Wayne Gomes to give the bullpen more depth. Then, he snagged the prized starting pitcher on the market, Jason Schmidt, along with outfielder Jason Vander Wal, from the Pittsburgh Pirates. Finally, he added left-handed specialist reliever Jason Christiansen from St. Louis.

In all, Sabean added six new players in the month of July.

Schmidt made his Giants debut on August 1, ironically enough, against his old Pirates teammates. The only players in the Giants starting lineup that night who started on Opening Day were Rich Aurilia, Barry Bonds and Jeff Kent, the three all-stars — a sign of the overhaul Sabean had done to the lineup.

Bonds was on the welcoming committee to Schmidt, hammering a first-inning homer off Joe Beimel: No. 46 on the year.

"When he hit that I thought, 'thank you,'" Schmidt said. "That's what it's all about. The past few days, it's been awesome just seeing what the guy can do."

What made the 46th most impressive was it soared through a strong cross-wind off the Lefty O'Doule Bridge and over the right-center seats, landing just shy of McCovey Cove. Two fans chased after it on the portwalk and collided into each other at full speed going after it.

The night before, Bonds had two potential homers that were taken away by the wind, there's no doubt in my mind. Both died at the warning track, one into the glove of Pirates center fielder Tike Redman and the other going off the top of the wall for a double.

Bonds was hot, once again, having homered four times in his last six games, a stretch that also included three doubles, a triple and a .545 batting average.

Schmidt, the hired gun, fired 96-mph fastballs, went seven innings, his only blemish was a solo homer to former batterymate Jason Kendall, and the Giants won 3-1 to extend their winning streak to seven games.

"We knew (Schmidt) was throwing the ball well," manager Dusty Baker said. "But we didn't know it was *that* well."

Baker gave Bonds another of his periodic days off August 2 and the Giants beat the Pirates, 3-0, to complete the series sweep and run the winning streak to eight games.

The Giants learned back in 1997 — when Sabean orchestrated the infamous "white flag" trade with the Chicago White Sox, landing pitchers Roberto Hernandez, Wilson Alvarez and Danny Darwin for six minor leaguers — not to take the team picture until after the trading deadline.

The date for this year's team picture was Friday, August 3. The time was 2 p.m. The game was at 7:35 p.m. Bonds requested the time of the picture get moved up closer to game time. The Giants didn't change the time.

Bonds didn't show up for the team photo.

He later explained his wife was having surgery at a hospital and wanted to take her home. That's why he requested the photo get taken closer to the first pitch. The no-show would prove more fodder for Bonds' critics.

That night, Baker filled out a lineup that resembled a game on ESPN Classic.

> CF Shawon Dunston, age 38
> SS Rich Aurilia, age 29
> LF Barry Bonds, age 37
> 2B Jeff Kent, age 33
> 1B Andres Galarraga, age 40
> RF Eric Davis, age 39
> C Benito Santiago, age 36
> 3B Ramon Martinez, age 28
> P Russ Ortiz, age 27

"It's no big deal," Baker said. "They can still play. Age is no thing."

The five oldest — Dunston, Bonds, Galarraga, Davis and Santiago — had a combined 16 Gold Gloves between them. All total, there were a whopping 26 all-star appearances by the players in the lineup.

It was one of those summer nights in San Francisco when it seems like there's a fog machine at the top of the ballpark blowing straight down. Maybe that machine was the fountain of youth because those old dudes had quite a game.

Dunston made a spectacular catch, crashing into the wall in center that ended up landing him on the disabled list. Santiago threw out Bobby Abreu trying to steal second, a crucial play in the ninth inning. And Galarraga hit a walk-off two-run homer to win the game in the bottom of the ninth and make the winning streak nine games. Arizona, Los Angeles and the Giants were all separated by a half-game in the standings.

"If this is a dream, I don't want to wake up," Galarraga said. "It's amazing. Sooner or later, I know we have to lose one game. But I don't want to think about that day."

Galarraga didn't just bring a hot bat to San Francisco, he brought quite a bit of karma. His father's name was Francisco and he would have celebrated his 85th birthday on the day the Giants traded for "The Big Cat."

The day of that trade, July 24, Andres' mother Juana prayed for her late husband to help her son. Stuck in Texas, on a last-place team, not playing every day and not happy as a designated hitter, Galarraga wanted out badly. He got his wish with the trade.

The winning streak ended the next afternoon, August 4, despite a two-run homer by Bonds off Nelson Figueroa that landed in McCovey Cove (Bonds' 12th to get wet in two years; the 14th by a Giants player). The 47th trimmed the Phillies lead to 5-2, but the Giants defense self destructed and the Phils won 12-2.

In the series finale, Aurilia continued swinging his lethal bat, hitting a three-run homer in the third in front of Bonds. An inning later, Bonds doubled home two runs, Aurilia added a two-run double in the eighth for insurance and the Giants won 8-4 to conclude a 5-1 homestand that left them one game out of first place.

———◆———

In the late-1960s and early-70s, black baseball players still weren't allowed inside all the hotels and restaurants and clubs as their white teammates. The discrimination bonded the minority players throughout baseball. It became a tradition for the minority players at home to invite the minority players from the opposing team to their home.

For instance, when Dusty Baker and Ralph Garr were roommates playing for the Atlanta Braves, they would arrive in Pittsburgh and Willie Stargell would pick them up at the airport. In St. Louis, it was Curt Flood and Bob Gibson. In Cincinnati, it was Joe Morgan, Ken Griffey Sr. and George Foster. In San Francisco, it was Gary Maddox, Garry Matthews, Tito Fuentes and Bobby Bonds.

It was through this network of friends the Griffey and Bonds families became close. The families first met in the early 1970s when Foster's mother would prepare lunch and dinner for the players and the kids. As the years went on, Birdie Griffey, the wife of Ken Senior, took over the food duties and became a legend for her cooking.

"We played together when our families were together," Bonds told me. "All the kids did. Tito Fuentes' kids did. Gaylord Perry's girls. Juan Marichal's girls. We all hung out together and grew up together. It's no different than anybody's kids nowadays. Junior's son, Trey, and my son, Nikolai, hang out together. Shikari and Junior's daughter hang out."

Even though they were separated by five years, Barry Bonds and Ken Griffey, Jr. knew each other well, bonded by their supreme talent at a young age and their famous fathers.

Junior was the first overall pick of the amateur draft by the Seattle Mariners in 1987. He made his major-league debut in 1989 at age 19 with a spring training so impressive the Mariners had no choice but to start him in the majors. Griffey Senior signed a contract with the Reds just before the regular season and they became the first father-son to play in the major leagues at the same time. In 1990, the year Barry Bonds was winning his first MVP, Ken Senior was traded to the Mariners and the father-son duo lived out the ultimate dream of playing the majors together. On September 14, father and son Griffeys hit back-to-back homers off Kirk McCaskill of the Angels.

In 1994, Junior had 22 homers on May 23 and became the latest player putting an early-season run at Roger Maris' record. By comparison, Bonds had 24 homers on the same day in 2001. Griffey finished with 40 homers in 111 games when the strike wiped out the regular season and World Series. (If he'd have continued at that dreaded word "pace" without the strike, Junior would have finished with 58 homers.)

In 1997, Griffey hit 56 homers. The next year, he hit 56 more. In both years, he was on pace early in the season and speculation was intense at the all-star break, but Junior wasn't able to "keep up the pace" in the second half of the season.

The similarities between Barry and Junior are staggering.

Both had fathers who were all-star major league players, but overshadowed by the superstars on their teams: Bonds by Willie Mays, Willie McCovey, Juan Marichal and Orlando Cepeda; Griffey by Johnny Bench, Tony Perez, George Foster, Pete Rose and Joe Morgan.

Both are the quintessential five-tool players: the ability to hit for power, hit for average, run, throw and catch. Both walk around with their caps on backward during batting practice, which still bothers some "old school" ballplayers to this day. It's an old habit from their childhood when they wore their dads' caps and the only way it fit was backward.

Both started their careers away from home, but returned to the city they were raised in highly publicized announcements: Griffey in a trade (he forced) to Cincinnati in 2000 after 11 years in Seattle; Bonds as a free agent to San Francisco after seven years in Pittsburgh.

Both have had their run-ins with the media, alienating some and inviting criticism because they aren't always available and are often curt in what they say. Both decide when they will run out grounders (not often) and when they won't.

Both have held the title of "highest-paid" baseball player in their lives: Bonds in 1993 ($7,291,666 average); Griffey in 1996 ($8.5 million average); and Bonds again in 1997 ($11.45 million average).

And both, throughout the 1990s, could lay claim to the title of "best player in baseball" in just about any given year.

At the end of the 90s, *The Sporting News* chose Bonds as its Player of the Decade. Baseball players chose Griffey as their Player of the Decade.

However, when the All-Century team was announced in 2000, Bonds received less than a third of the votes Griffey received. Griffey trailed Bonds in every offensive category, except batting average. Bonds also received fewer votes than even Carl Yastrzemski, and Bonds had already eclipsed all of Yaz's career numbers in eight fewer seasons.

Let's face it, Bonds' reputation was a major reason. Griffey could be just as surly, if not more, and fails to run out grounders just as often as Bonds. But Griffey has benefited by better public relations from heavyweights such as Nike and many still think of him as "The Kid" and fondly recall his youthful exuberance and personality and the smile from early in his career with Seattle.

Through it all, Bonds and Griffey remain close friends and soulmates of sorts. If anybody on this planet knows what one of them goes through, it is undoubtedly the other. They often stay at the other's house when their teams play each other — often playing video games into the wee hours of the morning.

"Birdie still does the cooking to this day," Bonds told me. "For Thanksgiving, I was there with Junior. We went to Disney World again with our kids, like we usually do. We go over to Kenny's house for Thanksgiving and his mom cooked."

If there is any jealousy between the two future Hall of Famers, it's never come out in public.

However, whenever they play against each other, they just can't help showing off.

⊷•⊶

The suddenly surging Giants arrived in Cincinnati for their only visit of the season August 6. The next day, with the scored tied 3-3, Bonds led off the 11th inning with a solo homer off closer Danny Graves to deep center, his 48th of the season, and told newly acquired reliever Jason Christiansen, "that was for you."

The inning before, Christiansen got out of a jam by getting Griffey to hit into a double-play and striking out Sean Casey to preserve the 3-3 tie.

"When you get a pitcher who does something like that, you want to do something for him," Bonds told reporters. "That was big when he got Ken Griffey to hit into a double play. You don't see that too often."

When told of Bonds' comment, Christiansen told reporters: "At least he wasn't yelling to the other dugout and saying, 'that one was *off* you.'"

Like most ballplayers, Bonds is superstitious. He honestly believed the reason for his slump was because he was talking about home runs too much with the media. Now that he was hot again, he wouldn't talk much about homers.

It wasn't surprising that Bonds bristled when a reporter from a Cincinnati radio station asked about the home run record.

"Anybody who talks about home runs, I'm walking away," Bonds replied.

The radio reporter tried again to ask about homers.

Bonds looked at him and said, "did you go to deaf school?"

None of the Giants beat writers used the quote, figuring Bonds was baited into a subject he clearly told the reporters he didn't want to discuss. The AP writer in Cincinnati used the quote though. It appeared in newspapers across the country — and again in numerous Sunday baseball notebooks.

It was another item for the "Bonds is a jerk" community. It wasn't entirely fair. But it was typical for Bonds in his relationship with the media.

The next night, Griffey answered with a big two-run single and a leaping catch at the wall of a Jeff Kent drive to preserve an 11-9 Reds win. Bonds walked twice and struck out three times. It wasn't often during the 2001 season you could accuse Bonds of swinging for the fences, but this night you could make a good argument that was happening.

In the series finale August 9, Griffey connected with his 450th career homer off Russ Ortiz in the first inning. Bonds answered by tying his personal season-high with his 49th homer of the season, and 543rd all-time, a low-line drive solo homer in the third inning over the right-field wall to give the Giants a 3-2 lead. They held on for a 6-4 victory.

"I think it's great what Barry's doing," Griffey said. "He's having a great year. If you look at every swing, it's quick and compact. As a hitter, you have to respect that. He's done it all year."

Birdie Griffey collects all of her son's homers in increments of 50, so the Reds public relations staff worked diligently to retrieve the home-run ball. The teen-ager who caught the ball just wanted to meet Griffey, but his dad held out for more.

Bonds' homer had bounced off a wall and back onto the field. Since that ball was available, Reds media relations director Rob Butcher grabbed his walkie-talkie and told his staff, "Tell that kid we'll throw in that ball Bonds just hit."

They ended up trading the Griffey baseball for five autographed baseballs, five autographed bats and assorted autographed photos.

The final game in Cincinnati ended at about 10 p.m., the Giants charter left afterward for Chicago and a Friday afternoon matinee that stated at 12:20 p.m., so manager Dusty Baker continued his pattern of well-calculated days of rest for his superstar, not playing Bonds in the Cubs 9-3 victory to start the series.

Bonds returned to the lineup August 11 and reached his goal for the season: 50 homers.

It was a three-run homer in the second inning off Joe Borowski, landing in the net above the ivy in left-center. There was some doubt. Bonds even ran hard out of the batters box. He stopped at second base, until an umpire gave the finger twirling gesture for a home run.

Finally, Bonds could get his godfather off his back for never reaching 50 homers.

"I finally accomplished it," Bonds told reporters. "Now he can leave me alone for awhile."

Minutes after the ball cleared the famous ivy at Wrigley Field, the *Chronicle's* John Shea (a fellow San Diego State brotheren of mine) got on his cell phone and called back to Atherton, Calif. to make sure Mays knew about it. It must be nice having Mays' home phone number, huh?

Mays was a little tired, having returned from Cooperstown and the annual Hall of Fame functions.

"Oh, he did?" Mays replied to Shea, perking up and energized by the news. "That's a little history for us. Only three guys with the Giants have done that. Johnny Mize, myself and Barry. I've been telling him about that. Whatever he does after this, it's gravy . . . With another month and a half to go, he should get past 10 more."

Mays' comment was shared by most of the Giants organization and traveling media. Few people were *expecting* Bonds to hit 70 homers. Conventional wisdom was 60 would be an incredible season and he might get close to 70, but opposing teams wouldn't pitch to him often enough for a realistic shot at 70.

Bonds considered his 50th the subplot to the afternoon, giving out props to Giants starting pitcher Livan Hernandez. A former third baseman/pitcher for the Cuban National Team, Hernandez went 4-for-4, including a no-doubt-about-it homer, and now had eight consecutive hits and was 12-for-13 over his last four starts.

"Livan's our hitting coach now," an amazed Bonds told reporters. "I've never seen anything like that. Eight straight hits! It ain't that easy. He's embarrassing all of us, but it's fun to watch. It doesn't matter what they throw; sliders down and in, fastballs . . . It was his day. Let him have it. I've had enough headlines in my day."

If something meaningful in a game happens, Baker always gives his lineup card to the player as a souvenir. On the day of Bonds' 50th homer, Baker gave his lineup card to Hernandez.

Bonds still had the baseball as a souvenir, although that wasn't an easy retrieval. After the ball bounced back on the field, center fielder Michael Tucker threw it back to the infield. Shortstop Ricky Gutierrez tossed it to the Cubs' bullpen. A security guard flung it into the crowd.

Russ Letourneau and his son David, 12, of West Lawn, Illinois, traded the ball for a tour of Wrigley's visitors' clubhouse, a bat and ball autographed by Bonds, plus tickets for the series finale.

Sammy Sosa continued to sizzle himself, blasting his 41st of the season. But the Giants won, 9-4, parlaying a six-run second inning into a comfortable victory.

"(Bonds) definitely has a chance for 70," Sosa told a crowd of reporters. "I don't know how many he's going to hit. He's such a great player, a great power hitter. If he's meant to be the man, he'll do it."

A mere 11 years ago, hitting 50 homers was a big deal. Cecil Fielder, in his first year back in the states after playing in Japan, hit No. 50 and 51 on the final day of the 1990 regular season for the Detroit Tigers.

"I'm in some good company," Fielder said that night. "It's unbelievable."

In the first 29 years following Roger Maris' 61 homers in 1961, only two players reached 50 in a season — Willie Mays (52 in 1965) and George Foster (52 in 1977).

After the 1990 season, 50 homers in a season had been accomplished 17 times. There were 12 members of the 50-homer club. (Babe Ruth did it three times, Jimmy Foxx twice, Mickey Mantle twice and Mays twice.)

After the 2001 season, 50 homers in a season had been accomplished 34 times. There were 20 members of the 50-homer club. (Among those not headed for Cooperstown are Greg Vaughn, Brady Anderson and the aforementioned Fielder.)

CHAPTER 14

The Suit Fits

August 14-20, Home Run 51-54

*"I'm happy that all you (media) are understanding
Barry a little bit. He's a hard kid to understand.
Sometimes, he thinks the world owes him everything.
Now, he's beginning to understand it a little bit . . . I
haven't seen a lot of negative stuff in the paper about
him. I hope you all understand, he's still just a
growing kid."*

Willie Mays, to the media.

WILLIE MAYS loves Barry Bonds. Loves him like a son. He still calls this 37-year-old man "kid." And Willie Mays loves reminding the kid that even if he's broken one of his records, he hasn't broken all of them.

It's been this way Barry Bonds' entire life. When Bonds won his first MVP award, Mays told him, "I won two."

So Bonds won two more.

Bonds has won eight Gold Gloves. Mays won 12.

Bonds reached his 10th all-star game in 2001. Mays went to 20.

This is what motivates Barry Bonds.

You can talk about contracts and money and best-player titles and Mark McGwire and MVP awards and critics and Babe Ruth and ballparks and a thousands other things. The biggest thing that motivates Barry Bonds is Willie Mays.

And Mays knows it.

"I tell him that all the time to keep him motivated," Mays said. "A lot of guys don't understand what Barry is all about. I joke around with him. I tell him all the time, 'you can't beat me. I don't care what you do. You can't do what I did.' That makes him mad. Just because you hit more home runs (in a season), you've only got one over me. I've still got triples. I've still got (career) home runs. I've still got 3,000 hits. I've still got stolen bases. That leaves a big gap. He's going to try. It's a mind thing that Barry needs to be aware of at all times."

The Mays and Bonds families have been close since Bobby Bonds was called up to the majors in 1968 and became Barry's godfather a year later.

"Willie just took to me ever since I was a baby," Barry told me, in a reflective moment after the season. "My parents asked him if he would be my godfather.

He said yes. I don't think there was one player in there, except (Willie) McCovey, who Willie didn't take under his wing. He was the focal point of that organization. He was the guy everybody wanted to be like as kids. We all wanted to be like Willie Mays. Willie had all the media around him all the time. He was always doing all the talking. He was the star."

Barry watched Mays do those interviews, the same way his son Nikolai does now.

"We used to hide on top of his lockers when he did interviews," Barry told me, a mischievous grin appearing on his face. "You used to be able to do that at Candlestick. We would hide in a bag and look down on him. He always knew we were doing it. He was cool about it."

Willie Mays, the *Say-Hey* kid, was 26 years old when the Giants moved from New York to San Francisco in 1958. He had 187 career homers. He hit a combined 63 homers in the two years (1958, 1959) the Giants played at Seals Stadium, a temporary home that was known as a pitchers park. He hit 29 homers the first year at Candlestick Park (1960), when the dimensions were an absurd 397 feet to the power alleys and 420 to center.

The fences were justifiably moved closer to home plate the next year: a very short 365 to left-center, 410 to center and 375 to right-center. Those dimensions remained until the Giants left Candlestick after the 1999 season. From 1961-71, Mays hit 367 homers, an average of 34 homers a year, with Candlestick his home park.

Mays was traded back to New York in the 1972 season at age 41, hit six in his final season with the Mets in 1973, and finished with 660 homers.

How many homers would Mays have hit if it weren't for the winds and other inclement conditions at Candlestick? That question has been asked a lot.

Roger Kahn, who covered the Brooklyn Dodgers as a beat writer for the *New York Herald-Tribune* in the 1950s and wrote the splendid "*The Boys of Summer*" novel, is often cited for an answer to this question based on what he wrote in his book, "*Memories of Summer*."

"Curiously," Kahn wrote, "Mays never hit a World Series homer, but despite the gales of Candlestick Point, his final total reached 660, third on the all-time list. Had Willie been permitted to play out his career in the Polo Grounds, like Mel Ott before him, he would have hit at least 800 homers and surpassed Babe Ruth and Hank Aaron. Or so I believe."

Rob Neyer, the thinking-man's numerical wizard who writes a baseball column on ESPN.com, shot down Kahn's theory in an exceptional column in April.

"First of all, it's fairly easy to estimate how many home runs Willie Mays would have hit if he'd spent his career in a 'reasonable normal' home park (assuming, of course, he didn't)," Neyer wrote. "We simply double his road home runs, and add a few — say two percent? — to account for the natural home-field advantage.

"Well," Neyer continued, "Willie Mays hit 325 road home runs in his career. If we double 325, and multiply that product by two percent, we arrive at 663 . . . which is exactly three home runs more than Mays actually hit. Oops."

Neyer's research showed that Mays hit four percent more homers at Candlestick than he did in road games. Willie McCovey hit five percent more at Candlestick. Their teammates hit two percent more at Candlestick.

So if Candlestick did take away that many homers from Mays and McCovey, so did other ballparks around the league. More than likely, Mays and McCovey benefited from the short fences in the power alleys for some of their homers. Sure, they lost some homers from the winds. But they also undoubtedly were aided by some of those winds. After all, the winds were not *always* blowing in.

Why is this important in a book about Barry Bonds?

Legacy.

The Bonds legacy will be written in great detail in the years to come. His numbers will be examined, crunched, scrutinized and downplayed. His numbers will be compared to Willie Mays and Babe Ruth and Ted Williams and Hank Aaron.

And, at some point, somebody will say, "well, Willie Mays lost all those homers playing at Candlestick. Bonds was aided by expansion, smaller ballparks and Pacific Bell Park."

Well, remember Rob Neyer's research, remember 365 to left-center at the 'Stick, remember the wind sometimes blew out, remember that all those old-timers never faced a left-handed relief specialist like side-winding Mike Myers in the late innings and remember that Pac Bell Park had the second *fewest* homers hit in it during the 2001 season.

———•◦•◦•———

Rick Reilly of *Sports Illustrated* approached Barry Bonds on Wednesday, August 15. Bonds was now at 51 homers. The day before, he mashed his latest into McCovey Cove, a grand slam on an 0-2 pitch off Ricky Bones in the sixth inning of the Giants 13-7 victory over the Florida Marlins.

The ball was retrieved by a man in a white boat with an American flag in the back. Bonds was now one away from tying his godfather for most homers in Giants franchise history for a season.

Bonds rejected Reilly's request for an interview before the game. He also turned down Reilly's request after the game, although he asked what subjects would be covered.

"Homers?" Reilly offered.

"I don't want to talk about that," Bonds replied.

And with that, Reilly left town.

Oh, yeah, the night before, the night Bonds hit No. 51, the night Bonds didn't talk to the press afterward, a night when all the local reporters had cleared from the clubhouse to file their stories on deadline, Reilly had a private conversation with second baseman Jeff Kent alone in the clubhouse.

———•◦•◦•———

August 16 was a Thursday afternoon business-persons special. It was overcast in the morning and a typically cool San Francisco summer day, a mere 71 degrees at first pitch. No matter. A sellout crowd of 41,804 blew off work to watch the finale of the three-game series against the Marlins.

A.J. Burnett, who pitched a no-hitter against the San Diego Padres earlier in the season, was starting for the Marlins. A hard-throwing power pitcher who had moments of wildness (including nine walks the night of his no-no), Burnett walked Rich Aurilia and Barry Bonds in the first inning. He escaped the jam by retiring Jeff Kent on a fly ball to right and blowing a 96 mph fastball by the recently acquired John Vander Wal to end the first inning.

In the third, Marvin Benard was thrown out trying to steal second base with Barry Bonds at the plate. So Bonds led off the fourth. On a 1-0 pitch, Burnett tried to throw a fastball inside passed Bonds. Like so many others, he failed.

It left the park in about two seconds. Another cannon shot. Pity the fans who sit in the first row of the bleachers in right field and actually think about catching the ball with their bare hands. The guy who tried on this one actually thought about getting his entire body in front of it.

At the last second, he evidently realized how quickly the ball was traveling and did a classic "*ole*" like he was battling a bull in Spain and reached out with his hands to the side. The ball might have gone through his hands for all I know. There was a mad scramble on the ground for the ball, although no high-stakes bidding would happen for this baseball.

By the eighth inning, the Marlins led 3-1 and Burnett had only given up one other hit besides Bonds' homer. Pedro Feliz pinch-hit for reliever Tim Worrell and doubled. Benard singled him home. Aurilia reached on an infield single. That ended Burnett's day. Interim manager Tony Perez went to Vic Darensbourg, one of the top-five left-handed relief specialists in baseball, to face Bonds.

The count was 1-2. Darensbourg tried to go away with a fastball. He left it up. Hitting a fastball up and away for a single isn't all that easy. Well, for mortals. Bonds crushed the pitch about 15 feet to the right of dead center for his 53rd homer of the season, passing Willie Mays on the franchise list and just about single-handedly delivering a 5-3 sweep-clinching win over the Marlins.

"It was," Darensbourg said, "like a nightmare."

How is this for eerie? Bonds' 53rd homer came in a game with a 5-3 final, on the 53rd anniversary of Babe Ruth's death. Ruth died at the age of 53.

For Bonds, the kid who grew up around legends, then chased their ghosts as a man, he could finally look into the eyes of godfather Willie Mays and tell him, "I caught you."

Well, the next time Bonds saw him.

Mays wasn't in attendance for the game.

"He'll probably congratulate me," Bonds said, minutes after the game in a crowded press conference. "But I'll have a few things to say to him. Like, 'I gotcha.' There are accomplishments you never think you can do. To try and reflect on it right now is very hard. When I hit 50 home runs I was surprised. When I had 39 before the all-star break, I was surprised. There's been a lot of surprises for me this year."

As he'd been doing all season, Bonds held back in getting too excited over regular-season homers. He'd rather save some of these for the postseason.

"I love this game, I love to win," Bonds said. "I've come up short a lot of times. I hope I can just carry this on, all the way through. That's on my mind more than anything. I've been able to help teams win divisions. I need to help a team win a World Series."

Bonds had 11 homers in his last 17 games. He was 24-for-60 (.400) with 18 runs, six doubles, a triple and 28 RBIs in that stretch.

His pace was back up to 71.

"He's hot now. He's been hot all year," Giants starter Shawn Estes said. "Most important, he's been clutch all year."

How clutch?

Of Bonds' 53 homers, 38 had either put the Giants ahead, tied the game, or put them within one run.

The Giants, who couldn't seem to win games when Bonds homered back in May, had a record of 9-1 in the last 10 games Bonds homered; and a 20-5 record going back further. Those wins were allowing Bonds to enjoy these homers a lot more.

"Oh yeah, without a doubt," Bonds said. "This is the time you have to excel. That finish line is getting closer and closer. You want to get as close as you can, give your team every opportunity to win."

In the greatest baseball family ever, full of legends and Hall of Famers — Bobby Bonds, Willie Mays, Reggie Jackson — Barry Bonds finally had bragging rights on at least one record.

"It's nice because my godfather held it," Bonds admitted. "It's something I will remember forever. But somebody will break it eventually."

The crowd that afternoon gave Bonds standing ovations following each homer and brought him out for a curtain call after the second.

Ann Killion of the *Mercury News* put it eloquently in her column the next day: "For years, the question has been whether Bay Area fans would embrace him. Right now, they are embracing him, adoring him, bowing to him, standing for him because they know they may never see anything like this again. It's a giddy kind of worship. The lust for a post-homer curtain call is frantic. There's Bondsmania in the air."

The day after Bonds finally caught his godfather for homers in a season, Mays showed up at Pacific Bell Park in a new suit.

Bonds saw him in a tunnel and told Willie, as planned, "I gotcha."

Mays smiled and laughed.

"He doesn't realize, that's just one record," Mays told the media in a press conference that afternoon. "I bought 12 suits the other day. This suit I've got on, I'm going to sign it and let him take it home. That will be one. I know Barry pretty well. I'll give him the coat and pants later. He doesn't know all this that I know.

"I've been preparing for this for a long time. He's the type of kid that needs motivation. I know what motivates him. He doesn't realize one year I got 20 triples. He has to get that. I got 3,000 hits. He's got to get that. I have 660 home runs. He has to get that. I'll put the suits in the closet and tell him, 'every time you do something, come pick one up.' That will give him motivation to do things I think."

During his illustrious career, Barry Bonds has passed Hall of Famers for a certain milestone and seemed indifferent about it. I distinctly remember the day in Houston that Bonds passed Lou Gehrig. Lou Gehrig! He was asked what it was felt like. Bonds looked at the reporter who asked the question with the "you don't have a clue" look on his face. He managed a smile.

"It's nice," Bonds said. "But I have much higher goals."

Some call this arrogance. Some accuse him of not understanding baseball history. But that's wrong.

Bonds understands baseball history. He doesn't need to pick up a book to learn about Willie Mays. He was there in his locker every day. There's one legend that causes Bonds to gasp in awe.

It's Willie Mays.

"He was like 4-5 years old, maybe 7," Mays recalled. "He used to come into the clubhouse. I never thought he would get this many home runs this quickly. I thought he would do it later. I think he can play 3-4 more years without a problem. He was a kid in my locker, day in and day out. (His mother) Pat used to bring him and he used to hang out with me all the time, go on the field with me.

"I knew he was going to do something. I told him you have to go to college first. Education is much more important than baseball. I think he can see why. He went down to Arizona (State). I thought we (the Giants) were going to get him. Now it seems like a blessing."

Mays, like so many others, was clearly in a nostalgic mood about "the kid" he's known for over 30 years.

"Every time he hits a home run, it reminds me of when he was 5 or 10," Mays said. "All those flashback in my mind. Here was a kid that was 7 years old. Do you ever think that kid would do all that? That flashes back into my mind a lot. Now, I realize that I'm not the only one. A lot of people realized he was a great sports guy when he was going to Serra (High School). I'm not the only one who realized he could do all these things."

Willie Mays was 37 years old during the 1968 season. He hit 23 homers, drove in 79 runs and finished the season with 587 career homers.

Barry Bonds, having turned 37 a month ago, already had 53 homers in the season and was up to 546 in his career. And it was still only August 16.

"This year, watching what I see, Barry is in much better condition than he was last year," Mays said. "That's what you have to do. You have to keep your body in condition to play. I hear this all the time, 'he can't do it at 37, he can't do it at 38.' Why not? Why can't he do it? I don't understand that. I'm not surprised . . . I think it's a great tribute to Barry and the short amount of time he's been in baseball. All records are made to be broken. It's right in the family. We're both Giants and I hope he stays a Giant all his life."

Mays called it a "special year for him and myself."

How come Mays wouldn't return Barry's phone calls earlier in the year, when Barry was hot?

"I only talk to Barry when he gets into a slump, when he goes bad," Mays said. "That's when I jump in. I make sure he's focused. You have to be focused when you play sports. You have to know what you're doing. You have to educate yourself on who is pitching. Sometimes, he gets out of whack and doesn't realize what they are trying to do to him. He'll try to pull every ball. That's when the focus leaves him a little bit."

Mays even had a message for the media.

"I'm happy that all you are understanding Barry a little bit," Mays said. "He's a hard kid to understand. Sometimes, he thinks the world owes him everything. Now, he's beginning to understand it a little bit. This is why you guys should put a little clap on your back. You've been with him all year. I haven't seen a lot of negative stuff in the paper about him. I hope you all understand, he's still just a growing kid. He should be rewarded."

The Barry Bonds home run victim list is quite impressive. Ten have won Cy Young Awards. Ten have won ERA titles. And at the top of the list, eight homers apiece, are Greg Maddux and John Smoltz, two of the best pitchers of their generation.

Smoltz' return from reconstructive elbow surgery was up and down in 2001. He'd been on the disabled list a couple times. The Braves decided to make him a relief pitcher in early August, taking some of the strain off the elbow and the results were promising so far.

On August 17, Maddux started against the Giants at Pac Bell Park. Bonds was out in front of a 2-0 changeup in first inning, grounding out to the shortstop on the right side. Bonds singled off Maddux in the fourth, stole second and was left stranded there. He popped to third in the sixth inning.

Smoltz took over in the eighth inning and Bonds was the first batter he faced. The at-bat went like this.

Fastball, 95 mph: strike one.

Fastball, 95 mph: fouled back, strike two.

Fastball, 97 mph: strike three looking.

Smoltz struck out three more batters in two innings of jaw-dropping, flawless relief to seal a 2-1 victory over the Giants.

The next day, the Braves pitching staff continued its dominance over a Giants lineup that consisted of Aurilia and Bonds and not much else on most days.

Jason Marquis held the Giants to just one run in 7 1/3 innings, but the one run was significant: No. 54 by Bonds. The ball bounced into McCovey Cove and was just about the only thing 41,722 Giants fans could cheer in the Braves 3-1 victory.

The 54th of the season was the 548th in Bonds' career. That tied Bonds with yet another Hall of Famer — Mike Schmidt, the premiere National League slugger in the 1980s.

The Bonds connection to Mike Schmidt goes back to Bonds' rookie year, 1986, when Schmidt was the NL Most Valuable Player for a third time. During a conversation around the batting cage one day, Schmidt, in essence, taught Bonds how to sleep before games.

Bonds is the undisputed champion at it now.

"Mike Schmidt told me to close my eyes and imagine positive thoughts in my mind," Bonds said. "A lot of times when you close your eyes and reopen them, the pitches are a lot clearer. I practiced that from the first time I ever met him on the field and when I was playing him. That was always something I kept up throughout my career."

Sometimes, Bonds just flat-out sleeps. Sometimes, Bonds visualizes that game's starting pitcher. Sometimes, he finds his happy place.

"Sometimes, I'm off on a beach, walking around," Bonds said. "I'm trying to take the intensity out of my body, trying to just be as relaxed and as calm as I can. A lot of times, when you get tensed up, everything slows down. There's a lot of things that . . . it's hard to explain. But it takes a lot of practice to be able to do it."

Bonds was sound asleep in the visitors clubhouse at Turner Field the night before his three-homer game in Atlanta. It happens so often, I can't even begin to count the number of times I've walked into the Giants clubhouse and seen Bonds sleeping in his reclining chair at Pac Bell, especially for day games.

Part of that, as any parent can confirm, goes with the territory of coming home from work late and having a 2-year-old daughter wake you up early in the morning.

Babe Ruth and Mickey Mantle, whose late-night partying was well-documented in their playing careers, probably did their share of sleeping in clubhouses in their careers. But those could have been alcohol-induced, not visualizing the starting pitcher or walking on a beach in their happy place.

Before the final game of the Braves series, yet another *ESPN Sunday Night Game of the Week* telecast, Bonds went up to starter Jason Schmidt and told his new teammate, "trust the ballpark."

Schmidt listened to his left fielder. He allowed one run in seven innings. Tom Glavine walked Bonds twice, the second an intentional walk in the fifth inning. Jeff Kent was then walked (not intentionally) and Andres Galarraga singled home two runs. The Giants won, 4-1, to prevent the sweep, another big-game victory by the hired-gun Schmidt to keep their deficit at 2.5 games behind Arizona.

"I like pitching here, how can you not?" Schmidt said. "It's a big left field. Every time I pitch here, Barry comes up to me and says, 'trust the park.' That's why I do."

CHAPTER 15

The Reilly Factor

August 21-27, Home Runs 55-56

"What do they think, that we're supposed to be break-dancing in here? Do you have friends everywhere you go where you work? I'm supposed to have friends all over the world all the time? What's the point? Doesn't it seem kind of strange? I've got friends in the game of baseball, but I don't have 700 of them."

Barry Bonds

LONG AFTER HIS career is over, it will undoubtedly happen to Jeff Kent. He'll be at an old-timers game. Or making some type of public appearance. Or he'll be in a restaurant and somebody will recognize him. And he'll get asked "The Question."

"How did you feel when teams walked Barry Bonds and pitched to you?"

I remember the first time I asked him the question. It was the second day of the 2000 season, Kent's fourth with the San Francisco Giants. Bonds was walked in the game and Kent made them pay with a clutch hit. I remember asking my fellow beat writers what Kent is usually like when he gets asked about the walks to Bonds. My colleagues decided to play a joke on me, the rookie beat writer, by telling me that he doesn't mind and I should ask him about it.

So I did.

"You guys have been asking me that for four years," Kent told me, his voice rising, his head shaking. "It just doesn't matter. They've always walked Barry. They always will. It doesn't matter."

It was a pretty good joke my fellow beat writers pulled on me (and the last time I trusted them). Actually, it was a good lesson. I felt pretty stupid afterward. But I've heard a lot of reporters ask the same question to Kent, phrased in a variety of different ways, and his response is the same.

"It just doesn't matter," Kent always says.

It took me a hundred times of hearing it, but I finally believe him.

Jeff Kent was born in Bellflower, Calif., a suburban city in the conservative Orange County area near Disneyland. His father was a police officer. If there was love in his family, it was certainly tough love. Kent never grew up a baseball fan. He didn't collect baseball cards. Didn't attend many games at nearby Anaheim

Stadium or watch many on television. And he certainly never read a baseball history book.

He was into motorcycles. He just happened to be good at baseball. In 1986, Kent batted .500 as a junior to set a school record at Edison High School in Huntington Beach. He was not drafted a year later and attended the University of California, Berkeley, on a partial baseball scholarship.

Kent was the starting shortstop on the Bears team that won the 1988 NCAA Central Regional in Austin, Texas, and advanced to the College World Series. During that Regional, the kid from Huntington Beach fell in love with Texas and the cowboy way of life. He made it a goal to buy some land and run a ranch in Texas one day.

Kent was drafted in 1989 by the Toronto Blue Jays in the 20th round. At that round you aren't considered a serious prospect. Kent, as he had always done, worked his tail off. He made the major leagues three years later in 1992, beginning his career as a reserve on a Blue Jays team that was *en route* to a World Series championship. Kent was never able to celebrate. On August 27, Kent and a player to be named later (outfielder Ryan Thompson) were traded to the New York Mets for starting pitcher David Cone, a key acquisition in the Blue Jays' stretch drive.

The next four seasons in New York were turbulent for Kent. He had a well-earned reputation for throwing helmets and never taking his outs like a professional. He was moved around the infield, playing some third base, because his defense wasn't very good and many felt at 6-foot-1 and 215 pounds, Kent lacked the range to play second base. In fact, when *ESPN The Magazine's* Jeff Bradley was a Mets beat writer, he would sometimes keep track of how many errors Kent made *in batting practice* and print them.

Kent was never liked by his teammates, considered a loner at best, a clubhouse cancer at worst. Much of that stemmed from simply not being "one of the boys" to go out and party after games. He was hated by the New York media — a feeling that continues to this day.

Before the 1996 trading deadline, Kent was shipped off again, this time to the Cleveland Indians with Jose Vizcaino for Carlos Baerga and Alvaro Espinoza. The Indians were essentially getting rid of Baerga, who had bulked up so much that he was no longer a competent second baseman. Vizcaino did most of the starting at second for Cleveland.

Kent didn't initially get much playing time and when he did, it was at third base. Most teams were of the belief that Kent was too big to play second base. Kent did hit .348 (16-for-46) in September as the Indians won another division title. Kent started twice in the division series and went 1-for-8 as the Tribe lost to the Baltimore Orioles.

Two months later, Kent was traded again, the third time in five years — the controversial trade that sent the popular Matt Williams to Cleveland and prompted then-rookie Giants general manager Brian Sabean to tell KNBR-AM listeners, "I'm not an idiot. I know what I'm doing."

Because he had nobody else to bat cleanup, Giants manager Dusty Baker inserted Kent into the fourth slot and left him there. Kent was allowed to play second base. Vizcaino was also included in the trade and he played shortstop, delaying the emergence of a youngster named Rich Aurilia for another season.

The combination of being older and wiser, plus getting a chance to play every day in the premiere lineup spot for RBIs (just behind Barry Bonds) helped Kent put together four of the finest offensive seasons by a second baseman in baseball history. His 475 RBIs from 1997-2000 were the most by any player who primarily played second base.

Baker attributed one of the reasons for Kent's success to no longer giving away at-bats as often.

"He learned how to hit that single the other way, instead of trying to hit the ball out of the ballpark," Baker said. "Now he's learned with two strikes to cut it down and go up the middle, instead of going for the pump. That's the difference. If Jeff was like that his whole career, it wouldn't have taken him as long to get to this point."

Along the way, Kent inexplicably turned into the "Go-To" quote for Giants beat writers. He came to town with a reputation of not getting along with teammates or the media, but Kent was nothing of the sort in the Bay Area. He was always at his locker after the tough loss, answering question after question, and became the unofficial team spokesman. His no-nonsense words and never-give-up attitude served as the consciousness of the team.

The four-year run was capped by a .334 average, 33 homers and 125 RBIs in 2000 — which earned him the Most Valuable Player award by the Baseball Writers Association of America.

The MVP award didn't change anything in Kent's life. He retreated to his

Diamond K Ranch in Texas and maintained his usual itinerary: running bow-hunting trips and raising cattle. In fact, the day Kent was named MVP, he was mowing the lawn. His wife Dana told him there was a phone call. He picked up the phone, received the news and returned to the lawnmower. His friends had to pry the news out of him. He celebrated the award at a barbecue restaurant where the most expensive item on the menu was under 10 bucks.

From day one, Kent and Bonds were never friends. That isn't exactly shocking. They both keep to themselves. Neither is considered "one of the boys." If they disliked each other, it never came out publicly, unless you happened to ask Kent if he saw better pitches hitting behind Bonds. The most telling sign, if any, was Kent's often indifference or token handshakes after Bonds hit a homer. In Kent's defense, you can make the argument he's simply putting on his game face and concentrating on his next at-bat.

During the stretch drive toward the 2000 NL West division, *Baseball Weekly's* Bob Nightengale did a profile on Bonds and Kent. It was terrific story, detailing the differences in their lifestyles and their indifference toward each other. (Bonds disputes some of the facts about the way he lives his life, insisting it's not very extravagant.)

The thesis, however, was that as much as Bonds and Kent might dislike each other, they desperately needed each other to reach their mutual ultimate goal — a World Series championship.

On the day Jeff Kent arrived at spring training in 2001, he moved his previous locker space to the far corner of the Scottsdale Stadium clubhouse. When asked why, the reigning MVP told us beat writers he wanted to have more of an influence and impact on the younger players whose lockers are in that area — the type of impact Dave Winfield, Tom Henke, Joe Carter and Pat Borders once had on him in Toronto.

It was suggested that Kent was really just trying to get further away from Bonds' locker. "The clubhouse isn't big enough for that," said Kent, before turning more diplomatic. "Barry and I are going down different highways. But we're both trying to reach the same place."

Four weeks later, as most of those rookies had been sent to the minor league camp, Kent had empty lockers all around him. Now *that* is a veteran move.

In May 1993, *Sports Illustrated* sent reporter Richard Hoffer to do a story on Barry Bonds returning to San Francisco to play for the Giants. Bonds put the interview off for days, stinging the ego of the reporter and the subject became an ongoing joke among the players. The reason was Bonds already felt slighted from previous encounters with the magazine.

"Dude," Bonds said, waving the writer away one day, "later."

Another day, Willie Mays volunteered to retrieve his godson from the trainers room. After a minute, Mays returned with the message: "Ice. He's getting ice."

On the seventh day of waiting, when Bonds had agreed to a specific appointment, he told the reporter: "Aw, dude! I forgot about stretching!"

The joke here is that Bonds rarely stretched with his teammates back then, and stretches with them about half the time nowadays.

Teammate Willie McGee walked by. "Man, dude's been here a week."

Later on the seventh day, and again the eighth day, Bonds agreed to the interview. But not until after Bonds had made his point to the reporter.

The reporter got even, of course, blasting Bonds in the infamous May 24, 1993 issue with the headline that endures to this day, "I'm Barry Bonds, And You're Not."

Bonds didn't talk to *Sports Illustrated* for seven years.

When he finally did, it was to, of all reporters, Jeff Pearlman, the author of the controversial story about John Rocker. It wasn't a cover story. It started on page 48. The headline was, "Appreciating Bonds." The subhead was, "Though obscured by the home run barrage, an older, wiser Barry Bonds is in many ways better than ever."

Pearlman's story was about an older Bonds who is mellowing out, maintaining his greatness, if not becoming greater, smiling more, laughing more, opening up to reporters more and not making them wait seven days for an interview.

Ahh yes, but that was 2000. And a year later, Bonds blew off Rick Reilly's interview request.

The headline on the back inside page, *The Life of Reilly*, in the August 27 issue of *Sports Illustrated* was, "He Likes Himself Barry Much."

Reilly's column begins this way: "*In the San Francisco Giants' clubhouse, everybody knows the score: 24-1. There are 24 teammates, and there's Barry Bonds.*" Kent is quoted in the article saying the following, "He doesn't answer questions. He palms everybody off on us, so we have to do his talking for him. But you get used to it. Barry does a lot of questionable things. But you get used to it. Sometimes it rubs the younger guys the wrong way. You just hope he shows up for the game and performs. I've learned not to worry about it or think about it or analyze it. I was raised to be a team guy, and I am, but Barry's Barry. It took me two years to learn to live with it, but I learned."

The issue hit newsstands when the San Francisco Giants were in Montreal. Beat writers found out when *SI* sent out advance notification to newspapers and the message was relayed by sports editors.

Something needs to be stressed here: Nobody in the Bay Area media thought this was a big deal. It was common knowledge. Most savvy Giants fans knew that Bonds and Kent weren't friendly. It was no big deal in the Giants clubhouse either. It was old news. Nobody blinked.

Oakland Tribune columnist Art Spander, who wrote about it first, summed it up best: "I've always believed Reilly was one of the cleverest journalists around, and this proves it. Bonds and the Giants will be going to New York in a few days, and everybody will be referring to the column. The only way Rick could get more attention would be to move in with Madonna. Reilly accuses Bonds of being selfish, egotistical and arrogant. He says Jeff Kent doesn't particularly get along with Barry, and Barry doesn't particularly get along with other players on the Giants. Hey, Rick, did you hear that Lindbergh flew the Atlantic?"

Still, a reaction from Kent and Bonds needed to be done.

It was Wednesday, August 22, and Bonds sat down before the game with Tim Keown, a former *Chronicle* columnist, now working for *ESPN The Magazine*. The interview lasted more than an hour, although as Keown explained in his cover story, an interview with Bonds is more like a verbal chess match. Bonds asks just as many questions as the reporter.

A sagging economy forced cutbacks to my newspaper's sports travel budget and this East Coast trip was deemed too expensive. Beat writers Joe Roderick of the *Times* and Dan Brown of the *Mercury News* were the first to approach Kent about the *Life of Reilly* column. They read some of the quotes to Kent.

"Ahh geez, he doctored up some of those comments pretty good," Kent told them.

Kent didn't deny making the statements. When Reilly asked him the questions, Kent felt the need to be honest. It isn't in his nature to say what he doesn't believe, and damn the consequences. Still, Kent thought Reilly would write a more balanced column. And he certainly didn't think his quotes would be the lone voice of discontent.

"I think most of those comments are pretty quotable, word for word, but taken way out of structure," Kent said. "I can't believe I used 'me' because I don't talk about me — you guys know that — especially to a *Sports Illustrated* guy. My comments to him were based on 'us.' He asked me questions about Barry's routines and so forth and I said, 'we don't worry too much about Barry off the field. We worry about what he gives us on the field.'

"He wanted to pull the trigger big-time," Kent continued. "It sounds like he did. I tried to show that there is not a personal problem between me and Barry on the field. There's not a personal problem with me and Barry or this team off the field. We just don't deal with Barry's extracurriculars. I told him it's just not a big deal because we just don't deal with it. It's been that way for years. It took me two years after I came over here to find his routines and deal with his routines. He's not a perfect player. You guys know that. He's not a perfect human being — nor am I. I don't think any of us are excluded from that conversation. But his article on it, he wanted to run with 'Us against Barry.'"

Bonds hadn't read the article yet. During batting practice, he approached Kent about it. Kent suggested he should read it. Bonds didn't read the entire article. But he got the gist of it and responded.

"What do they think, that we're supposed to be break-dancing in here?" Bonds told beat writers. "Do you have friends everywhere you go where you work? I'm supposed to have friends all over the world all the time? What's the point? Doesn't it seem kind of strange? I've got friends in the game of baseball, but I don't have 700 of them."

Bonds' response was quite telling. He could have further fueled the fires. He could have attacked Kent and tried to fight him. He could have ripped Kent and called him the problem. It could have turned into a divided clubhouse that would have looked like this: Bonds supporters (1 or 2); the Kent supporters (1 or 2); those totally indifferent (21-23).

Instead, Bonds continued his answer like this: "You know that's not the truth. I don't have any comment about it. If you know what is true, why would you even care? I don't care. I don't read *Sports Illustrated*. You don't even know what (Kent) told (Reilly). He could have taken those comments way out of context, you know what I mean? Go ask Jeff what he meant by it."

Manager Dusty Baker wasn't thrilled about the article, of course. And his biggest complaint was the following line by Reilly: *"There are 24 teammates who get on the players' bus at the hotel to go to the park, and there's Bonds, who gets on the bus with the broadcasters, the trainers and the manager who coddles him."*

Baker admitted he gives Bonds some leeway, as he does other veteran experienced players, but disagreed vehemently that he "coddles" his superstar.

"It sounds like you're guarding a kid," Baker told reporters. "How can you coddle a guy who's 37 years old? You treat your prize racehorses differently than you do one of your other horses. I was one of those prize racehorses. Certainly, my rules, guys are going to bend them, but nobody's going to break them. Sometimes you let them run. Sometimes a thoroughbred horse, he doesn't want to be saddled and he doesn't want a bridle in his mouth. Sometimes you let him be free."

Baker added, "I don't tell him anything. He's 37 years old. How many people in here can tell Barry anything? He is who he is."

What did the public think?

Rick Alber of San Carlos wrote this in a letter to the editor in the *Chronicle*: "Will somebody please find Jeff Kent's security blanket and remind him that Barry Bonds is never likely to warm up to a good 'ol son-of-a-cop whose hobbies are ranching, hunting and dirt-bike riding? I certainly thought an MVP would have the sense to not trash-talk a teammate in the middle of a tight pennant race."

And Kent Merrigan of Burlingame wrote this to the *Chronicle*: "The timing and motivation of Rick Reilly's 'column' on Barry Bonds in this week's *SI* is so obvious it's pathetic. Is it a coincidence that a rip job on the guy who is the biggest story in baseball this year appears as the Giants are set to arrive for their only visit to New York this season? The Giants don't pay Barry Bonds to be Mr.

Congeniality, and while Barry may be yet another example of a star athlete who acts like a jerk, this is not anything new (see Ty Cobb).

"Barry has said all along he doesn't care about the home-run record, he wants a World Series ring, which is the only piece missing from his resume for being considered among the greatest players ever! Is this another example of Barry being selfish? Probably, since I'm pretty sure his incentive is not to make Jeff Kent's career complete. But if he can accomplish it, I know I would be very happy, along with a few million other people who live in the proximity of the Bay Area."

As for author Rick Reilly, he was contacted in his Denver home by Tim Kawakami, a columnist at the *Mercury News*. Reilly stood by his story and the Kent quotes.

"I half-think Jeff Kent knew this was coming," Reilly told Kawakami. "I half-think that Jeff Kent knew, 'hey, we're going to New York, I just want my feelings known on it.' He's put up with a lot. It's not like he's just up from Topeka. I think sort of in the back of his mind, he knew what this would do. It was like he was ready to burst to me. I think he found himself in an empty clubhouse and maybe he saw a way to do it one time and get it over with. He looked like a guy who'd had it up to his eyebrows. I don't think he's jealous or anything. I just think he's sick of it."

The Giants clubhouse is truly unique. It isn't "run" by anybody. If pressed, the leaders are veterans Shawon Dunston and Eric Davis, but neither is an everyday player. Kent talks to the media when necessary, but never gives a rah-rah speech to his teammates. He's just as much a loner as Bonds is. Bonds would also never give a speech to his teammates.

The Giants had players from Nicaragua (Marvin Benard), Venezuela (Andres Galarraga), the Dominican Republic (Felix Rodriguez, Pedro Feliz), Cuba (Livan Hernandez) and Puerto Rico (Benito Santiago, Ramon Martinez and Edwards Guzman), mixed with players from Nebraska, California, Washington and Missouri on their 2001 team.

Veteran Mark Gardner is a leader among the pitching staff, but some of the younger pitchers tune him out. Benard is a leader among the younger Latin players, but more based on his talking to them in Spanish when needed and helping them out financially. But he's not the team leader.

Shortstop Rich Aurilia, who grew up in Brooklyn, one of the most racially mixed neighborhoods in the country, has a background that suits him well as the *de facto* team leader. He plays everyday. He talks to the media. He talks to all his teammates, including Bonds and Kent, regardless of race. But even Aurilia is not one to call a team meeting (that was Dunston in June) or make the big rah-rah speech.

So would the public airing of Bonds and Kent's relationship become any type of distraction in the Giants clubhouse?

"None whatsoever," Aurilia said. "I think we've always been a club, that no matter what happens off the field or in the press, it doesn't affect what happens on the field. I don't think any article is going to change the perception of the way we play together."

This can't be stressed enough: For all the fuss it made around the nation, the column was treated with mostly indifference in the Giants clubhouse. Baker talked with Kent and Bonds separately, but didn't feel the need to call a team meeting — and neither did Dunston or any other player.

"The guys looked at it like a writer was stirring it up because Barry wouldn't talk to him," Baker reflected to me, after the season. "They just let it roll off their back."

What I found most curious were the examples Reilly used in his column. Trust me, there's plenty of material out there to be used in a bash-Barry column. The items he used were laughable.

Reilly chastised Bonds because he rides the bus for broadcasters, trainers and manager. (A moot point because most players take a taxi to the park.) Reilly also wrote that Bonds eats special meals prepared by his nutrutionist (I've seen postgame spreads; more players should do this) and Bonds keeps his hands on his knees when a Giants pitcher gives up a monster homer (like it's going to make a difference?)

Then there was the column of the *Chronicle's* Bruce Jenkins, who, once again, was right on target with his opinion.

"Crazy as it might seem, Bonds could become a sympathetic character in the wake of this mess," Jenkins wrote. "OK, now it's all out in the open. Big deal. Bonds is smiling a lot more this year, conducting more meaningful interviews when the mood strikes him, connecting more with his teammates in the dugout. Typical fan's reaction: 'This guy has been raked over the coals during one of the greatest seasons anyone ever had. Let's cut him some slack. He can't be that bad.'"

As usual, the Giants and Bonds responded in the face of controversy. On August 23, in the final game of the Montreal series, Kent launched his 18th homer off Tomo Ohka in the fourth inning to tie the game and he exchanged a lengthy smile and laugh with Bonds in the dugout.

The message was clear: We might not love each other, but we're still brothers on this team.

In the top of the eighth, Galarraga hit a two-run homer to tie the score at five. Bonds hadn't started the game. But he was summoned to pinch-hit in the top of the ninth and Galarraga told him, "now it's your opportunity to go out on the field and be a hero and win the game."

Bonds blasted a pitch off left-handed reliever Graeme Lloyd into the right-field bleachers, his 55th home run of the season, to give the Giants a one-run lead. Bonds did a small and quick fist pump as he jogged around the bases. Kent gave Bonds a more pronounced high-five than usual. Bonds got a big hug from the Big Cat.

"Cat and I go back a long way, back to 1985, we've been friends a long time," Bonds said. "It's good for him. I'm glad to see him playing. He wasn't too happy (in the American League). He's really happy over here in the National League. He's really enjoying it."

Bonds' only two previous pinch-hit homers, oddly enough, were at the expense of the Giants: Joe Price in 1988 and Steve Bedrosian in 1989. Bonds was blunt about his abilities off the bench though.

"I'm not good at it, I stink at it," Bonds told reporters. "There's no doubt about it. I haven't been very successful in that role. I haven't been able to figure out how to prepare for that role. It's not something I'm really accustomed to. I don't know what I really have to do. Am I supposed to run up and down the hallway? Get loose?"

If the Bonds-Kent, Bonds-Galarraga, Bonds-homer chase, Giants-win stories weren't enough, one more behind-the-scenes story was taking place. Even this one evaded the beat writers, who could be excused because of all the other events involving the team. It was reported a month later by Keown.

It involved Aisha Bonds, the only 2-year-old in the country with the attention span to watch nine innings of a baseball game. Aisha was heartbroken because her dad wasn't playing in the game. Bonds came to the plate as a pinch-hitter and, as usual, looked into the stands and waved at his daughter and saw she was crying. Aisha pointed at right field. She was demanding a homer. Talk about pressure, huh?

Barry Bonds once told a teammate that when he's at home plate, he imagines his daughter is standing behind the plate and if he doesn't make contact with the ball, she's going to hit. That way, he's motivated to hit that ball.

With one swing, Barry made sure his daughter didn't get hurt and delivered the homer she was demanding.

He now had 55 homers in 127 games. A pace of exactly 70.

And now it was onto the media capital of the world.

———

The Giants woke up the morning of August 24 in their New York hotel rooms, 1.5 games out of first place, and the story on the front of *The New York Times* sports section was about steroid use. It quoted two unnamed baseball officials expressing concern over the size of modern-day hitters.

It did not mention Bonds by name. But it wasn't the first time Bonds' name was implied in stories about steroids.

C.W. Nevius, who penned the infamous "nice numbers" column three years earlier, wrote a column in the *Chronicle* about steroids two months earlier that mentioned Bonds' name in the lead paragraph as somebody whose body type has change dramatically over the years, but never directly accused him of being a steroid user.

It was just a matter of time before steroids, or the use of supplements, became part of the Barry Bonds Homer Story — since it was such a part of the McGwire story.

In case you forgot, a newspaper reporter looked inside McGwire's locker one day in the summer of 1998 and grabbed the bottle of androstendione from the top shelf. He did a little investigation and wrote a story that was the talk of baseball. Called 'andro' for short, the substance is a testosterone-boosting drug that is used by athletes to help recover quicker from a workout. It is banned by the NFL and the Olympics. It is legal in hockey and basketball. It is also perfectly legal in baseball, although if it wasn't legal, it wouldn't make a difference because baseball does not test its players.

McGwire endured a firestorm of criticism about his use of the substance. As his fame intensified that summer, more people began calling him a "hero" and it was only natural that teen-age kids started buying andro and using it. The opinion of doctors wasn't universal about whether andro was a steroid or not, and what type of effect it had. Many users have said, in fact, the biggest effect of andro is it makes you horny.

The year after shattering Roger Maris' single-season homer record, McGwire stopped using andro.

In July 2001, a Seattle all-sports talk radio station called me for a radio interview. And based on the Nevius column, one of the questions host John Clayton asked me was about Bonds' weight gain from 1986 to 2001.

This is my opinion: I do not know if Bonds uses steroids. Anything is possible. But I highly doubt it. Bonds doesn't smoke. He rarely, if ever, drinks. He does take supplements, like many athletes. Given the measures Bonds takes to maintain his body, it's doubtful to me that he would risk putting anything into his body that would hurt him. I've seen an offseason Bonds workout. I'm not close to a medical expert, but he seems legit to me.

Regardless, people are justified in wondering if Bonds — or hundreds of other players in major league baseball — are on steroids. Until Major League Baseball begins testing for it, you will never know for sure. But, also, until MLB tests for it, it's a moot point.

Baseball's hierarchy choose to not care. The increases in attendance, fueled by the fascination with home runs, give them reason not to care. The baseball players union is way too strong to ever allow random drug testing to occur. So don't expect testing to begin anytime soon.

Steroids was one of many topics discussed as Bonds did yet another lengthy Q&A with the media at Shea Stadium before the series in New York.

"People make up things just to have something to do," Bonds responded.

"If somebody does something good, there has to be a reason why. Why can't he do it just because he's talented? I don't think it's fair."

The New York media was eager to hear Bonds' desires for where he would play next season. It was asked if he's still willing to give the Giants the so-called "hometown discount" to remain in San Francisco.

"I want to be on a winning team," Bonds told reporters. "That's the key. Money is not the issue . . . My family's there (in San Francisco). All my roots are in San Francisco. I have a good relationship with the owner. I never play baseball for money. I play for the love of the game."

Owner Peter Magowan, the native New Yorker, accompanied the Giants to the Big Apple as he usually does. He listened to the press conference and talked to reporters outside the interview room. Magowan's words would be the strongest that anybody with the Giants had said since spring training. He indicated a lot of Bonds' future would depend on whether the team receives the financial windfall of reaching the postseason.

"The farther we go, I think the better chance there might be," Magowan said. "If we make an offer to him it would be an offer we can justify financially and still give us the best chance to win. If that's not enough for him, that's not enough for him . . . I hope he understands that. I hope his agent understands that. There's a big difference between giving a guy $10 million more than we can afford and what we can afford.

"Making the playoffs is a big thing," Magowan continued. "Certainly, there are some dollars involved in making the playoffs. You do an awful lot of making sure that our season-ticket renewal — which is the highest in baseball — is renewed. If we don't make the playoffs, we can't make that kind of statement with credibility. If we don't win, then we have to ask ourselves, 'why didn't we win' and 'what's it going to take to sign him' and 'will our chances be better to win in the future if we sign him or don't sign him?'"

Once the group was done, Nick Peters of the *Sacramento Bee* talked to Magowan and obtained this nugget.

"It will be resolved quickly," Magowan told Peters. "I'd like a decision, one way or another, within three weeks after our season ends. I don't want this to drag on. If our season ends September 30, we want to get it done before the end of the World Series. If we make the playoffs, I want a decision a few weeks later."

A few weeks later? With Scott Boras the agent? Now *that* was wishful thinking.

The talking could have lasted a couple more days, but a game needed to be played. Bonds doesn't have a great history of success at Shea Stadium. He came into the series with a .259 career average (97-for-375), nine homers and 52 RBIs in Flushing Meadows. Bonds also went 0-for-9 (three strikeouts, two walks) at Shea during the 2000 division series, including the final out in the decisive Game 4.

Bruce Chen started for the Mets and walked Bonds in the first inning to load the bases, but all the Giants could show for it was an Andres Galarraga sacrifice fly.

Todd Zeile and Edgardo Alfonzo hit homers off Giants starter Kirk Rueter, Jay Payton added a solo shot off reliever Brian Boehringer for a 4-1 lead. In the eighth, Brooklyn native Rich Aurilia hit a two-run homer off fellow Brooklyn native John Franco — imagine the discussion that ensued back in barber shops and the streets — to trim the lead to 4-3.

Mets closer Armando Benitez, who bragged to New York reporters the Mets could beat the Giants whenever they wanted, closed out the ninth flawlessly with two strikeouts to save the game. Bonds was 1-for-3 with a walk and a strikeout that brought 35,973 fans onto their feet to cheer.

Bonds was held without a homer again on the Saturday game, another Giants loss, and the Sunday game was switched to a night game for ESPN's national-television audience. Bonds took advantage of the free afternoon to watch the New York Liberty-Charlotte Sting WNBA playoff game at Madison Square Garden.

Back at Shea Stadium hours later, Bonds had finished taking batting practice and was walking back to the dugout when ESPN.com reporter Wayne Krehs observed the following scene. Hundreds of fans were yelling his name. One overzealous autograph seeker tossed a ball at Bonds, who never saw it until it pelted him in the chest. A New York City cop, at the other end of the dugout, sprinted over quickly and told Bonds he'd kick the teen-ager out of the ballpark.

"That's not necessary," said Bonds, who proceeded to pick the brand-new white baseball off the dirty ground, wipe it clean and ask the terrified kid for a pen. Bonds autographed the baseball, then told the kid "that wasn't right" and "most players wouldn't appreciate that."

Bonds handed the ball back to the kid and the fans around the dugout applauded the moment.

Al Leiter started for the Mets that night and purposely went after Bonds every at-bat. In the fourth, Bonds hit a ball off the left-center wall that just missed becoming No.56 for the year. Bonds ended up with a triple and winked at Leiter from third base, thankful for a pitcher challenging him.

"I think he appreciated that," Leiter said. "I took some pride in '98 that McGwire and (Sammy) Sosa didn't homer off me and I don't believe I walked either one of them. It's like a gladiator, competitive spirit."

Bonds remained at 55 homers. Two weeks earlier, he led Sosa 49-37 in the homer race. Now his lead was six, 55-49, on the charging Sosa.

The Mets won another nail-biter, 6-5, and the Giants fell back to 3.5 games out of first. The Giants needed a victory in the Monday finale to avoid a devastating four-game sweep.

The Little League champions from Japan were at Shea Stadium for the final game of the series. The U.S. Open tennis tournament was getting started across the street in Flushing Meadow.

But the biggest star was still Barry Bonds.

His personal Shea Stadium homer drought (going back to May 28, 1995) ended with No. 56 off Kevin Appier in the fifth inning, a solo shot that extended the Giants lead to 3-1. Bonds jumped on the first pitch from Appier, sending a towering blast over the right-center wall.

"I didn't know about a drought until someone came up and told me," Bonds would tell reporters. "It's one stadium. I don't hit well in Colorado, either. You get your hits, you just don't get it out of the ballpark. As long as you win the game, it doesn't matter."

The game was far from over. With thunder rumbling overhead, Bonds blooped an opposite-field double to left to lead off the seventh inning. Kent's grounder to the right side moved him to third and Bonds slid home on a Ramon Martinez sacrifice fly to re-take the lead at 4-3. The Mets tied the game 4-4, then as lightning crackled and the skies were moments away from dumping heavy rain on the field, J.T. Snow hit a go-ahead, two-run homer in the ninth.

Robb Nen came out of the bullpen and walked toward the mound, but never made a warm-up pitch. The umpires suspended the game for 54 minutes as rain pelted the field. Once the game was back on, Nen closed out the 6-5 victory.

"I don't know if you guys have ever seen, 'Escape from New York,' but now I know how Snake Plissken feels," Baker said. "It's one victory. It doesn't sound like much, but it was huge."

Bonds wasn't eager to help the anxious New York media write about the big homer-chase story. He was keeping the focus on the team's victory and his teammates performance.

"J.T. won the game for us and Robb Nen closed it out," Bonds told reporters. "The Mets came back to tie it up, so my home run doesn't mean that much."

CHAPTER 16

Devil of a Player

August 28-September 5, Home Run 57-59

"It depends on who we play, whether they are in contention or not. Look in the past at those numbers and see how many came against teams out of contention. You don't know if they will pitch to you."

Barry Bonds

NO PITCHER ON this planet is more intimidating than Randy Johnson. Ask the game's best hitters. Tony Gwynn and Wade Boggs both considered him the pitcher they least wanted to face. John Kruk, in a memorable All-Star Game moment, saw a Johnson pitch fly over his head and thought he was going to die. Larry Walker, a former Most Valuable Player, once asked out of the lineup when Johnson was starting.

For left-handed batters, Johnson evokes fear. He's 6 foot 10. He has long arms. He stands on the first-base side of the pitching mound. Earlier in his career, he was wild and had no idea where the ball was going. Batters never dig into the batters box against him. A famous chat with Nolan Ryan one day turned around Johnson's career starting in 1993. Since then, he learned to control his pitches better. He had four 300-plus strikeouts seasons and was working on his fifth in 2001. He would have six, but missed 300 whiffs by six in the strike-shortened 1995 and by nine in 1997.

Barry Bonds and Randy Johnson are not strangers. They both grew up in the Bay Area, Bonds along the San Francisco peninsula in San Carlos and Johnson in the East Bay suburb of Livermore. They both attended Six-Pac schools at the same time, Johnson pitching for USC and annually facing Bonds at Arizona State.

They even faced each other early in their pro careers, when Johnson, playing for the Montreal Expos, was still a wild pitcher, and Bonds was still coming into his own with the Pittsburgh Pirates.

Johnson took the mound at Bank One Ballpark on August 28 with a 17-5 record, a 2.45 ERA *and* 303 strikeouts. Giants manager Dusty Baker loaded his lineup with eight right-handed batters, plus Barry Bonds. Statistically,

Johnson isn't much different for lefties (.196 opponents average by year's end) or righties (.204 average). But most lefties are scared beyond belief to face him. Just ask John Kruk.

In the first inning, a runner at second base and one out, Bonds came to the plate. And Johnson, the most feared pitcher on the planet, walked Bonds — on *four* pitches!

By the fourth, Arizona led 4-0 and Bonds was leading off the inning, so Johnson went after him. Bonds grounded out to deep right, the exaggerated shift taking away a sure single. In the fifth, the score was now 4-1, Calvin Murray was at first base and Bonds didn't even represent the tying run.

Johnson walked Bonds. On five pitches.

In the eighth, Bonds again leading off the inning, the score still 4-1, Johnson pitched to Bonds and got a popup to second base. Still, the message was clear. Arizona was not going to let Bonds beat them or let Bonds put the Giants closer to beating them — even with the most intimidating pitcher in baseball on the mound.

Reggie Sanders and Luiz Gonzalez hammered two-run homers to provide the Arizona offense. Gonzalez was now up to 49 for the season. In Chicago, Sammy Sosa wasn't slowing down his own torrid homer pace. He'd hit three in his last four games and had passed Gonzo with 51 as the Cubs pursued the NL Central division.

With just over 30 games left, there were three races and they were all wide open: divisions, homers and Most Valuable Player.

"I'd like to split that one three ways," Gonzalez said of the MVP vote. "To be honest, I think the last month will dictate who wins it. All three of our teams are still in contention. Maybe the team that finishes on top, the guy on that team will probably end up with the MVP. If you ask Sammy and Barry, I'm the same way, I feel like, 'if the team wins, everything will take care of itself.' The bottom line is, you just want to contribute and produce any way you can for your ballclub."

At the all-star game, and again in late July, Bonds endorsed Gonzalez as the league MVP. The incredibly humble Gonzalez still couldn't believe he was even an MVP candidate, saying the last time he was considered, "I was about 10 or 11 years old playing in my backyard. I was the MVP of that league.

"It's been bad timing for me because the other two guys are having unbelievable years," Gonzalez continued. "It's just weird when you look back at guys who have won the MVP. Some of the numbers were almost passed at the (all-star) break. It's weird to see how the game has elevated to the next level with power numbers."

Look no further than Bonds as an example. When he won his first MVP in 1990, Bonds hit 33 homers. Bonds had 39 at the break this year.

Giants manager Dusty Baker, whose endorsement of Kent weighed heavily with voters debating between which Giants star to select a year earlier, felt Shawn Green and Gary Sheffield shouldn't be forgotten in MVP talk either.

"Right now, it would have to be Barry," Baker said. "I'm pulling for my guy, naturally. But you have to respect the others."

Barry Bonds hears voices in the stands calling his name all the time during batting practice. Like any big leaguer, he's learned to tune them out. But as he walked up from the visitors clubhouse tunnel to the dugout at Bank One Ballpark on August 28, he knew this voice was familiar.

It was Patsey Brock, the wife of Jim Brock, his late baseball coach at Arizona State University. Bonds went over and gave her a big hug and talked for a few moments. She showed him a button that read, "JB 33" in honor of Jim, who died of liver cancer in 1994.

"His eyes lit up," Patsey Brock told *The Arizona Republic's* Richard Obert, who wrote a series of fascinating stories in 2001 that chronicled Bonds' career at Arizona State and his 2001 season exploits. "He said, 'I'd like to have that.'"

Patsey quickly handed the button over to Barry. He signed a baseball for her, which would be part of a silent auction. Patsey said goodbye and told Bonds good luck.

"You know better than that," Bonds told her. "It's going to take more than luck."

Bonds proudly pinned the button to his cap, walked into the dugout and grabbed his bat. As always, Bonds wore his Giants cap backwards that day.

I remember standing in the dugout, seeing the button on his cap as Bonds walked by and asking him what it was. A huge smile was on Bonds' face as he displayed it to me with pride and told me it was for his former college coach. Bonds walked over to the batting cage for a typical round of batting practice that demands attention.

"I always thought a lot of Barry," Patsey Brock told Obert. "It's never been easy to be Barry Bonds. He was so talented from the beginning. . . . Jim used to talk about the twinkle in his eye. That's what I remembered. He'd get into trouble from time to time and didn't always do what he was supposed to do. But most of them were like that. There was jealousy. It's hard for people to take. He had the body of an athlete. He was good at what he did."

Bonds arrived on the Tempe, Arizona, campus in the fall of 1982, the same school his cousin Reggie Jackson attended decades earlier and fellow-Riverside family friend and major leaguer Alvin Davis attended. Bonds was the hotshot kid from California, the son of a major leaguer, with the money and the beautiful big black Trans Am to prove it.

"How did Jim word it?" Patsey Brock remembered. "The biggest superstar out of ASU was Reggie Jackson. He said, 'Barry is going to make everybody forget about Reggie Jackson. He said he's going to be a superstar and we need him at ASU.'"

Jim Brock could be accused of coddling his young superstar. He couldn't help it. Brock took a quick liking to Bonds. In an interview for a 1993 *Sports Illustrated* article, Brock remembered the teen-age Bonds as a kid with a "twinkle in his eye, never malicious, but a kid who might say silly things at any time."

"There are some players who come and go here," Brock continued, in the *SI* piece. "And you never get to know them. Who is Bob Horner? He came here, he went. Now, Barry, I got to know him a lot better. It was attention I wanted to give him. I really like the hell out of him. In fact, you know what the other kids called him? Barry Brock."

Like the coaches at Serra High School, Brock knew there was inherent jealousy among other players and gave Bonds special handling.

"I had to talk to him a lot," Brock said. "He wanted to be liked, tried so damn hard to have people like him. Tried too hard. But then he'd say things he didn't mean, wild statements. I tried to tell him that these guys, 20 years from now, would be electricians and plumbers, but he'd be making millions. I didn't know how many millions, of course. Still, he'd be hurt. People don't realize he can be hurt — and is, fairly often."

Like everyone else, Brock saw the multiple sides of Bonds' personality. And he also ripped Bonds in the pages of SI another year.

"I never saw a teammate care about him," Brock told *SI*. "Part of it was his being rude, inconsiderate and self-centered . . . I don't think he ever figured out what to do to get people to like him."

Dave Graybill was a pitcher at ASU from 1983-85. He was a fireman in Glendale, Ariz. in 2001 and shared the following memories of Bonds with *The Republic's* Obert.

"He didn't necessarily fit in with the family, per se, but he was able to produce great numbers," Graybill said. "He was always dialed in (at the plate). He loved being on the front line of competing.

"Very few guys who were superstars, guys like Pete Rose and Cal Ripken, had to work hard all the time," said Graybill, who pitched as a replacement player for the Seattle Mariners in 1995 during the strike. "They were superstars, but they were natural leaders. I don't think Barry was ever a leader. I didn't think it was in his nature. If I had a problem on the team, I wouldn't go to Barry to tell him about it. He'd blow you off."

Bonds was overshadowed his first two seasons at ASU. The superstar on the team was Oddibe McDowell, a can't-miss prospect who could do it all, and was the 1984 collegiate Player of the Year. That summer, on an Olympics team that included Mark McGwire and Will Clark, the player that had the scouts drooling the most was McDowell.

As a freshman, Bonds hit just over .300 (which isn't spectacular for an aluminum bat) and had 11 homers. Still, he started. Reggie Jackson, Rick Monday and Sal Bando played at ASU and none of them started as freshman.

During the summer before his next year in school, Bonds lived with Mylie Davis, the mother of Alvin Davis. The Davis and Bonds families were very close in Riverside, to the point they considered themselves an extension of each other's families. Barry held one of the few "real" jobs in his life that summer, stocking shelves and putting up cardboard window ads at a nearby grocery store.

"I had to let him know who was boss," Mylie told Obert, who tracked down another great source for his story. "He was not a bad kid. I remember he was being teased and Barry saying, 'My dad is rich and I'm not.' I always felt

Barry wanted to be his own person. He didn't want to capitalize on his dad's fame. . . . He's matured a lot. I've noticed it in the TV interviews."

As a sophomore in 1984, Bonds hit .360 with 11 homers (again), drove in 55 runs and stole 30 bases in 45 attempts. In the College World Series, Bonds tied an NCAA record with seven consecutive hits. But the Sun Devils fell short of winning it all, a prequel, if you will, to his professional career.

The third outfielder on those ASU teams was Mike Devereaux, who also made the majors, but never lived up to the high hopes the Dodgers had when drafting him.

By his junior season, Bonds moved to center field as McDowell was working his way up through the Texas Rangers organization. Bonds hit 23 homers his final season and was named a second-team All-American.

Louie Medina was the Sun Devils first baseman that season and a scout with the Kansas City Royals in 2001. He told a story to Obert of *the Arizona Republic* about a rainy day before the 1985 alumni game when a fearless Barry Bonds decided to show off.

With the pitching machine cranking out pitches in the 80 mph range, Bonds stepped into a batting cage and slowly moved closer and closer with each swing. Bonds ended up about 30 feet from the machine, whacking pitch after pitch all over Packard Stadium, eliciting awe from those watching the scene.

"He'd just turn on it," Medina told Obert. "None of the big leaguers would try it. He was a special talent . . . He always had a presence about him. Could you see he'd be this good? No."

———

Anything different regarding Barry Bonds consisted of news, including his jewelry fashion statements. So it was news when Bonds' earring was back in his left ear on August 29 in Arizona, even if the only reason it was out is because it was bleeding in New York.

Yes, the earring has a story behind it as well.

"The earring is for my father," Bobby Bonds said. "Every game Barry plays, his grandfather is with him. Barry is a very sensitive person. He put it in his ear a couple days after his grandfather's funeral. It's not a fashion statement."

It's the only piece of jewelry that Barry wears on a regular basis. He told me that friends have bought him gifts, such as rings and necklaces, to celebrate certain achievements in his life — a diamond-studded MVP ring, a 500-homer ring and 400-400 cuff links. Bonds usually wears them a day or two, to show his appreciation, then puts them away.

"I don't like jewelry," Bonds told me. "I did when I was younger, back in the day with Mr. T. But not anymore."

The Arizona Diamondbacks continued their pitching pattern the final two games of the series in Phoenix on August 29 and 30. They pitched to Bonds with nobody on base. They pitched around him with anybody on the bases.

In eighth inning of the second game, Arizona leading 2-0, Marvin Benard at second base, manager Bob Brenly issued an intentional walk to Bonds, earning him boo birds from his own crowd and putting the go-ahead run at the plate. Brenly brought in Byung-Hyun Kim into the game. Jeff Kent popped to second to end the threat and angrily slammed his helmet to the ground. Kim got the final three outs to preserve the 2-0 win and the Diamondbacks' lead was up to 4.5 games.

Once again, the Giants were in jeopardy of seeing the season slip away.

Gonzalez had gone deep again, crushing a 1-0 hanging slider back in the fifth inning off Kirk Rueter. Gonzo became just the 19th player in major-league history to homer 50 times in a season, the third this year following Bonds and Sosa. He'd become the most loved athlete in the desert and the BOB fans cheered their hero out of the dugout for a curtain call and the bleachers welcomed him back to the outfield with a boisterous standing ovation.

"I'll probably (think about it) when the season is over," Gonzalez said. "This is nice what I did, but we have a big game tomorrow. I'll go home and I have triplets, so I don't have a lot of time to sit back and enjoy what's going on. I'll enjoy everything at the end of the season, if we have a successful season. It's not over yet. We're still trying to push ourselves away from the pack."

Most frustrating for the Giants was Bobby Witt — not Randy Johnson or Curt Schilling — had shut them out.

"The playoffs started for us yesterday," centerfielder Calvin Murray put it. "Every day is do or die."

On the finale of the three-city, 10-game road-trip, Baker moved the slumping Kent down one place in the batting order to fifth. Andres Galarraga batted cleanup instead.

Kent was 7-for-38 on the road trip at the time. His recent struggles had been amplified because so many outs had come in RBI situations, which was uncharacteristic because those are the situations in which he'd thrived in years past. Kent batted a robust .338 with runners in scoring position during his MVP year of 2000. Since the All-Star Break this year, however, Kent was 7-for-44 (.159) with runners in scoring position.

"When you have a series of negative events, sometimes it's cool to be removed from the situation temporarily," said Giants manager Dusty Baker, who used 'temporary' repeatedly for the lineup switch. "When you are doing well, things can snowball. When you're not, things can snowball that way also. I just want to stop the snowball."

What had made Kent a better player since his turbulent years in New York was his ability to keep an even keel, turn the page — as Kent always says — after the good days and bad days. But lately, he'd been a little more animated in heaving bats and helmets after making outs.

"It eats at you," Baker said. "You can tell on his face. I've been there before. It eats at you. I don't want him to get to the point where you blame yourself (for the team losing)."

Nobody would admit this, but Kent was surely feeling some heat from his comments in *SI*. The proverbial cat was out of the bag in the Bonds-Kent relationship. It was in the open. And, for some, Kent was a heel, the teammate bashing Bonds during this historic season. Kent was pressing. And it was showing at the plate.

Kent was still on pace for 102 RBIs, which would be his fifth straight over the century mark. However, Kent was the first to admit he was capable of more. With Rich Aurilia second in the league in hits and Barry Bonds first in walks, Kent could easily have more RBIs. His 137 at-bats with runners in scoring position are the second highest, one behind Albert Pujols of St. Louis.

"He's still having a good year," Baker said. "But he raised the bar by having great years. . . . Who's been more clutch than Jeff around here the last few years?"

The lineup juggle had mixed results. Galarraga was 0-for-4 with a double play and four runners stranded after six innings.

But thanks to Rich Aurilia, continue to sizzle with the bat, especially in importantt games against the D'backs, the Giants had a much-needed 3-1 lead after his clutch three-run homer. Jason Schmidt, the hired gun, limited Arizona to two runs in 6 2/3 innings, added a homer, a sacrifice bunt that led to a run and an RBI single.

"We knew this was a game we needed to win," Aurilia said. "We hadn't gotten that big hit in awhile. I'm just glad we got it."

Bonds walked three times and singled once. Kent had a double in the seventh and an RBI single in the eighth. The Giants won a laugher, 13-5, headed home from a turbulent, cross-country trip with a 4-6 record, 3.5 games out of first and their famous slugger at 56 homers with 28 games left.

Barry Bonds will never be called Mr. October, like his cousin Reggie Jackson, but Mr. September would be accurate. Bonds' team has made the postseason five times in 16 years, plus a one-game playoff for the wild-card berth in 1998, and Bonds' performance in the stretch drive of the season was a major reason.

Here are Bonds' numbers during contending Septembers.

Year	Team	AVG	AB	H	HR	RBI
1990	Pittsburgh	.260	100	26	8	17
1991	Pittsburgh	.286	98	28	3	20
1992	Pittsburgh	.392	102	40	11	27
1993	San Francisco	.300	100	30	7	22
1997	San Francisco	.303	76	23	9	19
1998	San Francisco	.389	90	35	7	22
2000	San Francisco	.315	89	28	10	26
Totals:		**.321**	**655**	**210**	**55**	**153**

Stop and think about those numbers for a moment. Those seven Septembers are roughly one full season (and maybe an additional month).

Manager Dusty Baker likes to say of the final month, "it's where the strong get stronger."

The final month of the season — with all the pressure involved of a playoff chase — is when Barry Bonds has done his best work. Fifty-five homers? One hundred and fifty-three RBIs? That's simply astounding!

Bonds got an early start on his latest September stretch drive on August 31. His 57th homer came on an 0-2 count, in the eighth inning, off Colorado's John Thomson. Otherwise, Thomson was dominant as Bonds' two-run homer accounted for the only runs in the Rockies 5-2 win at Pac Bell Park.

Even with that homer, Bonds still didn't have 60 at the start of September — the magic figure, according to McGwire, for when it was officially a story. The Bonds homer race was still questionable. But with the Giants four games out of first, the divisional race was undeniable.

Baker was looking to give Bonds another day off, but knew it couldn't happen against first-place Arizona. The four-game Rockies series was sandwiched around six games, three home and three away, against the D'backs. And these were their final meetings of the year.

The next Bonds non-start was Saturday, September 1. The clubhouse was buzzing that morning as rosters had expanded and the minor league call-ups arrived, trying on uniforms, moving into lockers and basking in the glory of being in "the show."

Despite all the commotion, Bonds had no trouble sleeping in his reclining chair that morning, clinging to a towel to help stay warm.

The offensive explosion from the final game in Arizona hadn't carried over. On the heels of Thompson nearly shutting them out, the Giants trailed Mike Hampton 1-0 in the eighth inning. Benito Santiago doubled. Rookie Pedro Feliz doubled him home to tie the score. Curiously, Baker then pinch-hit Bonds for the pitchers spot, even though the obvious move for Colorado manager Buddy Bell was to intentionally walk Bonds — which he did.

Calvin Murray bounced into a double play and the inning was over. Aurilia saved the tie score with a spectacular defensive play in the top of the ninth. And Galarraga won the game with his second "walk-off" homer since joining the Giants, crushing a 3-0 pitch from Justin Speier deep into the left-field bleachers for the winning 2-1 margin.

The Giants were now 17-4 in games that Galarraga started.

Bonds was back in the cleanup spot September 2 as Baker continued to tinker with his lineup to find the best combination. Bonds didn't care where he batted in the lineup.

"It doesn't bother me," Bonds said. "Put me anywhere. As long as it isn't leading off."

Bonds was intentionally walked in the first inning of the game, just after Kent doubled home one run, and just before Galarraga doubled him home. Those season-long questions about whether opposing pitchers will even give Bonds the chance to swing the bat in September — first proposed by Mark McGwire back in June and now mentioned *ad nauseum* by fans and the media — were getting bigger.

"It depends on who we play, whether they are in contention or not," Bonds told me. "Look in the past at those numbers and see how many came against teams out of contention. You don't know if they will pitch to you."

Bonds cited Houston as an example. In the final month of the 2000 season, the Astros weren't in playoff contention. In three games at Enron Field, Bonds hit two of his 10 September homers.

"Houston pitched to me," Bonds told me. "This year, they are in contention. Right now, everybody is in contention. Everything is like a chess match. It's who can break who. It's exciting. But it can be frustrating."

———————

From the night the first Barry Bonds homer landed in McCovey Cove — May 1, 2000 — safety was an issue. Two motorized boats collided as they raced toward fetching the baseball, former Giants groundskeeper Joe Figone emerging with the ball in his net.

It's actually surprising it took so long, but on Monday, September 3, McCovey Cove officially became a motor-free zone. *Chronicle* news writer Steve Rubenstein had the story.

"It's going to be safer out here," Rubenstein quoted Sgt. Danny Lopez, the cop on the bay. "There's going to be less of a mad scramble."

Lopez was in a twin-engine police patrol boat, handing out yellow warning notices to all boaters in the cove, announcing the new law against using motors in the narrow strip of the bay. The Port Commission voted unanimously to ban the use of motors in the 70-foot-wide strip of water and limit the speed to six miles an hour, steps taken amidst concern and fear as the water crowds were growing larger as Bonds approached history.

Kayakers, rubber-tubers and other floating devices were still welcome. In fact, the new law was a way to protect them. The night Bonds put his 500th into the water, a man on a surfboard was nearly run over by a boat.

Back inside the ballpark, Baker was growing restless with the media's queries about his lineup maneuvering, growing testy when he was asked again before the final game of the series why Bonds was back in the third spot.

"I'm tired of explaining myself," Baker said.

I couldn't help but sympathize with him. I was tired of hearing the questions too, getting to the point when I only mentioned the lineup switch in passing in my game story.

An impressive Rockies rookie named Jason Jennings shut down the Giants offense on the Labor Day series finale. It was 2-0 in the fourth when Bonds connected on his 58th homer of the season, another dead center blast, cutting the lead to 2-1. Of Bonds' 58 homers, 42 had now either given the Giants the lead (22), tied the game (six), extended a one-run lead (eight) or brought the Giants within one run (six).

Jennings baffled the Giants the rest of the way, not allowing any further runs, and the Rockies won, 4-1, costing the Giants an opportunity to gain a half-game on the idle Diamondbacks. Bonds showered quickly and left the ballpark when the media was inside the manager's office.

There wasn't much for anybody to say, except to look ahead to the final head-to-head showdown of the season against the D'backs.

———————

Rich Aurilia's parents flew from Newark (NJ) to SFO on Flight 93, just over a week before that flight number would become memorable for all the wrong reasons. They came to see their son in a crucial division series and also to see their new grandchild.

In December of 1994, the Giants traded pitcher John Burkett to the Texas

Rangers for infielder Desi Wilson. As a throw in, the Rangers included Rich Aurilia. A 24th-round selection out of St. John's University, Aurilia is another player on the Giants roster who was never considered a can't-miss prospect.

A year later, Aurilia was considered the Giants shortstop of the future. But the Giants have a history of making their top prospects wait. Aurilia was understandably frustrated as the Giants signed Shawon Dunston, traded for Jose Vizcaino and signed Rey Sanchez to play shortstop, delaying his emergence as the everyday guy.

He finally got a chance in 1999 and Aurilia emerged as the premiere offensive shortstop in the National League. He led the circuit in homers (22 and 20) and RBIs (80 and 79) in 1999 and 2000. He was still fairly unknown, however, because those numbers paled in comparison to the spectacular trio in the American League of Alex Rodriguez, Derek Jeter and Nomar Garciaparra.

This season, Aurilia was joining the elite. He was moved to the second spot in the order, an assignment he reluctantly accepted, and thrived hitting in front of Barry Bonds. He isn't the first player to enjoy a career year hitting in front, or behind, of Bonds.

It couldn't happen to a better person as well. Aurilia is well liked by teammates, the organization and the media. He plays with a fiery demeanor on the field and is known for some legendary bat heaves after making an out. But he's laid back, honest, thoughtful and insightful with the media after the game. It's no wonder he's on the executive committee of the players association.

With his parents and other family in the stands September 4, Aurilia put on quite a show in the series opener against Arizona. Tied 1-1 in the fifth, Aurilia reached the 30-homer plateau with a solo shot off Bobby Witt for a 2-1 lead.

Arizona tied the score in the sixth, then Aurilia answered with a two-run homer in the seventh off Miguel Batista. Aurilia was a one-man wrecking crew against Arizona, hitting eight home runs in 17 games — all of them coming at crucial moments in the game.

The crowd didn't even have time to bring Aurilia out for a curtain call though. They were still on their feet, still clapping and celebrating, when Bonds swung at the first pitch from Batista.

In his chilling home-run call the entire country was learning from the background of *SportsCenter* highlights, Duane Kuiper screamed into the microphone: "*He Hits It High! He Hits It Deep! He . . . Hits . . . It . . . Outtttttttttttttttaaaaaaaa Here!*"

The Giants gave out white towels before the game and Pacific Bell Park was absolutely rocking. I remember just staring into the crowd, getting Goosebumps and chills as the place went simply bezerk. Robb Nen closed out another strong performance by Jason Schmidt, the DJ cranked the post-game music louder than normal and the crowd simply didn't want to go home.

Bonds now had 59 homers. He talked to reporters after the game, but deferred all the attention and praise away from himself and toward Aurilia.

"Hey, it's his night," Bonds said. "He's been playing like that all year. He's been clutch."

The Diamondbacks lead was down to 1.5 games. A pennant race, indeed.

"What's going to be the difference in September is defense and big hits," Aurilia said. "We haven't been getting too many big hits lately. To hit two home runs, and hold the lead the second time, was pretty big. Those are the moments you play the game for. I had some family here today and to have them witness it was pretty special. It's just a really good feeling."

The good feeling would be short-lived. Curt Schilling was back on the mound the next night, September 5, and extra determined after getting hammered by Bonds' two homers and the rest of the Giants lineup a month ago. Ever the competitor, Schilling wasn't going to be careful with Bonds and pitch around him.

Like he did in Arizona, Bonds went hacking on the first pitch. He fouled Schilling's first offering straight back, a sign a batter just missed the ball. Schilling continued to challenge Bonds, because he's way too proud to pitch around him, and Bonds ended up chasing a 96-mph fastball nearly in his eyes for a strikeout.

In the third, Bonds again fouled back a first-pitch fastball. He fouled back three more pitches and worked the count, a tremendous game-within-the-game duel between two of the best in the business. Ultimately, Schilling missed with his ninth pitch of the at-bat and Bonds walked.

In the sixth, Bonds continued his first-pitch swinging strategy. The crowd was teased by the chance of seeing No. 60 by a drive with high trajectory, but it turned into a routine out. Schilling allowed one run in eight innings, Arizona knocked around the usually stingy Russ Ortiz and won 7-2 to inch their lead back to 2.5 games.

"It's the biggest game I've pitched in a long, long time," Schilling said. "It was like a playoff game. There was some extra there for me and I tried to use it."

CHAPTER 17

Anything's Possible

September 6-10, Home Runs 60-63

"Say, 'I love you mommy.' Say it dad. Say, 'I love you mommy.' "

2-year-old Aisha Bonds, to her dad

SAY WHAT YOU will about the reason for this era of inflated homer totals —
diluted pitching or smaller ballparks or juiced baseballs or workout programs —
but 60 in one season is still special. The club is real short: Babe. Maris. Mac.
Sammy.

When the Bambino did it first in 1927, breaking his record of 59 set in
1921, the public was fascinated, but couldn't grasp what the number would
later mean. Ruth hit 54 again the following season and nobody else was in
Babe's class.

It took 34 years for somebody to reach 60 homers again. And 37 years after
that for a third member. And less than a week for the fourth member.

Barry Bonds became the fifth member of the club on September 6, an
afternoon game and the final of the homestand against the Arizona Diamondbacks. The crowd at Pac Bell wanted to see the 60th and Bonds wouldn't
disappoint.

Seventy-four years after Babe Ruth set the bar in 1927, Bonds joined the
60-homer club by crushing a salivating hanging curve from Albie Lopez over
the right-field wall, just missing McCovey Cove. ESPN had been cutting into
its broadcasts each time Bonds strutted to the plate, ensuring a big audience.

"My heart was just racing going around the bases," Bonds said. "To be with
people of that caliber is something you never think will happen in your lifetime.
You couldn't write anything better. You couldn't dream anything better. It's just
unreal."

Unreal, indeed. The scoreboard had Barry and Babe's picture side-by-side,
a chilling reminder of just what hallowed territory had now been entered.

"It almost made me cry," Bonds said.

"That's when it hit me," Giants reliever Tim Worrell said. "You know what Barry's doing, and you see all the home runs. But when he hit the 60th, I looked on the scoreboard and saw Barry's picture on the left and Babe Ruth's on the right. I just thought, 'wow, that is awesome. I'm part of history. I was there. I'll be able to tell my kids and my grandkids about it.' And I know he's not stopping now."

The crowd's cheering was louder and longer. Bonds pointed to God after he crossed home (as usual), waved to his family behind the backstop (as usual) and was greeted by an eager and euphoric group of teammates on the top step of the dugout for hugs, handshakes and high-fives.

Even Kent, who sometimes quickly gets into the batter's box after a Bonds homer, intentionally delayed getting to the batter's box, giving the crowd more time to cheer and roust Bonds up the steps for a curtain call.

"Sixty is a big deal for him," Kent told the *Chronicle's* John Shea. "He might not acknowledge it, but I think I helped him get there. For his bigger home runs, I've tried to stand back and let him have his glory. Today, before I got in there, I told the umpire it's going to be a minute."

The homer extended a two-run lead to 5-2. Dusty Baker managed like it was a must-win playoff game. It was as big a game you'll see for the September 6 day on the calendar. The Giants completed a 9-5 win to again get within 1.5 games of Arizona.

"My first thought was, 'hey, that's one more,'" said Baker, the manager who has seen just about everything. "Then I thought about it being number 60. I've never been around someone who has hit 60 before. I was with Hank Aaron, who had a lot of 40-home run seasons, but I haven't seen someone hit 60."

For 140 games and over five months, Bonds refused to acknowledge his chance of breaking McGwire's record. But after his 60th in 141 games, needing 10 in the final 21 games — which would still be an incredible feat — Bonds finally seemed willing to accept his chance at history.

"Anything's possible," Bonds said. "I never thought I'd hit six in three games in Atlanta, so anything's possible."

By Kent's even-keel standards, he was bubbling in his praise of Bonds.

"Heck, I think Barry can do anything he sets out to do," Kent said. "He's that talented and that gifted. He's done some remarkable things. I wouldn't put it past him. He's getting pitches to hit and he's depositing them over the wall.

I've hit behind him for almost all of those home runs, and it's amazing to see him able to stick it to them continuously and hit them a long way."

Even on the day of his 60th homer, Bonds was upstaged in his post-game news conference. Bonds brought 2-year-old daughter Aisha to the interview room and she simply stole the show, melting hearts and showing Bonds to be just another father bursting with pride.

Pointing at the microphone, Barry told his daughter to talk as a joke. She took it literally. Aisha definitely isn't shy around a microphone. Sitting on her dad's lap, she grabbed hold of the microphone and started talking, not even waiting for Dad's approval.

"Now batting for the Giants," Aisha said, auditioning in her role as a future public address announcer, "number 25, Barrrrrrry Bondssssss. And the crowd goes wildddd!"

It was simply adorable. Once she got started, Aisha couldn't stop hamming it up for the cameras and reporters.

"Excuse me, daddy," Aisha kept repeating as Dad tried to answer questions.

With an amused smile, Bonds said, "I should have left her with her mommy."

"This is my daddy," Aisha said, proudly, several times.

"I'm going to put her in acting classes," Barry said, equally proud.

A little later, Aisha turned a little bossy.

"Say, 'I love you Mommy.' Say it Daddy. Say, 'I love you Mommy.'"

Bonds had the biggest smile on his face I've ever seen.

"I love you Mommy," Bonds said.

The next day, in *The Oakland Tribune*, columnist Dave Newhouse put it beautifully when he wrote: "The daughter's presence was perfect, for baseball is a connection between parent and child — fathers playing catch with sons, and now a father holding a daughter on his knee, making her a part of the family's newest baseball treasure."

Bonds was still smiling the next afternoon. He was sitting on a metal chair at his locker inside the visitor clubhouse at Coors Field in Denver. In his hands were the daily clips from the Bay Area papers — which are printed out from the internet by a team official and distributed to writers, broadcasters, team officials and players on a daily basis.

Usually, if a player is going to read these clips, they do it in the trainers room — not in the open. Few players want the press to know they care what gets written about them or the team.

Bonds didn't care. He was reading and smiling. Occasionally, he would tear a page off the stapled pile of clippings. Somebody asked him why he was so amused that day and what he was saving.

"I'm saving all the stories that mention my daughter," Bonds said. "There's a lot of 'em in here."

Aisha Bonds was a certifiable star.

Before leaving San Francisco, Bonds warned people not to expect much from him at Coors Field.

"You look at my stats, and that's the one ballpark that's been able to dominate me," Bonds said. "I don't know why. I'll be rooting for the other guys in Colorado. I'll be on defense patrol."

Bonds paused and added, "Wait until I get to Houston. In Houston, I have a good chance."

The day before, when the Dodgers were at Coors Field, Gary Sheffield was sitting in a locker about four down from where Bonds' would be and talking about his favorite pseudo-big brother. On the MVP subject, which many in baseball were waffling on, Sheffield said it was a no-brainer.

"It's Barry Bonds. Hands down," Sheffield said. "You can't even describe his season. Barry Bonds has been pitched around his whole career. Barry Bonds makes his teammates better. People overlook that. That's why he should be MVP *every year* the last decade. You can make your teammates better and their numbers better. That's an MVP. When people talk about the best in the game, they just look at stats. But that's not how you judge stats. You have to look at when he got his hits, what part of the game. He's the one getting pitched around at the same time. That's how you judge who is the best in the game. You don't judge by just numbers straight up. Because if I was pitched, or if Barry Bonds was pitched like everybody else, then it wouldn't be any comparison."

Nobody in baseball history has ever won four MVPs. On the day Bonds won his third, back in 1993, Bonds told reporters his goal was a fourth.

"I'm just afraid the media is going to make me do inhuman feats to win four," Bonds said, at the time.

Uh, does hitting 71 homers constitute an inhuman feat?

Sheffield told Jason Reid, the Dodgers beat writer for the *Los Angeles Times*, that he wants Bonds to join him in Los Angeles the next season. Sheffield revealed he'd already pitched the idea to their mutual agent, Scott Boras, and Dodgers CEO Bob Daly.

Sheffield had it all figured out: He would restructure his own contract, freeing up money for the Dodgers to pursue Bonds; he volunteered a move to right field and figured Shawn Green could play center, so Bonds could play left field.

Bonds laughed when told of Sheffield's plans: "He's been saying that for years."

That night, September 7, Bonds' greatness was on display and it seemed the ghosts of Candlestick Park followed the Giants to the Rocky Mountains.

Bonds singled twice, walked three times — and in a classic at-bat that displayed his greatness — doubled home the tying run in the eighth inning off side-winding lefty reliever Mike Myers, who is nearly unhittable for left-handed batters.

It was still 2-2 in the ninth, an extremely rare pitchers' duel at Coors, when at 9:39 p.m. local time, an incredible windstorm arrived in an instant. The 33,473 fans either headed for the exits, headed for cover or cheered wildly. Ramon Martinez made the second out of the ninth inning, an extremely adventurous fly ball to left. Pinch hitter J.T. Snow singled to center as papers, napkins and wrappers bombarded the playing field.

Marvin Benard, who had to call time before one pitch, had the right idea by getting the ball up in the air with a towering blast to right. But the wind actually kept it in the ballpark.

"I've never been here when something like that happens," said Benard, who told Aurilia and trainer Stan Conte before his at-bat that he was going to homer. "I guess that's part of the game. I thought I hit it good enough, but the wind got it. I thought I had it."

Between innings, stadium workers tried in vain to pick the trash off the field, a hopeless exercise considering the volume of trash that continued to make its way on the field. Giants catcher Benito Santiago called time in the bottom of the ninth to put on clear sunglasses, keeping the wind and dust from his eyes. The game was never suspended though.

The windstorm settled down a little and the Rockies won the game in the 11th inning, 3-2, a game that took nearly four hours. Arizona also lost, so the Giants didn't lose any ground in the standings. Still 1.5 games out.

"We lost, bottom line," Bonds said. "It's 11:15 right now and we have a game at 1:05. I just want to get eight hours sleep. That's all I care about right now. Get out of here and get some sleep."

Added manager Dusty Baker: "We got beat by the elements. Marvin's was a home run, no doubt. But you can't do anything about that."

Jeff Kent, who had played in 138 of 141 games, got a much-needed day off by the skipper. He used the extra time to rest himself mentally and work on some things in the batting cage. Baker's timing, as usual, was perfect for giving his starter a rest.

The next day, September 8, Kent singled home a run in the first inning, a two-out hit he'd been lacking. First baseman J.T. Snow, who'd struggled all year, took three trips to the disabled list, and was the target of boo-birds whenever he started over Galarraga, doubled home Kent for a 2-0 lead.

In the third, after Aurilia and Bonds singled, Kent doubled home Aurilia for a run and Snow scored Bonds on a grounder for a 4-0 lead. Bonds just missed an opposite-field homer off the side-winding Myers in the sixth, Kent added a solo homer in the seventh and the Giants won, 7-3, in a game with a starting temperature of 42 degrees.

Kent spent an extra long time in the trainers' room and eating after the game. There was a crowd of reporters waiting for him at his locker, so he stopped near a table where there was more room for everyone and started talking.

The questions started slow, but everybody knew where this was headed. Kent had been feeling the pressure of being the MVP, the guy who criticized Bonds in *Sports Illustrated*, the guy who wasn't getting as many clutch hits, and it was time for him to unburden himself to the media.

"I thought I've done a pretty good job this year," Kent said. "I'm not a typical number four hitter. But I think I've played well this year. We, as baseball players, have emotions. It hurts a little bit when you get criticized over things we feel we can't control. Players set themselves up for falls sometimes. You deal with it.

"This ballclub is a different ballclub than in the past," he continued. "Barry Bonds is having one heck of a year in front of me. Sometimes that pisses the pitcher off, when Barry does the things he does, and then he doesn't want to give it to me. And I want to get it, because I see Barry getting it, and I want to get it too. Sometimes that can make a player too selfish. I'll take that this year. I've been a little too selfish. A little too greedy. Not too much. But at times."

It was a telling statement.

It isn't often any player, especially Jeff Kent, admit he was selfish.

Truly, things were changing in the Giants clubhouse.

Most of the other Giants players had left the clubhouse by then.

Earlier, Bonds had kept his comments brief: "We won. That's all that matters." And on the need for Kent to hit like he did in this game, "Yes we do. No doubt about it. The way he hit today, I like our chances."

The feeling of many players and coaches was the Giants needed Kent to hit like this the rest of the season if they were going to make the playoffs.

"To be honest, we need him to get hot," Benard said. "I know that he knows that he needs to get hot to help us out more. I don't know, he might be trying to do too much at times. We all do that when you know your team needs you. You try to do a lot more. We definitely need him to get hot and be the Jeff Kent that we know."

Kent didn't like the concept of one player making that big a difference.

"Guys are putting pressure on individuals and they shouldn't," Kent said. "We need everybody, period. Just look at last year in the playoffs. It's not just me. Our pitching staff has been phenomenal for us this year. They've done a great job. Pitching is a bigger key than offense in the playoffs. Obviously, they will need me. We need everybody else, too. Those are the types of things you need. You can't pin it on Barry, like people have done in the past. You can't pin it on me or Rich or J.T. or Big Cat. You need everybody on the same side."

Jason Kundtz, a 24-year-old mutual funds analyst from just outside Philadelphia, was in Denver for the weekend with his buddy, a diehard Denver Broncos fan, because they wanted to catch the opening of the new Mile High Stadium on Monday Night Football.

Realizing the Giants were in town playing the Rockies, Kundtz and his buddy decided to take in a game at Coors Field and purchased tickets in right field — just in case Barry Bonds hit a home run their direction.

But what are the odds of something like *that* happening?

Kundtz and his buddy settled into their seats for the Sunday, September 9 game. The temperature was back up to 68 degrees by first pitch and the ball was traveling again, like it normally does at Coors. Aurilia started the scoring early, mashing his 33rd homer of the season into the left-center bleachers off Scott Elarton.

Bonds was up next. On a 1-1 pitch, Bonds unloaded. The ball erupted off his bat and screamed over the fence and over the Giants bullpen in deep right-center, bounced off the enormous Coors billboard and bounced somewhere around the rocks and trees out there. The estimated distance was 488 feet, which many considered a conservative guess. Including me. Similar to the ball Bonds launched off Schilling in Arizona back in May, this was still rising when it hit the billboard.

The Coors Field crowd was on its feet. Bonds was now at 61 homers. I remember calling my sports editor at home, telling him to stay tuned, because I had the feeling Bonds wasn't done on this afternoon.

Finding the 61st homer wasn't easy. Bonds had told Giants officials he wanted as many of the final 20 baseballs as possible. The relievers in the Giants bullpen were searching and couldn't find the ball. Groundskeepers couldn't find it. Neither could security guards.

Finally, it was determined the ball must have landed in a small water fountain about five feet deep and just beyond the Giants bullpen in center field. So closer Robb Nen said they should get clubhouse attendant Ken Garibaldi to jump into the freezing cold water. Mark Gardner called the clubhouse and told Garibaldi to put on some shorts and go out to the bullpen.

Garibaldi, 20, attends a junior college in Arizona. He works for the Giants in spring training, then drives with a friend to San Francisco and works for the team during the season once his school year ends. He didn't have the foggiest idea why Gardner was calling him, but dutifully came out there wearing shorts.

Once he was out there, Gardner pointed to the water and told him to get the ball. Garibaldi knew the water was cold. But he's a trooper. He didn't care. He took off his shoes and socks and slowly entered the water. Finally, he took the plunge and dove to the bottom of the fountain as the Giants relievers laughed hysterically.

Garibaldi emerged with a ball alright. Problem was, he found seven in the water. How were they supposed to know which was the ball Bonds hit?

Well, four of the baseballs had the 1996 all-star logo on them, which are used for batting practice. Another had the Jackie Robinson commemorative logo, which is also used in batting practice. The sixth ball had no logo, was extremely heavy and so water logged it could be easily squeezed.

The seventh wasn't water logged and had the normal logo on it. That was the 61st homer.

For his heroic efforts, Garibaldi was nicknamed "Scuba Steve" by the bullpen.

A couple innings after Garibaldi had dried off and put on warm clothes, Bonds was up again in the fifth inning. On a 2-2 pitch, Elarton came inside and Bonds sent a low-line drive toward the right-field wall. The ball stayed up long enough, cleared the wall, bounced off the area between the fence in stands, hit a fan in the chest, bounced back toward the playing field and was snatched by . . . Jason Kundtz.

Talk about fate, huh?

After securing the ball, Kundtz let some fans hold the baseball. Some people yelled at him with offers of $5,000. Blake Rhodes, the Giants baseball information manager, had a security guard bring Kundtz to the press box. Negotiations took place behind closed doors for nearly two innings.

Kundtz, a former All-American Division II tight end at Lock Haven University, didn't ask for much. Rhodes offered him a couple autographed baseballs, an autographed bat and the chance to give the ball back to Bonds. Kundtz, a diehard football fan, asked if he could get an upgrade on his tickets for the following night's Broncos game.

Rhodes didn't have that kind of clout. But he did have an ally in Raul Velez, the radio engineer for the Giants radio broadcasts. Velez was going to engineer the football game for CBS Radio and figured he could sneak Kundtz and his buddy into the booth for five minutes.

That sealed the deal for the ball.

"Money comes and goes," said Kundtz, startled at the crowd of media interviewing him in the back of the press box. "I didn't want much. This ball means a lot more to him than me. I just want an opportunity to meet him."

Bonds now had two more homers, 62 for the season, and the editors back in all the Bay Area's papers had decided Bonds was going on the front of the news section.

Tied 4-all, neither team could capitalize on scoring opportunities and it went extra innings yet again. Bonds had walked in the eighth inning, drawing boos from the Colorado fans directed at their own team. In the 10th inning, the fall shadows had crept onto the field, the pitcher was in the shade and the left-handed batters box was directly in the sun.

The Rockies had summoned lefty Todd Belitz, a September call-up, into the game. Bonds looked at one pitch, a called strike, stepped out of the batters box and his lips could be read by television cameras saying, "I can't see."

Bonds somehow made contact. He popped out to the third baseman. The game went to the 11th inning. Snow, who entered the game in the ninth, hit a two-run homer to give the Giants a 6-4 lead. Much like his go-ahead homer in New York two weeks earlier, it was about to be forgotten.

Benard walked. Aurilia singled. And Bonds came to the plate, the sun gone and the shadows now allowing him to see. Belitz threw an 0-1 curveball down and inside. Bonds golfed it, a low 3-iron shot that cleared the wall and landed in the Rockies bullpen.

As Bonds rounded the bases, the entire stadium was on its feet. They cheered like Bonds was a Rockie. Belitz was removed from the game, giving the crowd time to stay on its feet and begin a chant of "Bar-ry, Bar-ry, Bar-ry, Bar-ry."

A bit shocked at the love he was receiving on the road, Bonds had no choice but to emerge from the dugout for the rarest of rarities: a curtain call on the road!

"Yeah, that was fun, a lot of fun," said Bonds, sitting in a chair without a microphone in an interview room outside the Rockies clubhouse after the game.

It was tough hearing him. I asked Bonds if he ever received a curtain call on the road before.

"I think in Atlanta, they gave me a standing-O," said Bonds, whose memory was correct. "This is the first curtain call. It's tough because they are trying to win. It's hard doing it on somebody else's turf . . . I'm just glad we won. It wasn't looking good early. It was looking gloomier and gloomier."

This was the first day I honestly felt Bonds was going to break Mac's record. Not that he had a *chance*. That he *was* going to do it.

In Barry's own mind, this was also the day he knew the home-run record was reachable; but not a foregone conclusion. He wasn't about to share those feelings with the media, weary of saying he can do something and then the backlash if he didn't do it. Still, his emotions were everything you would expect from somebody with 63 homers and 18 games left. The questions asked don't even matter. This is what Bonds said.

* "I don't know what to say right now. I'll have time later on today on the plane to reflect on what just happened."

* "Everything around me is unreal. I can't explain anything."

* "I'm just happy the way we are playing. I enjoy being in pennant races. It's a lot of fun. But it's also hard."

* "I got better pitches to hit. You have to tip your hat to them. They came right after me. You don't know you're going to be able to do those things."

Back in the Giants clubhouse, there was giddiness and laughs all around. Ken Garibaldi, the clubbie, was conducting his first press conference in one corner.

"Jay Leno wants you next," teased reliever Jason Christiansen.

"Scuba Steve," who rides motorcycles with Bonds from time to time, didn't know what to think when he was informed the Rockies groundskeepers found a dead cat in that water fountain a couple weeks earlier.

Kundtz and his friend gave the ball to Bonds, shook his hand, got their autographs and left with memories to last a lifetime.

There were heroes all around in the Giants clubhouse. Snow for his homer. The bullpen's five scoreless innings. Benito Santiago's spectacular catch of a throw to the plate and tag for a double play. Most of the talk, of course, was Bonds' three homers and the road curtain call.

"It just goes to show people appreciate what he's done," Baker said. "I'm sure they were applauding Sammy and Big Mac a couple years ago. People appreciate excellence."

Colorado manager Buddy Bell, ejected in the first inning, said the feeling was just like Mark McGwire in 1998.

"It seems like every time he's up, you think he's going to hit a home run," Bell said. "He's an incredible player. Incredible players do incredible things. I'm rooting for him."

Giants reliever Wayne Gomes — who had brawled with Snow and the Giants three years earlier in the series against Philadelphia that triggered Curt Schilling's negative comments on Bonds — was the winning pitcher in the game. Gomes had quickly gained friends in the clubhouse, including Bonds, in the five weeks since he'd joined the team.

His view from the bullpen of Bonds' three homers and explanation was classic.

"I didn't even see that (first) ball go," Gomes said. "I saw the camera shot. I don't think he saw it either. I still haven't seen it. I just know it went over my head. 62? Yeah, that scud left kinda quick too. I saw the last missile. I didn't think it would go over the fence. I thought it would hit the yellow line and knock the fence over."

Snow showered and changed without much fanfare, asking his teammates about scores in the opening round of the NFL schedule until reporters made their way over to his locker and asked if he felt overshadowed.

"It doesn't matter to me," Snow said. "We won the game. That's all that matters. Barry deserves the credit and attention he's getting. I've never seen a visiting player take a curtain call. Give credit to the fans. They're aware of what's going on and they know they might be seeing history. They were a part of it today. It's great for baseball."

The Bonds transformation with teammates wasn't complete. But it was getting there. If his teammates truly didn't like him, if it was truly 24-1, then 24 players have future careers in Hollywood. Noses were not growing. Bonds' teammates were genuinely excited and thrilled for him. There was no reservation in their words. Their first thoughts were squarely on the playoffs, no question. But they weren't holding back admiration and respect.

"This is my fifth year playing with Barry," Kent said. "I've said from the get-go, he's the most talented player I've ever played with. One of the most gifted. He's having the best year I've ever seen him have. I've never known him to be the dominating player he is now . . . It's awesome, ain't it? It's pretty neat. Especially when you win a game.

"It's special for him," Kent continued. "It's his time. I get criticized for not running up there and giving him a big bear hug after his home runs. But it's his time. He likes that. It's always neat to hit behind him. To watch him work pitchers and take good swings and be patient. It's been pretty incredible to watch this year."

It was September 9.

Bonds had just passed Babe Ruth and Roger Maris in one afternoon.

He now had 63 homers.

Next stop was the hitter-friendly Enron Field.

Some call it Home Run Field.

Others call it Ten-Run Field.

Bonds had four career homers in 12 at-bats there. He was absolutely on fire.

The Giants were on a roll. They left Denver that night and enjoyed a day off September 10.

They were greeted with an A-1 story on the front page of the *Houston Chronicle* about Bonds' arrival in town.

Nothing, it seemed, could stop Bonds from breaking the record.

CHAPTER 18

Fear

September 11-23, Home Runs 64-66

*"People want to know what our leaders are thinking,
what our President is thinking. They want to know
more what their plans are than what our plans are.
That's why we have a President. We have our leaders
to answer these questions. That's their job. Our job is
to back their decisions and give what we can, in all our
hearts, to help in any way, shape or form."*

Barry Bonds

BARRY BONDS was just another American, in some ways, on September 11. He was glued to his television set. His 63 homers no longer mattered. Baseball did not matter.

In another way, any fear he felt was double that of most Americans.

The day before the country was changed forever, San Francisco Giants manager Dusty Baker, general manager Brian Sabean, assistant GM Ned Colletti, a Houston police department officer, and an official from major league baseball security knocked on the door of Bonds' hotel room.

The news to Bonds on that Monday morning was chilling.

A man left a message on a Houston television station's voicemail that said he was going to shoot Bonds. It wasn't a black thing. It wasn't a money thing.

He just didn't like Bonds.

He didn't want him to break Mark McGwire's home run record.

Baker had been through this before, having gone through racially motivated death threats with teammate Hank Aaron nearly three decades earlier as Aaron neared the all-time homer record of Babe Ruth.

"I was surprised something like this didn't happen before now," Baker told me, in a reflective moment after the season. "Things haven't changed that much in society. There's all kinds of people out there. I told Barry to not stop living his life, but to be aware of it. I don't know if the guy was some kind of gambler or what because he said, 'if Barry plays . . . '

"This was just motivation for Barry to do even more."

The news of the death threat wouldn't reach the public until nearly a month after the season. In the final 30 minutes of a three-hour radio interview conducted by Hall of Fame basketball player Rick Barry on KNBR-AM, Bonds revealed the death threats.

"I kept that completely secret from everyone," Bonds said on the radio. "When they told me, I was like, 'you have to be kidding me. All this for a record?' I was more concerned about my children and keeping them at home or something. I didn't want anyone else on the team to know about this. And then, I didn't really want my wife to know about it. But I had to tell her for my little girls' sake."

The devastation from the events of 9-11 affected people throughout society and the Giants were no different. They had a couple close calls with relatives of players, but fortunately none lost their lives.

Shortstop Rich Aurilia, the Brooklyn native, told beat writers in the lobby of the hotel his mother's normal route to work is taking a bus from New Jersey, catching the subway at Battery Park — which is right next to Ground Zero — and riding that to her job in Brooklyn.

As fate would have it, Aurilia's mother didn't go to work on September 11.

Outfielder Shawon Dunston's parents still live in Brooklyn. Ash, papers and debris ended up in their backyard. They called Shawon in his hotel room and told him to turn on the television.

"I turned on the TV and saw a plane hit the building," Dunston said. "I thought it was a cartoon. But it was real. We aren't playing baseball for awhile. We can't think about baseball. Baseball is a game. This is life. This is serious . . . A little tear came to my eye."

There was high anxiety for Giants bullpen coach Juan Lopez, who Bonds took with him to Seattle for the home-run hitting contest at the all-star game. Lopez's sister-in-law is a flight attendant on American Airlines and frequently works the ill-fated Flight 11 from Boston to Los Angeles. However, she was not aboard the hijacked plane that crashed into the World Trade Center.

Baseball commissioner Bud Selig canceled all games on 9-11, then 9-12, then 9-13. The Giants voted unanimously as a team to not play the weekend of September 14-16. Shortly thereafter, Selig canceled the weekend games as well.

"It's just not that important," said Bonds, still visibly shaken and moved, when he made his first public comments inside the visitor dugout at Enron Field on September 13. "We have to move on eventually. But it just seems too early right now."

Selig decided the six games missed would be made up after the season was normally scheduled to end. However, even if they weren't, and the season was shortened to 156 games, Bonds said he would have "no regrets" over missing on a chance to break McGwire's record.

"People want to know what our leaders are thinking, what our President is thinking," Bonds said. "They want to know more what their plans are than what our plans are. That's why we have a President. We have our leaders to answer these questions. That's their job. Our job is to back their decisions and give what we can, in all our hearts, to help in any way, shape or form."

The Giants held workouts on September 12 and 13, then got on their charter plane and flew home once the FAA allowed planes in the air once again.

"I just feel for those people," Bonds said. "Innocent people are gone. It's devastating. It's just not right."

The sports world vocabulary changed September 11. When you think about it, the use of war references that have become so common in sportswriting these days was never appropriate. Football players are "warriors." Coaches are "generals." The playing field is a "battle ground." Linemen play in the "trenches."

Baseball players, especially hitters like Barry Bonds, hit "bombs" and "missiles" and "scuds" and "rockets." They are blasted, shot, scorched, rocketed. They explode off the bat.

Watching the scenes from New York, over and over, I couldn't help think how utterly ridiculous it was to ever use such descriptions — and the importance of rethinking how to describe future Bonds homers.

The Giants held a workout open to the media on Sunday, September 16, and I talked with chief executive officer Larry Baer about this. The game-day operations crew spent the day reviewing the song lists they play.

Closer Robb Nen comes to the mound with Deep Purple's, "Smoke on the Water" playing and the scoreboard showing fire behind him. That would be gone. Jeff Kent's entrance song is AC/DC's, "TNT." That was gone. Following a Giants home run, "You Dropped a Bomb on Me" is sometimes played. Again, gone.

The Giants were planning a celebration for the 1951 New York Giants pennant winner, a historic comeback capped by Bobby Thomson's game-winning homer in the ninth inning off Ralph Branca in the final game of the three-game playoffs series. It's been called, "The Shot Heard 'Round The World."

In these times, that phrase didn't seem appropriate. The ceremony was renamed, then later shelved until the following season. Baer also promised the volume and tone of between-inning promotions would be toned down to the appropriate level.

The mascot, Lou Seal, was given the first night off. Extensive security was added at Pacific Bell Park. All bags would be checked thoroughly. Coolers and backpacks were no longer allowed inside, a mandate from the Commissioner's office. Media members had their laptop bags checked extensively before coming inside. Photo identification was needed and had to be worn at all times.

As the country started to heal, the games returned on Monday, September 17. And the biggest question for Barry Bonds and all teams in a pennant chase was: What impact would the week layoff have, emotionally and physically?

The Giants first game following the tragedies was Tuesday, September 18. The team passed out candles and American flags, which made for a moving and touching scene as the candles were lit before the game. If this were still Candlestick, wind would have blown out all the candles. Pac Bell Park was different though. Players were lined up on the field like it was Opening Day, except they didn't line up on separate sides of the diamond. They lined up together, a Giant, an Astro, a Giant, an Astro, all the way through every player — a sign of unity.

A touching pre-game ceremony honored the victims and heroes of New York City, and video tributes continued throughout the game.

As "God Bless America" was sung, cameras zoomed in on Barry Bonds' face and showed him clutching an American flag and fighting back tears.

Once the game started, it seemed that everything was back to normal: Bonds was walked in the first inning. Both the Giants and Houston Astros played with playoff-like intensity.

In the second inning, Andres Galarraga hit what previously would be described as a bomb. It was estimated at 485 feet, beating Bonds' longest in the ballpark's brief history. Bonds was 0-for-3 with a walk and the Giants led 2-1 into the ninth inning.

Nen entered and the Led Zeppelin song "Kashmir" was played, instead of

"Smoke on the Water." The Astros scored two runs, a devastating loss for the Giants because Arizona had lost and they blew a chance to pick up a game in the standings. They remained two behind Arizona and 2.5 behind St. Louis for the wild card.

"That first game was really tough," Bonds told reporters, who were unaware of the death threats that had his mind racing. "Everyone is trying really hard to put it aside for a moment. There are a lot of emotions going on right now. I'm just glad to be an American citizen . . . It's tough to cheer and be happy right now. There's no way to tell how every (player) is feeling. It's so hard to tell. I'm sure it's mixed in every clubhouse."

Bonds later told me, as this book was nearing its end, he found himself looking into the stands frequently during that first game and was freaking out about how close the fans were to him on the field. He was thinking where he would run, if somebody came after him. He'd hear something loud in the stands and jump. His heart would start racing. His mind wasn't on baseball whatsoever.

At the plate, Bonds watched hittable pitches cross right down the middle of the plate. In the outfield at one point, he looked at the scoreboard and saw the count was 0-1. The next thing he knew, the scoreboard showed a 2-1 count.

"I just totally missed two pitches," Bonds told me. "That's when I told myself I have to concentrate."

Bonds considered himself fortunate the first games after the death threats were played at the comforts of Pacific Bell Park, instead of a unfamiliar ballpark.

"I looked around and I could see where all the security and stuff was located," Bonds said. "It was scary at first. I didn't start hitting again because I was more nervous. It was like, 'I'm going to get shot out here.' I'm thinking, 'did I tell my mom I love her? Did I tell my dad?' All these scary thoughts were going through my mind."

The Giants were routed the next night, 10-3, by the Astros. Bonds singled, walked and popped out twice. Only 16 games were left. And Bonds was still at 63 homers.

Bonds said his manager told him, "don't give them the satisfaction. If it was going to happen to anybody, it was going to happen to Hank."

In the nine years they've spent together, their complex relationship has never been considered tight. But in this time, Bonds leaned on Baker more than any other moment in his life — and, after the season, Bonds couldn't stress this enough in numerous interviews.

"Dusty coaxed me through it," Bonds told Rick Barry. "He made me feel better. Then I just started playing again and feeling better and hitting again. I thought, 'if this is what's going to happen to me in life, if this is how I'm going to go, I went doing something I loved.'

"Nobody understands what you actually feel in your heart," Bonds continued. "Just how scared you are. Even though you try to blow it off, it's in the back of my mind. I was like, 'wait a minute. This is just a game.' It was a very, very, scary feeling. But I did not want to take any focus off what we were trying to do.

"And I did not want people feeling sorry for me."

Nobody found out until after the season.

And, once again, Bonds persevered.

On September 20, the finale of the series against the Astros, Bonds hit back-to-back doubles with Rich Aurilia in the first inning for a 1-0 lead. Trailing 4-2 in the fifth inning, Aurilia singled and Bonds hit his 64th homer off Wade Miller to dead center to tie the game. A fan stretched as far as he could over a railing to make an amazing catch.

Only Aurilia and Bonds were hitting, though. The Giants stranded nine runners over the next five innings. In the ninth, Bonds walked, moving Calvin Murray into scoring position. Jeff Kent, again, couldn't deliver the big hit. He grounded out to send the game into extra innings — and the Giants would lose it when slumping closer Robb Nen allowed the winning run to score for the second time in three days.

"I don't know whether Jeff is pressing, but I know he wants to come through badly," Baker said.

Kent's take: "I think all of us want to do well too much in a game sometimes. I've been faulted for that quite a few times this year. I'll never put this on me. I didn't take us to the World Series last year and I'm not going to do it this year. There's more to this ballclub than just me. I think I'm doing all right. I'm hitting .292 and I'm watching Barry hit 70 home runs. I always want to do better. I would have liked to have done better last year."

After the game, in another press conference room after his 64th homer,

Bonds pledged to donate $10,000 to the United Way — targeted for the rescue efforts in New York City — for each homer the rest of the season.

"I've been thinking a lot about what happened," Bonds said. "There are a lot of emotions going on right now. The United Way is a great organization. I just hope I'm able to bless others in some way."

The emotions were still strong. Bonds recalled the mammoth homer by Galarraga two nights earlier and said, "I was hoping that over there, the ones who caused this tragedy, could hear that."

Fighting back tears, Bonds continued, "I believe in this country, in this presidency. I believe he knows we're behind him. We don't give up . . . I'm glad to be an American citizen. I'm glad to see people in the stadium, the turnout we've had, the cheers. And everyone just trying really hard in their hearts and minds to put things aside for that moment. It's a difficult thing. But everyone's trying."

Ask anybody in the room that day. Bonds was 100 percent genuine.

Just over two weeks were left in the season and Bonds was starting to get sentimental, realizing that his time playing in his hometown could be running out.

"I have 15 games left here," Bonds said. "I don't want 15 games to be it for me here. I want to have a 16th, 17th and 18th. I don't know how to feel. I have to think of the worst and prepare for the best."

———

Barry Bonds sat in a metal folding chair in the visitors clubhouse at Qualcomm Stadium the next day, his chin and head resting in the palm of his hand as he read the *San Diego Union-Tribune*. He had plenty to read.

Splashed across the top of the sports page was an enormous photo of Tony Gwynn, proudly wearing a San Diego State cap as he was introduced as the future Aztecs head baseball coach. Gwynn was retiring from his playing career in a couple weeks, but simply moving his address down Interstate 8 to the campus where his greatness was first on display.

Bonds read the paper almost cover to cover — including a lengthy "good and the bad" feature about himself.

Afterward, I sat down with Bonds for a rare pre-game interview and talked to him about Gwynn, figuring I would get some quotes this weekend and write an off-day feature about Gwynn the following weekend before his final trip to San Francisco.

I remembered Bonds telling Roy Firestone in his "Up Close Prime Time Special" interview that he would want to coach collegiate kids, so it was good timing to ask Bonds if he was serious and would he ever go back to Arizona State, his alma mater, the way Gwynn was doing.

His response was classic Barry.

"I told him I wanted to be his hitting coach," Bonds told me. "He said he's the hitting coach. He fired me. I was the first person he fired. I told him I'll move to San Diego. He didn't even give me the chance. I got an interview that didn't even last a minute. I didn't even get a chance to give my hitting philosophies."

I told Barry that being a pitching coach must be out of the question, too.

"I can barely throw from the outfield," Bonds replied. "I know I can't be a pitching coach."

With the Aztecs not in his future, Bonds didn't lobby for a job at his alma mater Arizona State. Instead he lobbied for rival Stanford.

"I don't want to be a head coach," Bonds said. "That's too much work. I just want to be a hitting coach. And I'll coach the outfielders. I'll just hit balls and make them run all day."

Just making sure, I asked if Stanford interested him because it was closer to home.

"Who knows, that may not be home," Bonds said.

Bonds truly has deep respect for Gwynn and stopped kidding around enough to praise him.

"Tony ended one chapter of his life and now he's starting the next chapter," Bonds said. "He always wanted to be a baseball player and he always wanted to coach at San Diego State. Tony's doing both. There's not too many people who can say that. It will be great for the kids to have a player of his caliber coaching them.

"But I have a message for them: Don't try to trick him. He's already been there. He knows every excuse. He's going to be a Hall of Famer. It's hard to tell him something he hasn't heard. You better be ready to just play baseball."

Bonds' favorite memory of playing against Gwynn?

"Stealing all his hits," Bonds said. "He brought out some of my best defensive plays when he hit."

Coaching was evidently still on Bonds' mind about 30 minutes later. The Giants had finished stretching (Bonds joined his teammates) and Gwynn was doing — what else? — an interview in the Padres dugout with John Saraceno of *USA Today.* Bonds made one last attempt to become Gwynn's hitting coach by interrupting the interview.

"I've got power," Bonds pleaded. "I can run. I can jump. I can tell them how to defend Punch-and-Judy hitters like you."

Gwynn laughed hysterically. But once again, Gwynn shot down Bonds' application. The future Aztecs head coach used Bonds' words as examples of what rival college coaches will tell recruits to persuade them to avoid San Diego: He'll turn you into a singles hitter; he can't coach power hitters.

"I can do both," Gwynn told Bonds. "I've waited long enough for this. I'm doing it my way."

Gwynn, already in full college-coach mode as a beggar for his financially-strapped program, extended an offer for Bonds to donate equipment or money or be a guest speaker.

The two traded some laughs and hugs and Bonds walked awake mumbling, "he *still* needs a power-hitting coach."

Bonds walked on four pitches in the first inning and tapped to first base in the third inning. In the fifth, Bonds hit one of those line drives that leaves the infield before he even finishes following through. The ball was down the right-field line and hit midway up fence as Bonds was just getting out of the batters box.

Bonds was held to a single, but it easily scored Jason Schmidt from second base, giving the Giants a 2-0 lead. In the seventh, Padres manager Bruce Bochy brought in lefty Chuck McElroy to face Bonds.

No pitcher has better success against Bonds than McElroy. Bonds made solid contact, hitting a low line drive to deep center that Cesar Crespo raced down at the warning track. Bonds was now 2-for-32 with one homer lifetime against McElroy.

The 2-0 score held up as the final, but Arizona won again and the Giants remained two games out of first.

Originally, this weekend was going to be Gwynn's final at home. But after the re-shuffling of the schedule because of the events of 9-11, Gwynn would still have three more home games. All the giveaways and festivities continued and it was called "Thanks, Tony Weekend."

A fireworks show, choreographed to video celebrating Gwynn's career, kept the record crowd of 60,066 in their seats for well after the game. Even Gwynn stuck around to watch the fireworks — the first time in his career he'd done that.

The next night, September 22, Bonds doubled in the first inning against Bobby J. Jones, the playoff tormentor from the previous season, but struck out twice and flied to left his next three at-bats. The Giants led 2-0 in the seventh, when Gwynn made his nightly pinch-hitting appearance. The Giants brought in lefty Jason Christiansen, giving the 60,870 fans at a sold-out Qualcomm Stadium extra time to stand and salute Gwynn.

Christiansen threw a fastball on the outside part of the plate. Gwynn took a self-admitted ugly swing on it, but hooked it enough between the first and second baseman for a game-tying, two-run single. The Padres scored another run to take the lead and the Giants tied the game in the eighth on a rare Calvin Murray homer. Mike Darr ended the game, 4-3, on the first pitch of the 10th inning with a homer.

It was the fourth time in five days the Arizona Diamondbacks had lost a game and the Giants failed to capitalize on it. They were still two games out, now 13 games left, and four behind St. Louis in the wild-card race.

The next morning, September 23, Bonds arrived at Qualcomm Stadium in a white limousine at 9 a.m. Bonds ran into Gwynn in the hallway on his way to the clubhouse. Bonds would later say that Gwynn "corrected my swing," but Gwynn said it was more like Bonds saying he was "trying to do too much" and Gwynn agreed wholeheartedly.

Bonds walked in the first off Junior Herndon, stole second and scored one of three first-inning runs on a J.T. Snow single. Herndon didn't make it out of that inning and Jason Middlebrook was pitching when Bonds came to the plate in the second inning.

On a 2-1 pitch, Bonds got a fastball and didn't try to do too much with it. He simply put a good swing on the ball and it went out of the park to deep center. Two innings later, the count was 2-0 and Middlebrook threw a fastball down and a little inside. Bonds went down and got it — hitting the ball over the *left* field fence.

Home runs 65 and 66 weren't tape-measure or anything spectacular. But they were the ultimate example of Bonds' greatness. He considered himself in a two-game slump (2-for-7, one walk), but knew exactly what he was doing wrong — and exactly how to fix it. He didn't pull either pitch. He didn't overswing. And he still hit two.

Personally, I had that same feeling from two weeks earlier in Colorado when Bonds hit three. I thought for sure he was going to hit a third, since it was only the fourth inning. It was already 8-1 (en route to an 11-2 final) and the Padres had no reason to pitch around him. Bonds grounded out his next two at-bats, then was lifted for a pinch-hitter in the eighth inning, so he could rest a couple innings and September call-up Dante Powell could get an extra at-bat.

This is all the pace you needed to know: Bonds was four homers shy of 70. Twelve games were left.

"What do I think about it?" Bonds said, looking out at a media group that had grown to nearly 30 in the San Diego State football team's locker room at Qualcomm. "I'll let you know if I reach it."

Bonds quickly told the media of his conversation with Gwynn and how it helped him.

"He kinda corrected my swing a little," Bonds said. "He told me to do the things I normally do. I was a little too aggressive the first two games here. I went back to doing things I've done my whole career, not doing too much."

The media asked Bonds more questions about exactly what Gwynn told him and how it helped him. Those are the questions Gwynn answers with joy, feeling that he can explain the baseball swing in a way that even a sportswriter can understand. Bonds, on the other hand, isn't much of a detail guy with sportswriters.

"We just happen to get here at the same time," Bonds said. "We were in the hallway. We have so much respect for each other. I've watched him my entire career. I've always admired his hitting and his approach. He always brought the best out of me defensively. He made some good valid points today and I took advantage of it.

"We just talked about hitting and the approach to hitting. Tony is a tactician when it comes to hitting. He's able to pick up things on other hitters, what you're doing wrong. If you're talented enough, you'll know what he's trying to say. He made some points today and I made good adjustments."

Bonds couldn't help adding, though, "he still needs me as a power hitting coach."

Breaking the record wasn't a foregone conclusion. But it was getting close.

"Slumps happen," Bonds reminded the media. "I don't want to assume anything or feel overconfident about anything. I just want to win this division. St. Louis just came from nowhere and tapped everyone on the back and went right by us. We have to win our division. That's what it comes down to."

The crowd of 35,247 booed heavily when Bonds was lifted for a pinch hitter. Plenty of sportswriters were wondering what Baker was thinking. A couple of innings off in May is one thing. A couple of innings off in September with a guy at 66 homers is another thing.

"You have to respect the other team," Bonds said. "I don't feel it's right to show up another team. We're trying to win a division here. We've got some guys on that bench that need at-bats. You have to look at the whole picture. Not just what one player is doing. It was Dusty's call with me . . . If it's close, I always play."

Bonds was now on the hook for a $30,000 donation to the United Way. "God willing," he said, "I can donate a whole lot more money the rest of the season."

Gwynn was getting dressed for the Padres flight to Colorado when the pack of media came his way. Gwynn couldn't understand why in the world they all wanted him. He struck out in his pinch-hitting appearance. Then he was told that Bonds gave him credit for the two homers.

"Oh great," Gwynn said.

Ever the trooper, Gwynn walked to the playing field and grabbed a seat in the makeshift bleachers so everybody could hear him easier.

"He didn't say that the other day," Gwynn said. "He came over and said I can't be the hitting coach of my own damn club. That's what he said. It's funny he goes deep twice. He didn't say squat to me for two days. Now today he wants to give me love. I'm punched out. Like I want to talk more."

If Gwynn was annoyed, and he probably was a little, he simply couldn't be too mad.

"That's how Barry is," Gwynn said. "I've known him since he came up. He's fire and fury with you guys (in the media). I spent about 15 minutes talking to him today. He's tuned into everything that is going on. He knows that some people want to see him do it and some don't. He knows his team is in the hunt and he has to carry a lot of the load.

"I think at times ya'll get on his nerves. Ya'll know what I'm talking about? It's happened to a lot of guys in this league. You just want to do your job. But when you're in the spotlight like him, sometimes you have to deal with it. I told him I thought he's handled it really well. Have fun with it, you know? He's one guy who doesn't care what people think when he's playing."

Gwynn compared the session to more like a psychological visit. Bonds talked about trying to do too much. Gwynn listened. And he agreed.

"I didn't say it, he's the one who said it," Gwynn said. "He said, 'I'm trying to do too much.' Usually, in this game, when you try to do too much, you get yourself out. But it's hard to stay patient when you only get 1-2 pitches a game to hit. I just told him to get in position and take a swing.

"The ball he hit to center he didn't hit good. It didn't sound good. But he still got it out. The ball to left he didn't hit good. But it still got it out. The difference between those two swings and the others he hit today was he didn't try to force it. That's the hardest thing to teach in the game."

Tony Gwynn couldn't coach power hitters?

Yeah, right.

CHAPTER 19

Money Talks

September 24-27, Home Run 67

"If I do it, I'll be excited. Don't worry. I won't hold back. I guarantee that. But right now, I'm in a quest to win a championship. If it means to hit home runs to help this team, then that's my job. If it means take a walk and get on base, that's my job."

Barry Bonds

THE FIRST CONTRACT Scott Boras ever negotiated was his own. Growing up, Boras' idol was Willie Mays. He was good enough to get drafted and negotiated a $7,500 signing bonus for himself in the late 1970s. He spent two years playing minor league baseball, making it as high as Double-A in the St. Louis Cardinals organization. A third knee operation in 1977 convinced Boras to return to college and concentrate on law.

Boras returned to the University of the Pacific in Stockton, Calif., located about a 90-minute drive south from San Francisco. Boras practiced law as a medical litigator in a large Chicago law firm prior to representing baseball players. His first client was longtime friend Mike Fischlin in 1983.

In the early 1990s, when Barry Bonds was winning his first two Most Valuable Player awards, the biggest agent in baseball was Dennis Gilbert of the Beverly Hills Sports Council. Gilbert's client list was impressive: Bonds, Jose Canseco, Bobby Bonilla and Danny Tartabull — who signed four of the biggest contracts from 1990-1993.

Boras was learning his craft and biding his time before he would become the best, and most notorious, agent in baseball. It was the summer of 1996 when Boras' name first started drawing the ire of general managers. In the amateur draft that season, Boras was the "advisor" of first-round picks Travis Lee and Matt White.

The term "advisor" is used because players aren't technically allowed to sign with an agent until after they are professionals. It's an old rule and not very fair, since it leaves mothers and fathers to negotiate signing bonuses with experienced general managers and scouting directors. The loophole is having someone "advise" a client, then become his agent once it's signed.

Another loophole is what Boras found in the draft rules that made Lee and White free agents. I followed the developments closely because I'd known Lee since 1994, when he was a true freshman at San Diego State and I was a third-year sophomore working for *The Daily Aztec* campus newspaper and writing a lot of baseball. (I've always told my parents that first year living in the dorms was my redshirt year.)

Travis was a very shy and humble young man. He sprinted around the bases after home runs, almost embarrased by his accomplishment and not wanting to show the other team up. He was drafted by the Minnesota Twins in June with the second overall pick, but it was common knowledge that Lee was going to play for the Olympic team and not sign a pro contract until after the Atlanta games.

The Twins knew this. As a result, they didn't offer him a contract within 15 days of the draft. Well, there's a rule that teams must do that. Boras exploited the rule, appealed to the commissioner's office and Lee was one of four players drafted in the top 12 overall who became free agents.

Half a dozen teams tried to lure Lee — winner of the Golden Spikes Award, the baseball equivalent of the Heisman Trophy — their direction with offers. He finally settled on a four-year, $10-million professional contract with the expansion Arizona Diamondbacks, even though they wouldn't play until 1998. The deal was worth $7.5 million more than first overall pick Kris Benson received from the Pittsburgh Pirates.

High school pitcher Matt White, who was drafted by the Giants, was another player who became a free agent. White signed with the Tampa Bay Devil Rays, another expansion team not beginning play until 1998, to the largest contract in baseball history for an amateur free agent ($10.2 million).

To this day, the Giants haven't drafted a Boras client.

J.D. Drew was the second overall pick of the 1997 amateur draft by the Phillies, but with Boras as his advisor, he held out all summer and never signed with the Phillies. He played for an independent minor league team as Boras tried and was ultimately unsuccessful at making Drew a free agent. Forced to re-enter the draft, Drew was selected by the St. Louis Cardinals with the fifth overall pick in the 1998 draft, finally signed and quickly rose through their minor league system and was in the lineup the night when Mark McGwire broke Roger Maris' record for homers in a season.

Following the 1998 season, Boras negotiated Kevin Brown's record-breaking contract. Boras reportedly had the Dodgers bidding against themselves, before settling on a record seven-year, $105-million contract. To sweeten the deal, Boras convinced the Dodgers to allow Brown the use of a private plane to shuttle his family back and forth between their Atlanta home and Los Angeles.

Boras had just broken his own record, a $57.5 million contract he negotiated for Greg Maddux the year before. But the *coup de gras* for Boras came after the 2000 season in his negotiations with teams for Alex Rodriguez. At 25 years old, Rodriguez was undoubtedly the most high-profile free agent in baseball history. No other player has ever had the power, speed, defense, charisma and youth of Rodriguez — and was available on the open market.

Very few teams could even get into a bidding war for Rodriguez and it was widely assumed the Texas Rangers weren't one of them. However, owner Tom Hicks decided he wanted A-Rod and kept bidding. And bidding. And bidding. Just like the Dodgers had done two years earlier, the Rangers owner bid against himself.

The final offer was 10 years and $252 million, exactly double the price of the previous highest salary in professional sports. The price was reportedly also nearly twice as high as any other team offered, although Boras denies that.

Boras smugly stood before a podium at the baseball winter meetings to announce the signing and answered questions all afternoon. As it has also been his custom after big signings like Kevin Brown, executive vice president of baseball operations Sandy Alderson stood before the same group of baseball writers and condemned the signing as horrible for baseball.

In his defense, Boras finds it ironic that Alderson makes such statements, since it was Alderson, as then-GM of the A's, who contributed to the system by signing Jose Canseco to the biggest contract in baseball history at the time (five years, $23.5 million in 1990).

The Scott Boras Corporation has a roster of players around 60. He is a rarity in the agent world in that he only represents players from one sport: baseball. Boras has a 15-person staff, which includes eight former major leaguers, a sports psychologist and a computer expert who once worked for NASA.

In the past 10 years, Boras has represented 30 first-round picks — and many more first-round talents who dropped to the second or third round because teams were scared to draft a Boras client and not be able to sign him — so it's clear he will be a force in baseball for many years to come.

Dennis Gilbert, meanwhile, had gotten out of the agent business after the 1998 season and was working as a special assistant to Chicago White Sox chairman Jerry Reinsdorf in 2001. After the 1999 season, Bonds left the Beverly Hills Sports Council (since Gilbert was no longer there) and hired Scott Boras to represent him.

From the outset, Boras worked on softening Bonds' image — skeptics would say this was strictly for endorsement opportunities — and implored him to be nicer with fans and the media. Bonds listened and has genuinely been more accommodating with writers, although he still has his moments and still remains the type of player who doesn't give off a warm image to writers looking for a pre-game interview. (Boras and Bonds have long maintained that pre-game interviews take away from Bonds' preparation for the game.)

As it was documented in chapter two, Boras came to Scottsdale, Arizona during spring training to talk with Giants general manager Brian Sabean and assistant Ned Colletti. Enough words had been spoken in the media. Boras felt it was best to talk in person. They talked at a picnic table for over an hour. They parted ways. Each side talked to the media. And each side told the reporters that no money was discussed.

<hr/>

It was now Monday, September 24, the Giants are in Los Angeles and Boras picked up Bonds at his hotel on Sunset Boulevard to have had lunch together.

Bonds arrived at the ballpark for his latest pre-series news conference with reporters. He didn't mind the group settings. In fact, he preferred it this way, instead of having reporter after reporter coming to his locker and having to repeat himself. That's what Roger Maris felt was the worst part of hitting 61 home runs in 1961. But back then, baseball PR staffs weren't as savvy in finding ways to protect the player and still help satisfy all the interested reporters.

Bonds liked the group interview settings because he felt it's safer.

"That way, nobody can lie," Bonds said. "Nobody can write bad stuff because everybody (has to) say the same thing. It takes a lot of pressure off me."

The first question to Bonds was about the tragedies of 9-11 and what impact they had on him.

"I don't want to talk about that," Bonds said, with a smile. "It's too depressing."

Bonds had talked at great length about the tragedies the past week. It wasn't like he was a Grinch or un-American. Like he said, it was a depressing subject and he didn't want to talk about it.

The person who asked the question was a columnist from one of a suburban Los Angeles papers. In his column the next day, he ripped Bonds and used Bonds' response to his question as another reason he's a jerk and why fans shouldn't cheer for him to break this record.

It's times like that when I'm ashamed to be a member of the media.

Boras is called by many in the LA media de facto general manager of the Dodgers. He represents seven of the best and highest paid players on the team: starters Kevin Brown, Andy Ashby, Darren Dreifort (a sub-.500 pitcher who signed a 5-year, $55-million contract the same day as A-Rod did) and Chan Ho Park; outfielders Gary Sheffield and Shawn Green; and third baseman Adrian Beltre (who Boras helped become a free agent by turning in the Dodgers for signing him before he turned 16, a no-no, then re-signed with the Dodgers).

Boras has season tickets behind home plate and is usually sitting in them during batting practice. We Giants beat writers often joke with our Dodgers colleagues that part of their pre-game ritual is not just talking to manager Jim Tracy, but also talking to Boras before games.

As you would expect, Boras was sitting behind home plate when the Giants were in town to play the Dodgers. After the Bonds press conference, I saw Boras and a group of Dodgers writers and went over to him.

The last significant news on Bonds' future came in New York nearly a month ago. Giants owner Peter Magowan said the further the Giants go in the playoffs, the better their chances of having enough money to re-sign him. Also, Magowan said he wanted to know quickly, within three weeks after the season ended, if the Giants were going to sign him.

Since Bonds didn't want to talk about contracts during the season, us beat writers respected his wishes and hadn't asked him about Magowan's comments. However, I figured I would run these comments by Boras and see what he had to say in response — well, once the Dodgers topics were done for the day.

"I don't think the ability to pay is an issue with the San Francisco Giants," Boras told me and a couple other national writers, who had started following the Giants for the Bonds Homer Chase. "They are in the top five in revenue in major league baseball. They are a very successful franchise. They're doing quite well. They are sold out this year and next year. Things have gone right. They are a well-managed team."

Somebody asked Boras if teams will be scared away by Bonds' age, since he's 37 years old.

"(Roger) Clemens and Bonds have taught us the book is being rewritten in the modern game," Boras said. "They are highly conditioned athletes. You can't look at the 1960s and 70s as a template for when optimum performance ends and mediocrity begins. Nobody in major league baseball at 36 and 37 has had the two years that Barry Bonds has had. Bobby Cox said something to me at the start of the season in Atlanta. He pulled me aside and he had Bonds in Japan.

"(Cox) said, 'I've never seen a guy more spirited and enthusiastic. I've never seen these things.' I kinda graded these things. This guy has a drive. He has that physical skill at such a high level. He's such a remarkably conditioned athlete and he never stops. The real issue for me is as much physical as it is mental. We all know the desire to do it will be overcome one day by physical inhibitions. No question. That's a grade that hits every athlete. When that comes, I would say with Bonds, the measurement stick is strictly his own."

It had been reported in *USA Today Baseball Weekly* a couple times in the season the Giants could have signed Bonds for four years at $16 million per. Another reporter followed up on that figure.

"In the spring, we went to the Giants and said four years and a lesser standard than (Jeff) Bagwell," Boras said.

Bagwell is signed to a contract for five years and $85 million (or $17 million, meaning Boras' spring training price had just magically gone up).

"I can't recall Bagwell's numbers last year," said Boras, meaning his homers and RBIs, not his salary. "Obviously, they were less than Barry's. We also told them, if they don't want to entertain it, the door is still open. We'd be willing to do that. Other than the fact we agreed to not discuss it during the season."

Then I asked Boras about the Giants having an answer on Bonds within three weeks.

"The player has the right to negotiate," Boras said. "He can allow the standard to be set. I think Barry will determine when the negotiations will take place and what he wants to do and what he wants to look at. Barry gave the club the right for a unilateral negotiation in spring training. They chose not to pursue that. I don't think they can create such a context later on."

Boras' translation: the Giants have plenty of money for Bonds; it doesn't matter how old he is; and the Giants will have to wait for everybody else in the offseason.

That night, after numerous celebrities, including Farrah Fawcett, stopped him to say hello during batting practice, Bonds came to the plate in the first inning and 38,849 fans at Dodger Stadium booed him. Then he was walked on four pitches. And then the crowd booed Dodgers starter James Baldwin.

It was the *bizarro* world.

In the outfield, the fans chanted "Bar-ry sucks, Bar-ry sucks" at Bonds. In the third, he was booed as he came to the plate. Rich Aurilia was at second with one out, first base open, and Bonds swung at the first pitch and fouled it back. The crowd went "ooh." Then he got jammed and flied to center. The crowd cheered.

In the fifth, a runner was at second again, one out again, the Giants led 1-0, and Dodgers manager Jim Tracy took no chances. Bonds was intentionally walked, which drew more booing from the crowd. In the seventh, it was still 1-0, two outs and nobody on base, so the Dodgers pitched to Bonds.

Baldwin missed with the first pitch, then he got careless. A 1-0 pitch was a slider down and inside. Bonds ripped it foul. Baldwin came back with the exact same pitch and — just like Ryan Klesko told me at the All-Star game, that Bonds is so good at doing — Bonds adjusted immediately. He lined the pitch down the right-field line and into the third row of the bleachers.

It was retrieved by James Malone of Simi Valley, Calif. Giants baseball information manager Blake Rhodes offered Malone four autographed baseballs and a chance to hand deliver the ball to Bonds. Malone said he'd think about it. Rhodes left and the chance was gone. Malone kept the ball.

Bonds was at 67 homers.

Eleven games remained.

Columnist Carl Steward wrote in the *Oakland Tribune*, "He's actually going to do this. Barry Bonds is actually going to hit 70 home runs, folks, and very likely more than that. All season long, as the hoopla of the Bonds Watch has mounted, most media observers, including myself, have held firm that it simply wasn't all that probable and even railed at the excesses of the homer hype. Bonds wouldn't get enough pitches to hit, let alone hit deep. He would hit a rough patch that would derail the pace. He'd get hurt just long enough, as he has over the past two seasons, to wreck the opportunity. And in the end, the daily pressure of the quest would ultimately wear him down. But what Bonds is doing now is what great athletes do: defy your beliefs and expectations."

The Bonds homer gave the Giants a 2-0 lead. Adrian Beltre trimmed the lead to 2-1 with a solo homer in the seventh off Livan Hernandez. But Felix Rodriguez retired Beltre on a fly ball to left with the bases loaded to end the eighth and Robb Nen pitched a perfect ninth to save the 2-1 victory.

In the ninth, Bonds hit a line shot the opposite field off Jesse Orosco that wasn't too far from being No. 68. After his at-bat, a startling number of fans left the park and went home. Granted, Dodgers fans are known for leaving early. They always leave early. Still, the Dodgers were still in a pennant race and it was still just a one-run lead.

Arizona was idle, so the Giants were within 1.5 games of first in the NL West.

"If I do it, I'll be excited," Bonds said. "Don't worry. I won't hold back. I guarantee that. But right now, I'm in a quest to win a championship. If it means to hit home runs to help this team, then that's my job. If it means take a walk and get on base, that's my job. Throughout this year, I haven't changed too much with my hitting. I've taken my walks. I've been patient. There was a couple games I got a little jumpy, like the first two games in San Diego. But I'm not gonna come out of my game for this record."

The homer was the 45th of 67 that had either given the Giants the lead (22), tied a game (7), brought the Giants within one run (6) or extended a one-run lead (10). And it was certainly needed.

"I hope people take into consideration that he's in a pennant chase," Aurilia said. "He doesn't get too many pitches to hit. That's what is most amazing. He won't see a strike, or a pitch he can hit for a homer, for seven innings. The one pitch he gets, he hits out of the park. I've seen it so many times."

Bonds went out to dinner that night in Beverly Hills and was mobbed. He vowed it was the last time he was going out the rest of the season. He was too tired and the attention was too much.

In the *Los Angeles Times* the next day, front office executive Derrick Hall was quoted as saying if Bonds ties or breaks the record at Dodger Stadium, they won't participate in any celebration. "We will not allow the game to be stopped or have a ceremony on the field," Hall told *Times* beat writer Jason Reid. "We're in the middle of a pennant race and the Giants are one of the teams we are battling. We would not recognize one of their players during that stretch run. We don't believe our fans want to sit through a ceremony for the Giants in Dodger Stadium."

Bonds dismissed the story quickly by saying, "It was a stupid story."

Perhaps the Dodgers were still fuming over the events of 50 years ago when the Giants won the pennant in dramatic fashion on Bobby Thomson's game-winning homer. It was revealed in a Wall Street News article nine months earlier the Giants actually stole the pennant. They stole the opposing pitchers' signs from their bullpen at the Polo Grounds and relayed them to their batters through an electronic scoreboard.

Or perhaps the Dodgers were still fuming because the Giants, in 2001, asked the Dodgers to wear uniforms from 1941 (which the Dodgers refused). Pitcher Ralph Branca, who gave up the homer to Thomson and has proven a great sport over the past 50 years, had agreed to attend the celebration, which was later postponed after the events of 9-11.

That afternoon, Major League Baseball officials frantically flew from New York to Los Angeles to take over production of the home-run race. With Bonds now at 67 homers, special media credentials were now needed to cover Giants games. Extra security would follow Bonds. Special baseballs with non-visible insignia — to help ensure the accurate retrieval of the ball — would be used when Bonds hits.

Bonds did some sleeping in the clubhouse before the game — or pretended to be sleeping to keep the media away. His chiropractor arrived in the clubhouse for a little "snap, crackle and pop" and Bonds headed out for batting practice. He returned and saw Dennis Gilbert, his old friend and former agent. Bonds signed the back of a Mickey Mantle jersey, alongside the autographs of the other 500-homer hitters that Gilbert has collected.

The figures that Boras told me (four years, less than Jeff Bagwell) the day before still didn't make sense. I wasn't feeling right about printing them. I approached assistant GM Ned Colletti and asked him if that was true or whether it was revisionist history.

Colletti couldn't believe that's what Boras told me. I couldn't print most of his response in my newspaper. I asked him for something on the record.

"Let's get Sabes for this," Colletti told me. "Go sit in the dugout. I'll bring Sabes over to you."

Sabean sat down with a half-grin and half-disgust look on his face. I sensed another Sabean blowup, but to a smaller extent since there were so many other reporters around. I asked Sabean if Colletti had filled him in on our discussion.

"Yep," Sabean said, "ask away."

I gave him a summary of what Boras told me.

"His version of our conversation is not even close to what Ned and I heard," Sabean told me. "He spoke in generalities. The one concrete thing was they would consider a four-year deal, contrary to popular belief. We never discussed money. His version of that conversation is far different.

"They gave us a chance to negotiate. They did not give us a chance to do a deal. They did not outline the limits of a deal. The only thing I can think is he's trying to make us look bad or trying to embarrass us, so the public will think there was a deal to be done. The specifics were never talked about. The only thing he mentioned is their willingness to do a four-year deal. Anything he claims that we talked about beyond that is non-existent."

Did Sabean regret not trying to get a new contract done, considering the season Bonds was having — home-run record or no-homer record?

"It wouldn't make a difference," Sabean said. "Scott was explicit in saying he didn't think it wasn't in anybody's advantage to negotiate in spring training. He would rather wait it out."

How would Boras' tactics and the Giants reaction hurt negotiations in the future?

"You have to hope they will sit down in spirit and negotiate in good faith," Sabean said.

On more than one occasion, Sabean would be in the middle of an answer and say, "look at me, Josh" like he was Tony Soprano.

"Once we say we're out of negotiations," Sabean said, "we're (expletive) out and I don't give a flying (expletive) what the consequences are."

Bottom line then, I said to Sabean, the only way Bonds returns to San Francisco is if he accepts less money than he could get elsewhere — just like what Kirk Rueter and Robb Nen did the year before.

"Exactly," Sabean said, "except to a higher degree . . . The more we pay him, the less we'll have to pay anybody else. That goes back to '96. We are not going to have two guys making up 40 percent of the payroll, or one guy making up 25 percent of the payroll. Not now. Not ever."

At that moment, I was convinced there was no way in the world Bonds was returning to San Francisco the next season.

That night, September 25, Bonds was walked on four pitches in the first inning by Chan Ho Park. He was walked on six pitches in the third inning. Two outs and nobody on base in the fifth, Bonds swung at the first pitch that was a little out of the strike zone and grounded out to second.

In the bottom of the sixth, the Giants committed a comedy of errors and passed balls, coupled with poor decisions and bad bounces; it led to a seven-run inning and a 7-1 Dodgers lead.

In the seventh, the Giants mounted a comeback. One run was home, two runners were on base and Bonds was coming up. Dodgers manager Jim Tracy went back to Jesse Orosco, another old nemesis of Bonds, and the strategy worked as an overanxious Bonds tapped out in front of the plate. Bonds stood at home plate, expecting the ball to roll foul, then started to run and was easily tagged out. Bonds was now 3-for-22 in his career against the ageless Orosco.

The Giants tacked on three more runs and were only down 7-5. But Matt Herges and Jeff Shaw put out the fire, Bonds grounded out to second to end the eighth off Herges, and the Dodgers scored two runs more and won the game, 9-5, to keep their slim division hopes alive. Arizona lost again, refusing to run away with the division, so their loss kept the Giants at 1.5 games out of first place.

The press box was filling up quickly with writers from across the nation. Baseball writers, in case you don't know, spend half their lives standing around and waiting — for a player or manager or somebody. We have a phrase for it. It's called "hurry up and wait" because that's what you are always doing. It's during this time that writers talk to each other, usually about Marriott reservations, United flights and dinner plans.

During the "Race For the Record II" — as it said on our special press credentials — reporters would pick the brains of the five traveling Giants beat writers, myself included, for story ideas and interview subjects. It's professional courtesy to help the out-of-town scribes out as much as possible. After all, it's not like you are competing with them for stories. And who knows, you might learn something from them about Bonds or a player from their part of the country.

This is when it really dawned on me that few writers really understood Bonds. Not that I understood him completely. But I had a better idea than most being around him every day, and writers from San Diego and Denver were picking my brain. One reporter, thinking about doing a story on why Bonds' teammates don't like him, asked me if it was true that Bonds rips his teammates a lot to the media.

Well, I responded, he's said some unflattering things about teammates years ago. Most of them were the good-natured ribbing that teammates give each other — or the type I say to my friends as a joke — in the clubhouse and are misconstrued when they get printed. I told them in the last two years, Bonds had never said one thing that was slightly negative about a teammate in print.

Bonds was stretching with his teammates as our conversation continued. The other writer commented to me, "I thought he didn't stretch with his teammates."

Well, I told them, Bonds stretches about half the time. He does when he feels like it. And he does it more often on the road. Bonds has long maintained that stretching four hours before a game is pointless. Most players in baseball just go through the motions. More talking gets done than stretching. Bonds does extensive stretching about 15-20 minutes before the game.

Bonds was relaxed, laughing and joking with friends Shawon Dunston and Eric Davis. At one point, he put his arms around head trainer Stan Conte and smiled. Cameras clicked away for this moment and I later joked to Conte that one of the photographers was from AP, and he was going to be on the front page of every sports section in the country tomorrow.

The cynics couldn't help wonder: Was this type of behavior from Bonds genuine? Or was he acting for the cameras? I couldn't help think he was acting in some ways. It's human nature to put on your best face knowing how many people are watching you. Bonds might not have mastered being a politician, but he's no dummy. Either way, he couldn't win. The critics would rip him for either being himself or not being himself.

Before the final game of the series, Bonds spent the afternoon at the 10,000-square foot Bel Air home of his old friend and pseudo younger brother, Gary Sheffield. Its estimated value is about $5.6 million.

Bonds had a similar house, a custom-built, 15,000-square foot home he described as his dream home. It was wired with computers and high-tech equipment in every room. Six months after moving in, a dot-com executive knocked on his door and made him an offer for the house. Bonds told him to get lost.

The dot-commer kept offering him more and more money. His final offer was $24 million. Bonds finally said yes and made an $18 million profit. He used the money to buy two vacation homes and a new 4,000 square-foot home in the Los Altos hills.

Sheffield's wife, DeLeon, cooked shish kebobs, turkey wings, collard greens and rice. Bonds finished eating at 2:45 p.m. and slept in the car as Sheffield drove them to the ballpark.

Before the game, Baker handed Bonds a good-luck gift from a friend's daughter. Bonds doesn't wear much jewelry (except the earring for his late grandfather), but he's a sucker for a gift from a friend. This gift was a wooden cross on a chain and Bonds put it around his neck. Bonds also put on a copper bracelet that read, "In memory of our fallen heroes: 9-11-01."

When I saw Brian Sabean before the game, I asked him if he saw a copy of my article with his harsh comments directed at Boras.

"Yep."

Got any problems with the story?

"Nope."

Terry Mulholland, a three-time former Giant and ex-teammate of Bonds twice, was starting the series finale. To his credit, he actually tried to get Bonds out. Bonds popped to first in the first inning and singled to right in the third. Mulholland was ahead of Bonds 0-2 in the fifth, then nibbled on corners and Bonds eventually walked.

The Dodgers had led 1-0, then 3-1, and it was 3-2 in the seventh. Marvin Benard started the inning with a single and Calvin Murray bunted him to second. That's normal protocol for manager Dusty Baker, who refused to change his strategy based on the likelihood of Bonds walking two batters later. Rich Aurilia grounded out and Bonds was issued the no-brainer intentional walk. Jeff Kent singled off Giovanni Carrara, but Benard was thrown out at the plate by Sheffield to keep the game at 3-2.

The Giants showed their resiliency in this game, though. J.T. Snow delivered a clutch pinch-hit single to tie the game in the eighth. The Dodgers retook the lead on an Eric Karros sacrifice fly, but the Giants had another answer in the ninth. Aurilia doubled and Bonds was semi-intentionally walked with first base open. That was walk 162, tying Mark McGwire's National League record set in 1998.

Kent grounded out, the runners advanced, Edwards Guzman was walked to load the bases and Benito Santiago just missed a grand slam, settling for a sacrifice fly to score the tying run. John Vander Wal followed with a pinch-hit, bloop single that scored two runs. The Dodgers put the tying runs on base in the bottom of the ninth with two outs. Adrian Beltre was batting third in place of Shawn Green, who was sitting the day out to observe the Jewish holiday Yom Kippur, and Beltre flied out to the warning track against Nen to end the game.

"We had to win," Bonds said. "This was a good game. A lot of pressure. But a lot of fun."

It was a crucial win because they remained 1.5 games behind Arizona in the National League and three behind St. Louis for the wild card.

"This was a huge game for us," Vander Wal said. "We knew Arizona won. We knew Arizona had RJ (Randy Johnson) pitching tomorrow. We couldn't afford to go three back with nine to play. This was huge."

CHAPTER 20

For Franklin

September 28-30, Home Run 68-69

"I really haven't had a lot of time right now to do anything, and every time I want to enjoy it for a minute, something else happens. When I really want to give you guys the story I want, it seems like I can't. I just can't. I haven't had time."

Barry Bonds

BARRY BONDS was being "Barry" once again. Or so it seemed. It was the next press conference, on September 28 following an off day, and it was proving a waste of time for reporters. Bonds had no interest in being there. His answers were short and without much feeling.

Then it was learned why.

On the ninth question before the game, Bonds was reminded of his comment that he was "star struck" as he approached 500 homers because of the people he was chasing. Bonds was asked what he's doing to maintain his focus.

"Right now, I'm trying to just relax," Bonds said.

He paused.

His eyes got watery.

And he opened up.

"One of my friends, I lost yesterday," Bonds said. "So it kind of added a little bit . . . Right now, I just have a lot of emotions right now about everything that's gone on for me off the field, and there's been distractions for us all. I'm just praying real hard that we get a chance to win here. I've got a lot of things in my mind right now, and I'm just trying to stay as calm as I can and as relaxed as I can and not cause any distraction amongst the team. I hope I've answered your question properly."

The next question was about Rickey Henderson and Tony Gwynn. And I don't think Bonds even heard it. You can tell he was distracted and his emotions were all over the place.

"Every time I have the opportunity to exhale or breathe, whatever you want to call it, something has come up that has been difficult for me," Bonds said. "I had a very disappointing article that came out, what happened with the tragedy and some other issues, and I lose one of my best friends yesterday. I haven't had time to think about anything right now. I really haven't had a lot of time right now to do anything, and every time I want to enjoy it for a minute, something else happens. When I really want to give you guys the story I want, it seems like I can't. I just can't. I haven't had time."

The friend was Franklin Bradley. Bonds had known him for 13 years, and hired him on occasion to provide security for himself and his family. Bradley played with Bonds' kids and was described by anybody who knew him as a wonderful man, a lovable and generous man, who was always giving of himself to others. Bradley also provided security for Jerry Rice and comedian Sinbad.

He'd gone into the hospital for what doctors thought would be a fairly routine surgery. Bradley's weight was near 400 pounds and he was going to get his stomach stapled to help him lose weight. Bonds was called at 9 a.m., put on some clothes and rushed to the hospital. Bradley died on the operating table. Bonds, who paid for the operation, was in his car on the way.

Bonds arrived at the hospital, saw his friend dead in a bed and started crying. Franklin Bradley was dead at 37 years of age. The same age as Bonds.

Around the same time, Bonds had also lost a cousin. She was a three-year-old girl and died in a fluke car accident. She was in the backseat and unhooked her safety belt. Her parents didn't even know she knew how to do it. She opened up the van door as it was traveling about 30 miles and hour and was flung out. She was a block from her house.

Bonds was devastated. The details hit home because his youngest daughter Aisha is about the same age and often tries to take off her seatbelt when the car is moving.

Bonds didn't tell any of his teammates about Bradley's death. Manager Dusty Baker knew about it. Baker always knows these things. So did a few others.

"We all knew the gentleman," Baker said. "It's tough when you lose a friend. I didn't say anything to him about it. The more you talk about it, the more it comes to the forefront of your thoughts. He just seemed a little quiet tonight, a little more stoic about things."

Pacific Bell Park, however, was electric that night. The fans did not know Bonds' close friend was dead. They were handed white rally rags as they entered the stadium and the crowd was rocking from the first pitch of the night.

In the first inning, facing Jason Middlebrook, the pitcher who gave up two homers to Bonds five days earlier, Bonds walked on five pitches. He didn't swing at any of the pitches. He now had 163 walks, breaking the National League record. In the second inning, Rich Aurilia hit a two-run homer to give the Giants a 3-0 lead. The crowd was still on its feet when Bonds came to the plate. Flashbulbs went off like crazy during each pitch to Bonds. Middlebrook wasn't coming close to a strike. The count went to 3-0, the crowd was booing the loudest I've ever heard, and Bonds still hadn't swung after eight pitches. Then Middlebrook decided to throw a fastball, perhaps thinking he could get an easy strike since Bonds would be taking. It proved a foolish thought. Flashbulbs lit up the ballpark as Bonds took his swing.

And absolutely crushed it.

Even in the damp thick air, the ball soared and soared to dead center in the ballpark and landed two-thirds of the way up the bleachers. The estimated distance of 440 feet was one of the longest of Bonds' season. The fans went ballistic. Bonds circled the bases and the emotions were already building inside of him. He stepped on home, high-fived a batboy and pointed into the sky — as he'd been doing all season.

But this time, he pointed longer than usual. He skipped a couple of times and kept pointing into the sky. It was obvious this homer was for Franklin.

Bonds received congratulations from his teammates, took a curtain call from the crowd and sat down on the bench by himself.

The tears started flowing.

And they wouldn't stop.

Bonds sat there by himself and cried as he thought about his close friend and the homer he'd just hit for him. Bonds just hoped the inning would continue. There was no way he could go out to play defense right then.

Jeff Kent cooperated by working a walk. Vander Wal struck out looking, but the length of the two at-bats provided enough time for Bonds to collect himself.

Bonds received another hearty ovation as he went to the field. Kent added a homer in the sixth — the fourth by the Giants that night — and the Giants rolled to a 10-5 victory. Bonds walked in the fourth, struck out on an 81 mph changeup in the sixth, doubled in the seventh and clapped his hands together with the crowd when the retiring Gwynn made his nightly pinch-hitting appearance in the seventh.

He went to a different interview room after the game. To handle the larger crush of reporters, the Giants set up a bigger interview room under the left-field bleachers — just like in the playoffs the year before — and talked about his most emotional homer of the season.

"It was hard to hold back (the emotions)," Bonds said. "I just said, you know, let God handle it. I've got to play the game. Let God handle all of the emotions."

I asked Bonds what made Franklin such a good friend.

"Everything," Bonds said. "He's done everything for everybody else. He's been around me ever since before my kids were born. And the one time he wants to do something for himself, something fatal happens to him. He was a real good friend of mine and I know my kids are going to miss him, too."

The curtain call was difficult for Bonds because all he wanted to do was cry at that moment.

"I just felt good because I just tried to do it for him, you know?" Bonds said. "Being able to do something on the day that you really wanted to do something for somebody . . . I lost one of my best friends. It's been a real tough year for me, but this — I think this was everything built up inside of me at once, and it just felt really good to be able to do something that I wanted to do for numerous different people."

How would this affect Bonds' perspective on the home-run chase and the pennant race?

"I got through today and that's the most important thing," Bonds said. "Yesterday was very, very difficult and today was another difficult time. But I got through it. I'm fine with it now and I can move on."

Then came another bizarre moment that only happens with Bonds.

A reporter from England raised his hand and said, "maybe I'm from England and I just don't get it, but why do you think some people give you a hard time and do you care about it?" The timing of the question was horrendous. Bonds was in the middle of talking about his friend dying and he picks that time to ask *that* question?

"I don't know what people you're pertaining to," Bonds said. "That's a broad question. I don't know who . . . "

The reporter from England tried again.

"Some of the media has been negative on what you've been doing and possibly some of your teammates?"

"That's America," Bonds responded. "Freedom of speech."

A few questions later, Bonds was asked if he's prepared to set the record.

"I'm prepared to win the division," Bonds said. "If Arizona ever decides to cooperate."

Arizona had won again and the Giants were still two games out. What about the NL walks record?

"That's not one record you want to be proud of," Bonds said, laughing.

Why not?

"Because, you know, it's part of this job to play," Bonds said. "Not observe."

———————

The first serious threat of Roger Maris' single-season home run record came in 1969. Reginald Martinez Jackson, then 23 years old, had 37 homers at the All-Star break for the Oakland Athletics. Jackson tailed off considerably, hitting five in August and two in September, finishing with 47 homers and didn't even win the home-run title (Minnesota's Harmon Killebrew hit 49).

Jackson won the MVP in 1973, thought he should have won the MVP the next year (Texas' Jeff Burroughs won it narrowly) and was the best player on the Oakland A's three consecutive World Series championship teams in 1972-73-74.

He arrived in New York in 1977, boasted that he "brought his star with him" to the Big Apple and proclaimed himself "the straw that stirs the drink."

Jackson fought with manager Billy Martin that season, but backed up his bold talk with a legendary performances for the ages in the World Series. In six games, Jackson hit five homers, including three in the clinching game, off three different Dodgers pitchers, as Dusty Baker watched helplessly from left field, and Jackson was nicknamed Mr. October forever.

Jackson's postseason statistics back it up:

	G	AVG	OB	SLG	HR	RBI
World Series Games	27	.357	.442	.755	10	24
All Playoffs Games	77	.278	.354	.527	18	48

Jackson's ego was enormous, something he does not dispute, and when Jackson finished in 1987 back in Oakland, his career home-run total was 563 — placing him sixth on the all-time list. Jackson was once an all-around talent early in his career, but turned into a one-dimensional talent even as early as that 1977 season, when his skipper pulled him from a nationally-televised game for his lackadaisical approach in the outfield, and routinely benched him in favor of better defensive outfielders.

Jackson spent more time as a designated hitter than an outfielder beginning in 1983 (at age 37). His final season playing mostly right field was his 39-homer season in 1982, his first with the then-California Angels. He was the DH in 134 games in 1984 and 121 games in 1986, the last of his five seasons with the Angels.

The Oakland Tribune's Dave Newhouse wrote, "Barry Bonds is the most complex baseball superstar since Reggie Jackson. Both are hard to like, both are hard to be around, both can be unbelievably rude to fans and the media, both can be excessively charming. Both will wind up in the Hall of Fame. Jackson's plaque already hangs in Cooperstown. Bonds is the better all-around player, which is no knock on Jackson. Bonds is generally acknowledged as the best left fielder ever. To be the best sets you apart."

Throughout the 2001 season, when Bonds talked about his famous family, he often included "my cousin Reggie Jackson."

New York Daily News columnist Mike Lupica caught up with Mr. October late in the season for an interview about Barry Bonds.

"He swears we're related," Jackson told Lupica, "that my family is somehow related to his mother. He says it all the time. I finally decided it's fine. Hey, the guy's got these home runs, he's going to win another MVP, he's a lock for the Hall of Fame. If it makes him happy to call me cousin, who am I to stop him?"

Jackson laughed and added, "I'd feel differently, of course, if he was hitting .240. Cousin? Get lost."

Bonds clarified to me after the season that his grandmother on his mom's side of the family is Jackson's cousin.

Jackson told Lupica that Bonds' arrogance is legendary. And when Lupica reminded Mr. October that his arrogance was legendary, Jackson said that's why you better listen to what he has to say.

"It's not just the arrogance in the way he's treated people," Jackson said. "He's brought it to the game. There's just been too many balls he didn't run out, too many times when he didn't run as hard as he could have after balls in the field. You know this isn't just me talking. There's certain obligations that come with having a talent for this game like he has.

"Listen," Jackson continued, "I know how many people out there thought I was a pain in the ass. How many people thought I was stuck on myself. But I just look at the way Barry has gone about things, and wish he had made things easier on himself. I wish he'd enjoyed himself more than he has. I don't know what's going to happen with Michael Jordan now that he's out of retirement. But I'll tell you something about Michael before: He enjoyed the game. He enjoyed being Michael. And he sure as hell enjoyed his greatness.

"I don't get the feeling Barry does. I never got the feeling that (Junior) Griffey did. Maybe it's because it's like they inherited the game from their fathers, that there were so many expectations. I also think there's an insecurity with both of them that's never left them, like, 'don't blame me if I screw up.'"

All that said, Jackson was rooting "like hell" for Bonds to break the record. He rooted for Sosa to beat McGwire in 1998, even though Jackson's final season with Oakland in 1987 was the same year McGwire hit 49 homers as a rookie.

"Why? Because he's a great player and the other guy (McGwire) wasn't," Jackson said. "I'm not sure (Bonds) is the best player (in baseball). I think Griffey, at his best, has a better arm and is a better fielder. But it's the two of them ahead of the field. I was at a signing with Pete Rose the other day, and we got to talking about Bonds and the home runs and all, and Pete said, 'at least this time, the record will belong to an all-around player.'"

September 29 started off as another day, another walk. Brett Jodie walked Bonds on four pitches in the first inning. Kent tied the game 1-1 with a solo homer in the fourth inning. It was still 1-1 in the sixth and Bonds was leading off the inning. Padres manager Bruce Bochy brought in another of those lefty nemeses of Bonds.

Chuck McElroy had allowed just two hits in 32 career at-bats against Bonds. The two were friendly with each other. Before games, they would talk and Bonds would inevitably remind McElroy that he's got his number.

Bonds thought to himself, "my day is over" as he saw McElroy coming into the game.

"He's always given me problems," Bonds said. "He's always pitched me well. Even when he makes a mistake, I still haven't had an opportunity to take advantage of it."

Well, he did on this day.

The count went to 2-1 and McElroy threw a mistake fastball. Bonds connected and it was another no-doubter. The ball whisked over the right-field wall, over the fans and into McCovey Cove. A mad swimming dash ended quickly as Scott Sicilliano, of Shell Beach, dove off his surfboard into the water and got to the ball first.

"I've challenged him since day one," McElroy said. "Today, he got me. It was the pitch I wanted. Just not the location I wanted. He's a man on a mission right now."

Bonds' 69th homer gave the Giants a 2-1 lead and tied his cousin Reggie Jackson on the all-time list with 563 homers. Jackson was the ninth Hall of Famer that Bonds has passed on the homer list during the 2001 season.

"I have a lot of family members that played professional baseball, and Reggie is another one," Bonds said. "It just feels good to finally get all those conversations off my back a little bit. I know he's happy for me, and I'm pretty sure he'll give me a call. It's good to be in that class."

In Bonds' final at-bat, he tapped in front of the plate in the eighth off Jeremy Fikac. The Giants won, 3-1, yet couldn't get any closer to first place because Arizona won again to maintain its two-game lead in first place.

Bonds showered after the game and started walking down the corridor toward the interview room. His daughter, Aisha, was ahead of him and implored her daddy to catch up with her.

"C'mon, daddy, c'mon," Aisha said, and by her request, Barry started to pick up the pace down the corridor to catch his daughter and face another room full of journalists.

"I don't feel any pressure with the home runs," Bonds said. "I feel pressure with the (pennant) race. Arizona, unfortunately, is not cooperating. Even though they had a short down-spell, we never had the opportunity to take advantage of it. When they lost, we lost. And it looks like they are getting hot again, and it could be too late. But we still have to keep trying to win games and hopefully they will hit a lull again."

One more game remained against the Padres and it was very conceivable that McElroy would face Bonds again the next day, this time with No.70 or No.71 a possibility.

"I'll be ready for the challenge," McElroy said. "I'll go right after him. You worry about it, you'll lose sleep. I'm not going to lose sleep. A lot of people don't have homes. A lot of people are still searching for their families. Today's game is over. We lost. They won. What else can you say?"

I thought Chuck McElroy was the classiest pitcher I interviewed who gave up a Bonds homer during the 2001 season. His perspective was needed with everything our country was going through.

⁕

Nikolai Bonds walked into the Giants clubhouse on September 30, the day originally scheduled as the final of the season, looked to the right for his dad and didn't see him. He walked over to Eric Davis, who was talking to Willie Mays, and asked him if he'd seen his dad.

"Yeah, he's over there sleeping," Davis said, pausing as Nikolai looked. "On the ground."

"Again?" said Nikolai, and he walked over and woke him up. Bonds' teammates laughed. Bonds was wearing a T-shirt that says "daddy loves me" with photos of his three kids.

Motorized boats were no longer allowed in McCovey Cove, so that made it safer and easier for anybody else to crash the party. And plenty took advantage of it. The scene outside the ballpark was the story of September 30. People showed up in yachts, innertubes, canoes, kayaks, surfboards, dinghies, cabin cruisers and just about any other flotation device they could find.

It was quite a scene.

If a Bonds homer went into the Cove, there's no way it would have landed in water. There was simply too massive a sea of humanity.

Not that Bonds had a chance. The record was not going to be tied before his home fans. Starter Brian Tollberg walked him on four pitches in the first inning. Bonds grounded to short on the first pitch he saw in the third. It proved to be his only swing of the day. Tollberg walked him on four pitches in the fifth inning. And rookie Jose Nunez plunked him on his protective elbow pad in the seventh inning.

Final tally for the day: 11 pitches, one strike.

The Giants couldn't take advantage of Bonds on the basepaths and lost a very winnable game, 5-4, to the Padres. It was a wasted "golden opportunity," as short-stop Rich Aurilia put it, because Arizona finally lost. The lead was still two games.

And this was the reality:

* In 1998, the Giants trailed the Chicago Cubs by four games with seven left. They went 6-1 down the stretch and forced a one-game playoff.

* In 2001, the Giants now trailed the Arizona Diamondbacks by two games with six left. However, the Cubs didn't have Curt Schilling and Randy Johnson on their staff in 1998. The Arizona Diamondbacks did. They had Johnson starting twice. And Schilling starting once, plus ready and available, if a one-game playoff was needed.

I told those facts to J.T. Snow.

"Really?" Snow said. "That doesn't help us out any."

Nope, it sure doesn't.

Bonds left without talking to the horde of reporters waiting at his locker. He put on his black leather jacket, leather gloves, hopped on his silver Harley Davidson motorcycle and left.

Shawon Dunston observed the scene and started talking out loud to no-body in particular.

"Barry's a class act," Dunston said. "All these people want him to talk about home runs. We're trying to get into the playoffs, man."

A few feet away, Davis summed up the Giants situation best: "It's like the NCAA Tournament. You lose one, you're out. So we can't lose anymore."

Quarterback Jay Fiedler of the Miami Dolphins was on the cover of the October 1 issue of *Sports Illustrated*. Inside, five of the nine letters to the editor printed were responses to Rick Reilly's column on Barry Bonds. The standing head was "Of Humane Bondage."

Letter one:

"Kudos to Rick Reilly for telling the rest of the country what we in the Bay Area already know. I got fed up with Barry Bonds' arrogant act a long time ago. For the amount of money he is paid you would think he could pose for a measly team picture, ride the team bus, stretch with the rest of the Giants and, most of all, run out all the ground balls he hits. Maybe then he would get a high five from someone other than himself when he hits a milestone home run. It would be nice if Willie Mays would pull him aside and tell him to 'get it, ASAP.' "

— Larry Becker, Danville, Calif.

Letter two:

"Since Bonds already had his own PR man, masseur and flex guy, maybe he should assemble a team of statisticians to document his postseason performance for Pittsburgh. This would provide excellent reading material for Barry in his recliner. Those rotten playoff numbers tell you all you need to know about Bonds."

— Cary Forte, Attleboro, Mass.

Letter three:

"I didn't expect my favorite SI writer to be a Barry Basher. What's the matter, Rick, Barry wouldn't talk to you?"

— Jim McGrath, Modesto, Calif.

Letter four:

"Last summer my husband, our 10-year-old son, Aran, and I were lucky enough to visit the Giants' locker room at Pac Bell Park before an afternoon game. To our utter surprise, Bonds stopped to have a few words with Aran and pose for a photograph (and was quite patient while I fumbled with the camera). As he was about to leave,

he gave Aran his batting gloves. Needless to say it was a day and a moment our son will never forget."

— Carolyn Tanaka Wilson, Honolulu.

Letter five:

"I was a Giants teammate of Bonds' for three years and saw firsthand what Reilly wrote about. What Reilly didn't write about was Barry's toughness. He plays every day. Even when Barry was hurting, he was not only on the field but also kicking butt. There were no excuses offered, no injuries hidden behind. Other things I remember about Barry: his picking up huge checks at restaurants; embarrassing a magician at a team party by yelling out the secret to every trick he had; getting down on his hands and knees and playing with my then four-year-old daughter at a kid's birthday's party and telling me, 'she's the cutest little girl I've ever seen in my life!' So Rick, Barry, isn't a villain in a Hollywood movie. There's good and bad in everyone. He wasn't the perfect teammate, but he's not a phony. He is who he is. More power to him — hopefully enough to get him to 71."

— Todd Benzinger, Cincinnati.

One week later, after Reilly wrote a column praising Ichiro Suzuki, and didn't seem to mind how infrequently Ichiro talks to reporters, another letter appeared in *SI*.

"Rick, Ichiro doesn't talk to reporters and he's a saintly Zen master, but Barry Bonds doesn't talk to reporters and he's the Antichrist?"

— Leslie Lewis, Palo Alto, Calif.

CHAPTER 21

Walk This Way

October 1-4, Prelude to No. 70

"Not since golfer Casey Martin took his case all the way to Supreme Court has the simple act of walking drawn this much attention."

Houston Chronicle columnist Fran Blinebury

THE MEDIA CREDENTIAL list was now over 250 as the circus moved to Houston, the place the Giants were stranded during the 9-11 terrorist attacks on America.

Some of the reporters from the East Coast might not have come to California, but they joined the circus in Houston. The headline read "Anticipation" on the front page of the *Houston Chronicle*, showing diagrams of where Bonds has hit most of his homers and the best place for catching the historic baseball.

Bonds faced another packed interview room before the game and most of the questions centered on how Astros would pitch to him. Bonds did his best to dare the Astros into challenging him.

"I've played against Houston a long time and I've never known them to bypass anybody," Bonds said. "They have too many quality pitchers on that side, going back to Nolan (Ryan) and Mike Scott and all the rest of them. They have pride, too. They have always been up for the challenge. When you look at some of the other teams, you can probably say, 'sure, they won't pitch to you.' But when you look at a staff like (Houston's), it would be kind of odd if they did (pitch around me).

"When you get the opportunity to play against the best, you want their best," Bonds added later. "I don't want to cheat them by not taking good swings, and I don't want to get cheated by them by not getting good pitches. I want their best . . . It's an inner feeling inside all of us, I believe, that you just want their best and you want to compete and you want to not feel cheated. I have a lot more pride to walk off the field and say, 'you won,' than to not get the chance."

Bonds also gave heavy respect to the man who still owned the record.

"I think everyone needs to understand, Mark set the table," Bonds said. "He's the first one and it's his record and he needs to be recognized for his record. (Roger) Maris is gone . . . and I think Mark deserves that respect, you know, being the single-season home run leader. He has put new hype on this thing and he deserves every amount of respect for being the man. It's really hard because he's the one that made the comment, 'records are made broken.' No one ever thought it would happen. I thought maybe Sammy (Sosa) might get close. He's the only one that ever hit 60 (three times). If Mark stays healthy, he might be able to do it again. But no one in their right mind would ever dream that anyone else even had a chance at this."

Following the press conference, I was in the Giants clubhouse and a television was turned to a local Houston station that was doing a live report from the field. They replayed Bonds' quote about not getting cheated. Bonds watched casually, while Eric Davis and Shawon Dunston laughed.

"Yeaaaaah," Davis said to Bonds. "You tell 'em, Dog. Go get 'em Dog."

That broke the tension, they all laughed and the three outfielders walked toward the field for stretching. Davis walked down the tunnel and into the dugout first. Dozens of cameras recorded his every move.

"Ya'll been waiting for me?" Davis said, giggling.

A little later, Bonds entered the batting cage. The cameramen and boom-microphone holders practically attacked the cage. One of them shoved Rich Aurilia out of the way. Aurilia drew a small box in the dirt and proclaimed, "this is my spot."

Coach Robby Thompson yelled at a Giants media relations employee to get the cameramen back so he could continue hit fungo grounders and nobody would get hit. They backed off a little. The circus was officially out of control.

On the other side of the diamond, in front of the home dugout, Astros general manager Jerry Hunsicker told reporters, "I think it would be pretty irresponsible to pitch to a guy when he's having the kind of year he's having. I'd be surprised and disappointed if that happened, unless it's a blowout game."

The Astros starter was Shane Reynolds. Here's a breakdown of the at-bats that night.

* First inning, one on, one out: strike one, hit by pitch.
* Fourth inning, Aurilia at second after a double ("I was thinking, 'should I hustle into second base or hold up so they can't pitch around Barry?'"), none

out: ball way outside, ball way outside, strike on the corner, ball outside, ball outside.

* Sixth inning, nobody on, nobody out: ball outside, single to center on a pitch probably a ball.

* Seventh inning: runners at second and third, two outs: ball outside, ball way outside, ball way outside, intentional ball four.

Fire-balling lefty closer Billy Wagner pitched the final inning.

* Ninth inning, nobody on, two outs: ball one, ball two, fastball fouled back, fastball grounded to first.

In all, Bonds saw 17 pitches and only five were strikes.

However, the fourth-inning walk put Aurilia in position to score and he did — on an infield groundout. Bonds scored after his sixth-inning walk on a double by Kent. The Giants won the game, 4-1, and remained two behind victorious Arizona in the NL West. It was the 16th consecutive day the Giants and Diamondbacks played on the same day and had the same result.

The Astros fans booed their home team louder after each ball. Astros manager Larry Dierker was grilled by reporters to defend his strategy after the game.

"Our strategy is not to talk about him anymore," Dierker said.

As for Bonds, he told a ridiculous pack of reporters near his locker, "(Reynolds) surprised me a little bit. He went after a guy with 57 homers (Sammy Sosa) against a team in his own division. I just assumed he'd pitch me the same way . . . He didn't challenge me at all. Not at all."

Reynolds defended his actions by saying, "The way he's swinging the bat, you can't let him win the game with one swing of the bat. If we have a big enough lead, two or three runs, maybe you give him something more to hit in this situation. No way could we give him a pitch to hit."

Tim Redding, a rookie, started the second game of the series on October 3 and the first inning offered promising hope for Bonds. Redding threw five straight fastballs to Bonds. On a 2-1 pitch, Bonds fouled back a 95-mph fastball and then swung and missed on a 96-mph heater.

Then it was back to normal. The next at-bat was four straight balls, the final three on fastballs away. That walk was Bonds' 170th of the year to tie Babe Ruth for the all-time record. Kent made them pay with a double to score Bonds and later scored himself to tie the game 2-2.

Redding was lifted for a pinch-hitter in the fourth inning and Nelson Cruz was the new pitcher in the fifth. Cruz walked Bonds on four pitches to start the sixth inning and that broke Ruth's record for walks in a season. Kent and Andres Galarraga followed with singles, and an RBI groundout by Vander Wal made it 4-2.

The Houston crowd was furious. And none more so than 10-year-old Shikari Bonds and 2-year-old Aisha Bonds. Shikari wrote messages on her erasable bulletin board and held them up for cameras that read, "Please pitch to our Daddy."

In the seventh, Mike Williams was the Astros pitcher. There were runners at first and second, two out. After falling behind 2-0, Williams didn't take any chances and made the next two balls intentional for a walk. Kent and Galarraga answered with singles again and the Giants led 7-3.

Growing more and more upset, Shikari scribbled another message that read, "Give our Daddy a chance."

It was 8-3 in the eighth and Mike Jackson, a former teammate of Bonds, threw a first pitch close enough to the strike zone and Bonds took a rip at it, singling to right and another run scored.

That night's final totals: 18 pitches, 14 balls, four strikes, five plate appearances, three walks, one single, one strikeout.

The totals from the last three games: 46 pitches, 37 balls, 0 homers.

The Giants ended up 11-8 winners, their seventh win in nine tries, but Arizona also won and it was now 18 consecutive days both teams played and had the same result. The Giants were still two games out of first.

And another day was wiped off the schedule — for Bonds and the Giants. Only four games remained now.

As the mob of reporters surrounded Bonds at his locker again, Bonds grew defensive at the scene, saying, "this is not right. (Jason) Schmidt pitched good. J.K. (Jeff Kent) came through. You have to give some respect to my teammates. This conversation is over."

Kent had finally delivered with clutch hits after Bonds walks, but refused to accept any extra satisfaction from it.

"I've played with Barry for five years and 99.9 percent of the time I've hit behind him," Kent said. "They're gonna walk him. They always walk him. It doesn't bother me. You've asked me that 100 times. Check your records."

Yeah, sure, Jeff, but there are an extra 100-plus credentialed media who don't watch every Giants game and they're here to chronicle history.

Even Galarraga was frustrated.

"I'm a fan," Galarraga said. "I want to see him tie the record. There's no doubt he will do it. But when?"

Even leaving the ballpark, Bonds was pestered with questions about the walks — from his son, Nikolai.

Bonds told his son the same thing he was telling the media: "It's not a big deal they are walking him because he's getting on base, creating runs and scoring runs and the team is winning. It's still a team game."

Nikolai still wasn't pleased.

But he accepted his dad's argument.

<hr />

You think it was rough on Barry Bonds?

Just wait until you hear the stories of Randy Bass and Tuffy Rhodes.

Bass was once a promising minor leaguer in the Montreal Expos organization. He wasn't getting an opportunity to play in the majors, so he went to Japan and became one of the first American stars. The Japanese were awed by the big American and his ability to hit home runs.

In 1985, Bass hit 54 homers for the Hanshin Tigers, putting him one shy of the Japanese record. The legendary Sadaharu Oh hit 55 homers in 1964 for the Tokyo Giants, the New York Yankees of Japan.

Bass' final two games were against the Toyko Giants, who were managed at that time by Oh. Under orders from Oh, Bass was walked six times in nine plate appearances during the final two games.

He was so furious that he held his bat upside down to protest during some of the at-bats. Many believed it was a conspiracy to keep an American from breaking the record.

Sixteen years later, Tuffy Rhodes was facing a similar situation. Rhodes was also once a promising minor league prospect in the Chicago Cubs organization. He hit three homers on Opening Day of the 1995 season, but never lived up to his promise in the states.

"He always had power," said Shawon ("I'm everybody's former teammate") Dunston. "But the United States baseball is a little different than over there in Japan. Here, if you have a weakness, they will find it. If you have a hole, they will exploit it. He was always a good clutch hitter. He hit for average and a couple home runs. Then he stopped working and thought everything was going to come easy to him. Now he realizes how you have to work hard, day in and day out."

Rhodes hit just 13 homers in six years in the major leagues, then went to Japan and launched into a home-run frenzy that rivaled Bonds' on the other side of the world. Rhodes tied Oh with his 55th homer for the Osaka Kintetsu Buffaloes on September 24.

In his third-to-last game of the season — the same Sunday that Bonds saw one strike in 11 pitches as an army of fans waited anxiously in McCovey Cove — Rhodes' team faced the Fukuoka Daiei Hawks.

Guess who was the Hawks manager?

Yep, the same Sadaharu Oh.

Rhodes went 0-for-2 with two walks. Even the Commissioner of the Japanese League criticized Oh for the way he managed that game. The final chance for Rhodes came on a Friday night in Japan, Thursday night in America, against a team called Orix.

Dunston, who has maintained a friendship with Rhodes and his family, said his former teammate didn't have any plans to return to the United States and play baseball. But if he did?

"If he were to come back over here to the big leagues, he would hit 30 homers — easy," Dunston said. "Because he was a good hitter then. And now, he's a much more disciplined hitter."

Dunston has the unique perspective of having been teammates with Rhodes, McGwire, Sosa and Bonds. Since his uniform number is one away from Bonds, his locker is usually right next to Bonds' on the road and has a front-row seat to the media circus.

Still, Dunston couldn't even imagine what it must be like for Rhodes, trying to break Oh's record, in Oh's country, with Oh managing against him.

"No way," Dunston said. "Way too hard. But I'm happy for him."

Rhodes ended up going homerless in his final two games — but at least the opposition pitched to him — and he settled for a tie of the all-time Japanese record with Oh.

———◦•◦———

What were the odds of this? In every sports section in the nation, a sportswriter was defending Barry Bonds, feeling sorry for him, and questioning the manhood of the Houston Astros pitchers and their manager.

"Not since golfer Casey Martin took his case all the way to Supreme Court has the simple act of walking drawn this much attention," wrote *Houston Chronicle* columnist Fran Blinebury.

For comparison, Mark McGwire was walked 19 times in the final month of the 1998 season — and only one was intentional.

But the most ridiculous aspect to this walking story was still to come.

Giants manager Dusty Baker found himself before the October 4 series finale against the Astros answering more questions about the Astros pitching around Bonds. Baker had known Houston manager Larry Dierker from their playing days and knew it wasn't in his nature to order his guys into pitching around somebody.

"I told people 100 times, Larry Dierker was one of the nastiest guys I faced when I came into this league," Baker said. "It's not in his personality to run from anybody. He was facing some of the baddest dudes in the history of the game . . . The only thing that surprises me is people looking for reasons why they are walking him. If these guys were seven games out, it wouldn't matter. Barry understands that. Nobody likes it. That's part of the game, too. I got booed in St. Louis in '98 for walking Big Mac with nobody on base. What will they say if Barry hits a three-run homer in the eighth to beat them and they don't go to the postseason? They've got to live here."

In 1998, manager Tony La Russa basically challenged opposing pitchers to come after McGwire. Baker was asked if he would do something similar.

"I don't believe in challenges," Baker said. "Every man can do what he wants to do. I issue actions. Dares went out when I was a kid. My momma whipped me for jumping in the canal because somebody dared me that I was too scared to jump in the canal. If you want a whipping, go jump in the canal.

It's slippery on the side and you can't get out, and they have to pick you up two miles down the road."

It was vintage Baker, using an analogy that would sound corny coming out of most people's mouths. But with Baker, it was real. And it was right on the money.

Dave Mlicki was starting the finale of the series for the Astros. In the first inning, with two outs and nobody on base, Mlicki threw four straight balls: a fastball up, a changeup away, a breaking ball low, a fastball away.

(The Astros were hot the home-plate umpire was squeezing the strike zone on them. Even Bonds admitted to me after the season the umpires were expecting balls so much they weren't calling any pitches on the corners against him and he could wait for a pitch right down the middle.)

Again, the boos cascaded down from the ballpark. Following Bonds' four-pitch walk in the first inning, Kent swung at Mlicki's next pitch and hit a two-run homer. It was still 2-0 in the third when Bonds came up, again nobody on base and two outs.

Bonds fouled off a pitch into the dugout and chased an 84-mph changeup in the dirt. Bonds fouled off a fastball, watched a changeup low and fastball away, then grounded out on a changeup to the right side for an out.

In the fifth, Rich Aurilia singled home a run for a 3-0 lead. There were runners at first and second, one out, and Mlicki was still pitching as Bonds came up again.

Mlicki threw four straight fastballs, in order: low and inside, low and outside, low, low and inside. It was yet another four-pitch walk.

In the stands, one sign read, "Sorry Bonds, We've Got A Division To Win." But most of the fans were booing. Kent plated a run on a fielders choice, Galarraga walked and Dunston singled home two runs for a 6-0 lead.

Once again, the Astros had become so consumed with not letting Bonds make history against them, they completely took themselves out of the game.

Then came the sixth inning. Rookie Ricky Stone was pitching. The score was now 8-1 after a two-run homer by Marvin Benard. Aurilia doubled with one out. First base was open.

And the Astros walked Bonds intentionally.

Again, remember, the lead was seven runs. *Seven runs!*

The fans were irate. I don't think a home crowd has ever booed its home team so loudly. Whatever insults you can think of, the fans were screaming them onto the field. First-base coach Robby Thompson, who isn't close with Bonds, was screaming profanities at the Astros pitchers and dugout in defense of Bonds. The press box was filled with stunned disbelief and furious fingers typing scathing insults directed at the Astros.

I looked over at general manager Brian Sabean. The Astros didn't give him a luxury box for the final game. So he was sitting in the press box, just to my left, flanked by trusty assistant Ned Colletti and director of player personnel Dick Tidrow.

"Can you believe this?" I said to Sabean.

Sabean shook his head, his eyes began to bulge. Colletti asked how many times Houston had walked Bonds in the series.

I quickly added up the totals, scribbled them on a piece of paper and showed the three executives: 14 plate appearances, eight walks, a hit-by-pitch, two singles, three outs.

Including the final game against San Diego, a whopping 51 of the last 64 pitches thrown to Bonds were balls.

"The baseball Gods will get them," Colletti said, shaking his head in disbelief.

Sabean got up from his chair, started pacing around, his blood started boiling and he walked next to me and the columnist from my paper, Monte Poole.

"Now I'm really starting to get (expletive) pissed," Sabean said. "This is (expletive)."

Sabean was steaming. He vented his frustration and defended his star.

"You can't tell me Barry only cares about the record," Sabean said. "He could have swung at those outside pitches and tried to hit them over that short porch in left. He's all about the team."

Aurilia started feeling guilty about going into second base and tried explaining himself to Bonds after the inning. Bonds cut him off.

"Dude, what are you mad at?" Bonds told him. "Don't put that much pressure on me. You hit the ball. Don't take away your game. That's your job. It would be embarrassing if you stopped at first when you could make it to second."

The worst part was the Astros strategy worked.

Kent bounced into a double play to end the inning.

When the game was over, J.T. Snow would call the walk, "a slap in the face."
Kent would say, "I thought the Astros had a little more class than that."
And Eric Davis proclaimed, "That's B.S. You don't play the game like that.
You are talking about the integrity of the game. Something like that is blatant
disrespect. I have been in this game a long time, but I have never seen a slugger
intentionally walked with an 8-1 lead. . . . That's not baseball."

Even Bonds, who was doing his best not to complain about the walks, said,
"Everyone could understand if the situation was a close game. After that, I just
went in the dugout and said, 'you know, it's tough being this patient.'"

Manager Larry Dierker's comments were vague: "I'm extremely angry. I'm
angry at everything."

Of course, keep in mind, that intentional walk in a seven-run game came in
the seventh inning. Bonds still had one more at-bat in the game in the ninth
inning.

And, well, you did read Chapter One, right?

As it turned out, all this made seventy all that sweeter.

And all the more dramatic.

CHAPTER 22

The Story of His Life

October 5-6, Home Runs 71-72

"I've seen a lot of changes out there this year, you guys, the fans of San Francisco toward me. It was really hard. Finally, things start turning around for me for the good. You don't know where you're going to be or what you're going to do next. It's tough. I think everyone worked hard to kinda mend things together."

Barry Bonds

NED WILLIAMSON was the first single-season homer king. He was the king for 35 years, in fact. You don't hear the name Ned Williamson very often. But somebody had to come before Babe Ruth. And his name is Ned Williamson.

Williamson hit 27 homers in 1884 for the Chicago Cubs. You can't excuse ol' Ned of benefiting from the prevailing winds at Wrigley Field. That ballpark wouldn't be built for another three decades. And this was back before the Cubs were lovable losers.

You could call Williamson a "one-year wonder" though. He never hit more than nine homers in a season the rest of his career after hitting the record 27. In 13 years, he hit a total of 64.

Still, he was the king. His total was *Ruthian* at the time. Well, *Nedthian* for its time. And he was the king until George Herman "Babe" Ruth stopped being a pitcher and started concentrating on hitting.

Ruth broke the record by hitting 29 homers in 1919 for the Boston Red Sox as a center fielder and pitcher. That offseason, Ruth was sold to the New York Yankees by Red Sox owner H. Harrison Frazee for $125,000 and the promise of a $300,000 loan to finance a Broadway show called *No, No Nanette*.

Ruth followed that with 54 homers his first season with the Yankees in 1920, concentrating exclusively on hitting. He topped that with 59 the next year. Six years after that, the Bambino hit 60 in 1927 for the Yankees.

For perspective, the Philadelphia Athletics hit 56 as a *team* that year — the next highest team total. Then again, the eight American League teams combined for 610 triples. Seventy-four years later, the 14 AL teams combined for 440 triples and 2,506 home runs.

Simply put, the game has changed.

The list of reasons would take another book.

Ruth's record became the landmark total and it lasted until 1961. That was an expansion year. Yankees teammates Roger Maris and Mickey Mantle pursued the record all season. Billy Crystal made a movie (61*) about that season for HBO. And since Crystal made a movie about it, I'll spare the details on Maris losing his hair and what he went through with the media — who ripped Maris when he didn't talk as much as they wanted.

Nobody really came close to Maris' record until Mark McGwire came along. Big Mac hit 49 as a rookie. He hit 52 in 1996. He hit 58 in 1997. And he didn't just break the record in 1998, he obliterated it. He bashed 70. In an expansion year.

Williamson's record lasted 35 years.

Ruth's record lasted 34 years.

Maris' record lasted 37 years.

Mac's record was about to last three years.

———•◦••◦•———

For those who witnessed the record-breaking game, the first word that comes to mind is surreal. The entire night was surreal. The night stretched into early morning and that was surreal too. It was a night like none other.

And, unfortunately for Barry Bonds, it was a night fitting for his career.

The Giants returned from Houston in the early hours of October 5, around 3 a.m. Bonds tried his best to sleep and get rest. He knew he was going to need it.

He returned to the Los Gatos Hills home and didn't sleep much. His afternoon was going to be busy. Franklin Bradley's funeral was that afternoon. Bonds paid for the entire thing. It was emotional, of course. Bonds had made peace with his friend's untimely death, though. He hit the homer. He cried. He was still sad. But he was moving on.

Bonds arrived at 24 Willie Mays Plaza and faced the media before the game, yet again. Based on the following answer, it was almost like he knew exactly what was going to happen that night.

"What's there to celebrate?" Bonds said. "I'm going to be happy, but I'm not going to have a party or anything like that. I'm going to move on and hopefully we are in the playoffs. And if we are not, I'm going to give my body a bit of rest. I'm going to go back into the training room and try to give myself another chance to go to the playoffs."

Bonds was operating on about 3-4 hours of sleep. But as he revealed recently, he'd been relaxed at the plate and maybe he plays better without sleep.

Asked to give advice to the legions of fans in McCovey Cove, Bonds replied with a smile, "Don't drown yourselves, man. It isn't worth it. That water is so cold, I didn't think anyone could even go swimming out there."

Dusty Baker, the deep and spiritual manager, had been dreaming about this night for some time. He told his longtime friend Lyle Spencer, a former Dodgers beat writer when he was a player, about the dream. Spencer is now a columnist for the *Riverside Press-Enterprise*, the paper for the hometown where Baker and Bonds were born, and Spencer elected not to print the dream out of respect to his friendship with Baker.

Baker also told the dream to Ray Ratto, a columnist of the *San Francisco Chronicle*, and gave Ratto the thumbs-up to print it.

"*I think he'll hit one tonight,*" Baker told Ratto, hours before Bonds tied the record in Houston. "*And you know what else? I dreamed he's gonna break it over the weekend against a guy whose been a real nemesis for him.*"

Keep that in mind when we get to the eighth inning of this game.

There is always electricity in the air for a Giants-Dodgers game. A game on a Friday night when it's chilly raises that electricity. The electricity for this game, of course, was off the charts.

"U-S-A, U-S-A, U-S-A," the fans chanted, before that morphed into something more normal for a Giants-Dodgers game. "BEAT L-A! BEAT L-A! BEAT L-A!"

Shawn Estes was starting that night for the Giants. It was a bit of a gamble. Estes was originally scheduled to start the night before against the Houston Astros. Baker and pitching coach Dave Righetti were constantly looking at the statistics for every possible advantage with their pitching match-ups and went with Russ Ortiz on his usual rest in Houston, pushing Estes back one day.

There was one problem with that decision. Estes had been shelled by the Dodgers all season. It was truly uncanny. In four starts against the Dodgers, Estes had allowed 35 hits and 19 runs in 19.1 innings. He was 0-3 and had an

ERA of 8.84. Against everybody else in baseball, Estes was 9-5 with a 3.06 ERA.

As beat writers, we couldn't help wonder if the Dodgers had spotted something that let them know what pitches Estes was about to throw. I asked him after a couple different starts. Estes vehemently denied it.

After giving up nine hits and five runs in 3.1 innings against the Dodgers on July 2, Estes gave us scribes the following quote: "Hopefully, I'll get them again at the end of the year. It will be awhile before we see them again. Hopefully, I'll catch them when they're not as hot."

Estes had his chance October 5. The Dodgers weren't hot. They were already eliminated from the playoffs. But it didn't matter.

On the sixth pitch of the game, on a 1-2 count, Marquis Grissom singled up the middle on a fastball up. Mark Grudzielanek singled to right on another fastball up. Estes was in troubled immediately. Estes was the master at getting out of trouble and the Giants were holding their breath that he could do it again. But Estes left another fastball up and Shawn Green ripped a single right back up the middle to load the bases.

Pitching coach Dave Righetti came out to settle Estes down. He reminded him to keep the ball down. Use all his pitches. Go for the double-play ball. They would trade two outs for one run right now. Just keep the game close. On a 2-1 count, Gary Sheffield nearly took Estes' head off with a rocket to center. Two runs scored. Still none out. The boo birds were out already. Mark Gardner started to warm up in the bullpen.

Catcher Benito Santiago tried to help his pitcher by picking off Sheffield at first, but Galarraga dropped the ball and Green advanced to third. The error was costly. Paul Lo Duca, who owned all Giants pitchers the entire season, hit a routine fly ball to left on another pitch up in the zone. Bonds caught it and threw to second base, allowing the third run to score and keeping Sheffield at first.

Then Estes struck out Adrian Beltre looking on a borderline 3-2 pitch. Three runs weren't so bad. It looked like Estes would escape further damage. Estes thought he had Jeff Reboulet on a 2-2 pitch, but it was called a ball, and on his 31st and final pitch of the inning, Reboulet doubled to the left-center gap on a fastball right down the middle.

Baker had seen enough. He couldn't afford to wait any longer. Even with

Estes — who Baker has often called "the master of getting into trouble and the master of getting out of trouble" — on the mound, that was it.

Estes was pissed. He would fume to reporters days later. He thought the timing of his hook was awful. The next batter, Chad Kreuter, was intentionally walked. And then it was the pitcher's spot. Estes reasoned that he could have gotten out of the inning. That he had a history of rebounding after rough first innings. Baker didn't feel like he could chance it. The season was on the line.

Veteran Mark Gardner came into the game. Gardner hadn't pitched much lately. He was a starter in the first half. But went on the disabled list to start the second half so he could attend to his wife Lori, who was ill. He'd pitched out of the bullpen since returning and not very often.

Choking up high on the bat, the pitcher Park blooped an 0-2 pitch down the right-field line for a single. Two more runs scored. Back to the top of the order, Grissom popped out. The inning was over. The damage was done. It was 5-0 already.

In the Giants half of the inning, Park felt a twinge in his back on the second pitch he threw. Park elected to stay in the game, but pitched out of the stretch — even with nobody on base. He stretched his back and tried to loosen it up. It wasn't helped by the cool night and long wait before the first inning. Despite feeling the pain and barely bending his back, Park struck out Marvin Benard and got Rich Aurilia on a ground out.

And here came Barry.

There was no reason to pitch around him. The lead was 5-0. Nobody on. Two outs. The Dodgers were out of the playoff race. Park didn't need to be told what to do. He was going right after Bonds. He was trying to strike him out.

Park had experience in such moments. He was the pitcher at the all-star game when Cal Ripken, Jr., led off the third inning in his final Midsummer Classic appearance. Park threw a first-pitch fastball. And Ripken clobbered it out of the park for a chilling home run that will be remembered forever.

Out at McCovey Cove, the occupants clutched their fishing nets. One man wore an Uncle Sam hat and grilled hamburgers on his seagoing barbecue grill. Two men, a couple of laid-off dot-comers, were dressed as Batman and Robin inside a Batboat. A girl in wet suit paddled through the crowd with a wine bottle on her surfboard.

(I couldn't make this stuff up if I tried. It was Halloween on the bay.)

The occupants inside 24 Willie Mays Plaza rose to their feet.

The bathrooms were empty.

The venders stopped.

Flashbulbs went off like crazy.

Dr. Dre boomed from the PA system.

And Bonds strutted to the plate.

Park's first pitch was a fastball low. Ball one. The crowd booed.

Two-thirds of the way across the country, Mark McGwire struck out in his game against the Cardinals. That he was batting at the same time was a bit eerie.

Park's second pitch was another fastball. Belt high. Tailing away on the outside corner. The time was 8:15 p.m. PST.

> *"There's a high drive . . . deep into right-center field . . .*
> *to the big part of the ballpark . . . Number seventy-one!*
> *And what a shot! Over the 421-foot marker! The deepest*
> *part of any ballpark in the National League! Barry*
> *Bonds is now the home-run king! Number seventy-one!*
> *And it was impressive!"*

Jon Miller's call on Fox Sports Net

Nothing cheap about it, either.

As Miller described so beautifully, it was hit to the deepest and highest part of the ballpark. It's 421 feet to right-center. The wall is 20 feet high. The air was thick with moisture, not conducive for a traveling baseball.

Sitting in Section 145, Row 1, Seat 1, 49-year-old Jerry Rose was probably the least likely person beyond a fence to catch the baseball. He's a season-ticket holder. He brought his glove. Rose reached out and caught the ball in the webbing, a little white showing as he squeezed it. It was the first ball he'd ever caught in his life. His $9 seat was going for $150 outside the ballpark.

Pacific Bell Park erupted. The fans jumped up and down, hugging complete strangers and jumping for joy. They cried. They screamed. They awed.

Fireworks erupted overhead.

Bonds kept a poker face after the ball left his bat and he started his trot. He gave a high-five to first-base coach Robby Thompson and rounded first. There was no fist pumping. There was no index finger raised. There was no pounding of his chest. It was one of his faster home-run trots of the season.

If this was a guy consumed with hitting 71 homers, he deserved an Academy Award. Sure, he was happy. But his focus was the game. And winning.

Bonds' teammates didn't wait to see if they were allowed to leave the dugout — like the 500th. Nikolai Bonds led the way, jumping up and down as he sprinted toward the plate. The players were right behind him. It was pandemonium at home plate. They slapped his head and patted his back. And, like the night before, they probably got in a couple shots for all those years of frustration.

Bonds picked up Nikolai and gave him a Giant bear hug.

On the left side of the scoreboard, an enormous banner was unveiled that read BONDS. On the right side of the scoreboard, the banner read 71.

Bonds went inside the dugout and was handed the cell phone of Debby Magowan, the wife of managing partner Peter Magowan. Bobby Bonds was on the other end. Bobby was in Bridgeport, Connecticut for his annual charity golf tournament. The date was chosen well in advance, knowing the regular season would be over. But after the events of 9-11, the schedule was altered and Bobby chose his golf tournament over his son's biggest moment.

The crowd kept cheering. Jeff Kent wasn't going anywhere close to the batters box. Bonds came out for a curtain call. He walked behind home plate and his wife Liz came down from the stands. Barry Bonds has called his wife Liz, "the best thing that's ever happened to me."

Liz came down and hugged and kissed her husband. Bonds also kissed his daughters and mother and hugged his "three angels," the female friends who handle the PR of his charity endeavours. Bonds waved to the crowd again and returned to the dugout quickly, eager to restart the game. He told his teammates, "all right guys, we have to score more."

Total delay: four minutes.

There were still eight innings left.

Nine minutes later, the Astros took a 2-1 lead over the Cardinals. Arizona was already winning easily in Milwaukee. The Giants were fighting for their playoff lives. If they lost, the season was over.

Gardner gave up another run in the second and it was now 6-1. In the bottom of the second, Eric Davis pinch hit for Gardner and delivered a three-run double. Now it was 6-4 Dodgers.

Wayne Gomes was the next Giants reliever. He gave up a two-run homer to Marquis Grissom. The lead was 8-4 Dodgers.

Bonds led off the third inning. With a four-run lead, Park once again went after Bonds. On a 1-1 pitch, Bonds crushed a hanging breaking ball to center. It was a towering, majestic blast. Grissom gave chase, but it landed in the second row of the bleachers, hit a fan's glove and bounced back onto the field.

Number 72!

"This begins to leave the realm of reality," ESPN play-by-play announcer Gary Thorne said on the air.

Note that it was 8-5. It was already 9:07 p.m., the game wasn't yet one-third over and the early editions for the West Coast writers were approaching in one hour. It was past midnight on the East Coast and the final editions of the morning paper were minutes away from hitting the printing presses. There simply wasn't enough time for the newspapers to put together as spectacular a display in the morning papers as everyone would have wanted.

In the top of the fourth, Shawn Green hit a solo homer off Gomes for a 9-5 lead. Wasn't Pac Bell supposed to be a pitcher's park? What in the world was going on?

Real simple: a classic Giants-Dodgers game in October.

In the bottom of the fourth, the Giants put runners at second and third with one out. Aurilia was at the plate. A walk loaded the bases for Bonds. The count went to 3-2. The crowd pulled for a walk, knowing they couldn't pitch around Bonds with the bases loaded — and knowing he was red hot.

Park, still pitching out of the stretch, saw Aurilia foul off two pitches. Aurilia then flied to left, not deep enough to try and tag up. First base was still open. So this was a no-brainer for Tracy. He held up four fingers. A homer trims the lead to one.

The crowd booed, of course, as Bonds was intentionally walked for the 35th time in the season.

Kent ripped a shot into the right-center gap. Two runs would score easily. Bonds was at full speed after two steps. Underrated for his base running, the way he cuts the corners on bases and doesn't take a wide turn, Bonds motored around the bases and scored. Kent was thrown out at third base to end the inning on a bang-bang play, but now the lead was down to 9-8.

Anything, indeed, was possible.

And by now, a victory was needed. The Giants trailed Arizona by two games in the NL West and Houston by two games in the wild card. Arizona had won in Milwaukee. Houston had won in St. Louis. The Giants not only needed a victory that night to stay alive for the postseason, they needed to sweep the series and hope either Arizona or Houston lost the next two.

Aaron Fultz, the fourth Giants pitcher, restored some sanity to the game. He retired the Dodgers 1-2-3 in the top of the fifth, the first half inning without a run in the game. But the Giants were also held without a run by new Dodgers pitcher Giovanni Carrara. In the sixth, Gary Sheffield hit a solo homer for a 10-8 Dodgers lead.

In the bottom of the sixth, Benard singled and Rich Aurilia turned on a 1-1 pitch from Carrara. If it stayed fair, the game was tied.

The ball stayed fair — the sixth homer of the game — Aurilia raised his fist above his head as he rounded first and Pac Bell was absolute bedlam again.

This game was blowing my mind in more ways than one. Myself and the other sportswriters were filing, or already filed, the early "pre-quote" edition stories on the game and Bonds' record. But many of those stories, certainly mine, were focusing on the Giants getting eliminated from the playoffs on the same day as Bonds broke the record.

My *Oakland Tribune* colleague Carl Steward told me, "this is the story of Barry's life" and wrote his column with that theme in mind.

"Welcome back to the strange saga of Barry Bonds' life: Tremendous, unparalleled individual achievements, coupled with mortifying shortcomings within the framework of a team," Steward quickly typed into his laptop. "It's the paradox of greatness that Babe Ruth, Mark McGwire and even Roger Maris never had to contemplate. Bonds, on what should have been the greatest night of his baseball life, still couldn't escape the shadow of career-long mixed blessings."

It was at deadline now. The editors didn't want to hear this, but the outcome was necessary in this story because a loss would end the Giants season. For six months, I'd listened to Bonds talk about how badly he wanted another trip to the playoffs, and how he would gladly trade 71 homers for a World Series ring in a fraction of a second. Now he'd broken the record and the team was scratching and clawing, fighting for its collective life to win the game and keep the dream alive.

In the press box, it wasn't the ideal circumstance for writing a memorable story that will be remember for years and savored forever. What can you do?

Well, you do the best you can. You keep writing furiously. You write something and hope it happens, and send it to the office. Then when something does happen, you write quickly and send it again. I can't even tell you how many different versions of stories I filed that night.

Oh yeah, and did I mention, Barry was up again!

Carrara, to the surprise of many, didn't pitch around Bonds with the game tied. He came after him. And this is what people will probably forget in the years to come. At that point, in the sixth inning, Bonds had homered on each of his last three *swings*: the 70th in Houston, the 71st in the first inning, the 72nd in the third inning.

The count went to 3-1 and Bonds nearly hit No. 73 right there. When the ball left his bat, I thought for a split second that he really was Superman and he'd just given the Giants the lead.

Can you imagine what kind of story *that* would be? Three homers on the night to break the record and keep his team alive in the playoff race?

Alas, the man is human. He got the under the ball and grimaced immediately, knowing he uppercut too much and just missed it by fractions of an inch. Sheffield caught the ball in left.

Still three innings left, at least one more at-bat for Bonds, and the game was tied.

But not for long. Tim Worrell was now pitching for the Giants. Reboulet led off the seventh and hit a grounder up the middle. Aurilia raced far to his left and snared the ball on the outfield grass. He should never have thrown the ball. He normally eats the ball in that situation. One of his strengths as a shortstop is knowing his limitations. But he was caught up in the moment and tried to make an impossible play. His throw wasn't close. It went into the stands. And Reboulet was at second to start the inning.

Reboulet went to third on an infield groundout. Pinch-hitter Dave Hansen was walked intentionally. Grissom hit a chopper toward third base. Backup catcher Edwards Guzman was playing there because regular starter Ramon

Martinez injured his hand the game before and Baker had double-switched to remove Pedro Feliz an inning earlier.

Guzman couldn't make the play and the Dodgers had the lead again, 11-10. Grudzielanek singled to right and Dunston gunned down Hansen at the plate to keep it a one-run deficit. Worrell struck out Green to end the inning.

Rubber-armed reliever Matt Herges entered the game for the Dodgers in the seventh and retired the side in order. Felix Rodriguez set down the Dodgers in the top of the eighth. And now came the Giants half of the eighth, the top of the order due up.

This was it. The Giants best chance to win the game. Herges retired the first two batters and Dodgers manager Jim Tracy went to lefty Jesse Orosco to face Bonds.

Bonds in his lifetime against Orosco: 3-for-22, nine strikeouts.

Take a quick breather right now. Remember Baker's dream now? "*I dreamed he's gonna break it over the weekend against a guy who's been a real nemesis for him.*"

This couldn't be, could it? I looked down to the right in the press box at Ratto and he was stunned at the possibility. I turned around and looked at Spencer behind me in the press box and he actually wasn't all that shocked. He's known Baker for over 20 years.

"Dusty is a deep man," Spencer told me. "A really deep man. He's always been that way. It's really eerie."

The Dodgers and Orosco weren't that foolish though. Sure, they weren't going to intentionally walk Bonds, but they weren't going to serve it up right down the middle for him, either. Orosco worked Bonds away for ball one, away for ball two. The crowd was on its feet and booing heavily. Bonds took a mighty cut at the 2-0 pitch, chasing a rare pitch out of the strike zone, and missed.

Bonds wanted a pitch to hit so badly it was killing him. He was making an exception and coming out of his game. Orosco wouldn't give in. Another two pitches missed way out of the strike zone. It was a five-pitch walk. The crowd was booing heavily once again.

Tracy returned to the mound, grabbed the ball and brought in closer Jeff Shaw. The stage was set for Jeff Kent. The ultimate chance to make an opponent pay for walking Bonds. The ultimate spotlight moment.

Kent swung and hit a ball hard into the right-center gap. It was a good swing. It came off the bat well. It had good distance to it.

But it was hit to the wrong part of Pacific Bell Park.

Right-center is death valley, especially for righties like Kent.

Shawn Green hauled it in. The rally was over. Robb Nen, the 12th and final pitcher of the night, kept it a one-run lead in the top of the ninth and the Giants still had once more chance. The bottom of the lineup would have to do it. Bonds was due up eighth.

Galarraga started the inning with a walk. Dante Powell ran for him. Calvin Murray, who entered on a double switch, was asked to bunt. He didn't get the ball on the ground. It was popped up and caught by Lo Duca at first. Murray slammed his bat into the ground in frustration.

Baker was going to empty his bench. J.T. Snow pinch-hit for catcher Benito Santiago. Snow is the owner of the most dramatic non-Barry homer in Pac Bell's brief history. It came in game two of the division playoffs the previous year, a game-tying homer off Armando Benitez that was a classic October moment. Snow did a Carlton Fisk-like impression, trying to keep the ball inside the right-field line. He walked halfway toward the mound, the ball stayed fair and it was bedlam.

Could he do it again?

Almost. Snow hit a fly ball to right, but this one didn't have the distance. It was caught by Green. Two outs. Bonds put a knee on the top step, praying for a miracle, wishing so badly he could be at the plate and the other team would pitch to him. Four batters needed to reach base for Bonds to get to the plate though. Instead, it was up to Dunston.

Dunston isn't much of a patient hitter. His favorite line is, "I've got a bat in my hand to swing and that's what I'm going to do." The book on Dunston is never throw him a first-pitch fastball for a strike. If so, he's going to hit it. Dunston swung at the first pitch and fouled it back. He looked at ball two. Then he grounded the third pitch up the middle. Grudzielanek gloved it, stepped on second and the game was over.

So was the season.

The time was 12:06 a.m.

The game set a record for nine innings, lasting four hours and 27 minutes. Whew.

The night, make that morning, was far from over. There was a ceremony to be done. Even if the Giants were gone from the playoffs. Even if Bonds was a free agent and had possibly taken his last swing as a Giant. Even if it was past midnight. Even if the ferries were making last call. Even if the muni trains were making their final runs of the night. Even if it was past the deadlines for everybody who doesn't work for the Internet.

Surreal, indeed.

I'd estimate half the capacity crowd of 41,730 stuck around for the entire game and for the ceremony. Dusty Baker didn't stick around. He retreated into his office.

"I probably should have stayed on the field," Baker would say later. "But I was just too emotionally devastated. I watched from the TV."

The rest of the Giants stayed in the dugout as a stage was brought out and microphones were turned on. Jon Miller was the master of ceremonies for the ceremony. The crowd kept itself busy with chants of "M-V-P, M-V-P" as Bonds emerged from the dugout and tipped his cap.

Paul Beeston, the chief operating officer and number-two man in the Commissioner's office, announced a $100,000 donation from the MLB players association disaster relief fund will be donated in Bonds' name. Beeston invited Bonds to throw out the first pitch in Game One of the World Series and told him he'll be given the Historic Achievement Award by the Commissioner.

Rich Aurilia was called from the dugout and gave Bonds a big hug. He was recognized for teaming with Bonds for the most homers by teammates in baseball history. The rest of the Giants players followed and stood at the back of the stage.

"What's there left to say? Wow!" Aurilia said. "Barry, you didn't need this to get into the Hall of Fame. But this solidifies it."

Next was Magowan. You couldn't hear what he said. He was drowned out by the fans chanting "sign him" and "four more years." Rumor has it, he announced the Giants were matching the $100,000 total to the relief efforts. Rumor also has it, he mentioned Bonds' donation that was now at $90,000 and counting.

Then Willie Mays stole the show.

"You gotta shut up now," he told the crowd on the mic.

And the crowd shut up.

Only Mays can get away with telling a crowd to shut up.

"This is a special moment," Mays said. "Barry talks a lot and backs it up. A lot of people didn't think he would do this. He made a liar out of a lot of you. I know. I'm one. I didn't think so either. I didn't think he'd get there."

It was cold and Mays shivered under his Giants parka jacket. He continued to address the crowd and Bonds: "As a kid, Barry was five years old and I remember telling him, 'Boy, get out of my locker. Stop chewing my gum and go out on the field.'"

The crowd laughed. Bonds laughed. Mays was just getting warmed up.

"I know Bobby couldn't be here, but I'll be on the phone to tell him he should have been here," Mays said. "Don't worry. I will."

Mays continued by saying he wants Bonds to obliterate this record, hitting 73 and 74 and 75 in the next two days. "It will be a long time before anybody breaks this," Mays said. "I want him to put it where nobody can get it."

Looking at the players standing behind Bonds in support, Mays said, "I think that if Barry looks around and sees all the guys behind him, that should tell him they all appreciate what he's done, not just on the field but off the field. It's important sometimes to make people believe that you can do both."

Mays then looked at Peter Magowan and said, "Barry belongs here in San Francisco."

The crowd went nuts and the "four more years" chant re-started. Now it was Bonds' turn on the microphone. He thanked his family, mom, dad, wife, children.

"I'm going to miss you Franklin," Bonds said. "You believed in me and I did it."

Bonds turned to his teammates still standing behind him and told them, "we worked real, real hard and we're gonna work real hard again. I love you all. I know some of you took cheap shots on me. I know who you are. I love you very much. I'll play with you any time, any day, any hour, any year."

Bonds then informed the crowd of the bet he made with Dunston back in Phoenix in May.

"Dunston told me I was gonna hit 71," Bonds said. "I told him he was crazy. I made a stupid bet. So Shawon . . . the CL500 Coupe . . . you've got it."

The crowd cheered, Bonds giggled, laughed, and not missing a cue, added, "and you guys thought my divorce was bad."

It was 12:47 a.m. now. The "Keep Barry" rally was still going strong. More chanting of his name. Bonds was trying to think of what to tell the crowd. He didn't want to say goodbye. He didn't want to promise he would be back. The crowd kept cheering and the emotions started to get to Bonds. The emotions overwhelmed him and Bonds broke down into tears. He started crying and he couldn't stop.

Mays came over and whispered into his ear, "just try and get through it."

Bonds needed time to collect himself. Mays told Dunston to take over.

"I just want to thank everybody for coming out and supporting the Giants," Dunston said. "Barry really loves you. He really does want to come back. What do you think?"

As the crowd cheered, Dunston turned to Magowan and said, "I'm coming back, why not Barry?"

The doors to the clubhouse were open, but nobody was inside. I was standing down the third-base line, above the dugout about 20 rows. A fan standing a few feet from me yelled out "sign him now" and "I've got a pen" and the crowd continued to cheer. Magowan handled the situation about as best as an owner could.

"And he *will* buy me a new Mercedes Benz," Dunston said.

At this moment, it's important to note who was holding Aisha Bonds.

It was Jeff Kent.

Yeah, Jeff Kent.

Indeed, a very surreal night.

Bonds had wiped the tears away and collected himself. "He's right. I do love San Francisco and I love you fans. And my family knows, and God knows, I'm proud to wear this uniform."

The DJ turned on the Tina Turner song, "Simply the Best" as the field and ballpark emptied.

There was no press conference for Bonds. It was past 1 a.m. by now. He was surrounded by waves of reporters at his locker.

"I still don't know what to say," Bonds said. "I have to soak in what happened."

Asked about the emotional ceremony, Bonds talked about the changes he witnessed this season.

"I've seen a lot of changes out there this year, you guys, the fans of San Francisco toward me," Bonds said, sounding a lot like Rocky Balboa in his speech to the Russian crowd at the end of Rocky IV. "It was really hard. Finally, things start turning around for me for the good. You don't know where you're going to be or what you're going to do next. It's tough. I think everyone worked hard to kinda mend things together.

"I'm a forgiving person and I saw a lot of changes in how the media treated me and how the fans treated me. It was really nice. I don't think I've changed. But we've been winning and doing well."

Bonds didn't know what to feel — how do you celebrate on the night your team is eliminated from the playoffs? — but his teammates had no trouble finding the correct words.

"As time goes on, we'll be able to appreciate what we just witnessed even more," outfielder Eric Davis said. "He should be elated. He should cherish it. It's an individual accomplishment. He's earned that. He shouldn't be criticized for being elated. It's like if a guy gets 3,000 hits and the team doesn't win. Should we not celebrate? Of course he should be elated. He shouldn't have to apologize. We didn't get it done as a team. But he got it done as an individual."

Shawon Dunston added, "Babe Ruth started baseball. Ted Williams, Mickey Mantle, Willie Mays. I was a kid watching Reggie Jackson. Now Barry does this. It just doesn't seem real."

Dunston has seen a lot of homers before, from Mac and Sammy, but still nothing quite like this.

"Barry could hit 50 home runs every year," Dunston said. "He's hitting a baseball like it's a golf ball. He makes it look easy. It's not that easy. This is a hard game. And he always gets walked. I have 200 in my career. He has 180 in one year. He stayed in his strike zone. He never went out of his zone. He stayed the same way, just like Big Mac did. I'm honored to play with Mac and Barry. It's kinda funny, I ground out and the Cardinals are in the playoffs."

Dunston left with this parting shot, "don't be surprised if Sammy breaks the record next year."

CHAPTER 23

The Spirit of 73

October 6-November 20, Home Run 73

"Winning is going to come first for me. That's going to be the key, putting a team together that's going to win and then I'll make my decision."

Barry Bonds

THE CHANTS of "Bar-ry, Bar-ry" re-started around 11 a.m. the next day. Well, the same day. On Saturday, October 6, Bonds requested to be out of the starting lineup, even if his godfather Willie Mays was hoping he would end the season with 75 homers. He was just too drained.

As the chanting got louder, Bonds went to manager Dusty Baker and reminded him, "you better pinch-hit me or something."

Bonds pinch hit in the ninth inning and singled to right field off reliever Matt Herges. Bonds was lifted for a pinch runner and received another standing ovation. The Los Angeles Dodgers won the game, 6-2, a game that wasn't memorable for anything except the overcast skies and hangover feeling.

Bonds, as you might expect, slept before the game in his recliner. He received many phone messages from friends around the country.

"Bobby Bonilla, my best friend, called me on the phone and tried to explain what I did," Bonds said. "But I still haven't had a chance . . . I still don't know what to say."

Mark McGwire, who said back in June he would congratulate Bonds, reportedly left a message with Robb Nen for Bonds to call his cell phone number.

Bonds said he hadn't received the message.

On Sunday, October 7, the final day of the regular season, knuckleballer Dennis Springer was the starter for the Dodgers. Bonds was laughing as he watched eephus-like pitches dance and float to the plate and break in all different directions. His biggest laugh came on a 3-2 pitch, when a Springer knuckler dropped into the bottom of the strike zone, Bonds shifted his feet a few times, took a mighty swing . . . and added to his new record with one more homer: number 73.

Bonds laughed at himself, in complete disbelief he even made contact on the pitch — let alone hit yet another home run.

The ball landed on the small arcade level of the ballpark in right field. It was a mob scene of humanity trying to get the historic baseball. The joke in the press box was the ball probably changed hands a couple times and the strongest would emerge with it. The joke turned out to be real.

Patrick Hayashi, 36, from Santa Clara County, emerged with the baseball. A videotape from a KTVU-TV cameraman showed the ball initially landed in the glove of Alex Popov, before the swarm of people took him to the ground and the ball came free. Popov ended up claiming rights to the baseball, hired a lawyer and a judge put the historic ball in a safety-deposit box until a custody trial could be held in 2002 to determined the rightful owner.

By hitting 73 home runs, Barry Bonds passed everybody in the pro baseball record books: Babe Ruth, Roger Maris, Sammy Sosa, Mark McGwire and even Joe Bauman.

Huh?

The final name on that list is the least known, even to seamheads and baseball historians, including diehard baseball fan and Giants owner Peter Magowan, who never heard of Joe Bauman.

But in 1954, playing for the minor-league Class-C Roswell (N.M.) Rockets, the 6-foot-5, 235-pound Bauman, a left-handed hitting first baseman, smashed 72 home runs — in 138 games — for a city best known for a rumored 1947 alien landing.

If you've heard of Bauman, it's probably because you saw the "X-Files" episode in 1999, written by series star David Duchovny, that centered around Bauman's feat in Roswell and suggested the baseball player might have been an alien.

My *Oakland Tribune* colleague, Carl Steward, gets 100 percent credit for uncovering this gem of a story. I must confess that I never heard of Bauman or his record, either. Carl told me about it the day before the game and I eagerly told him he should write a column about it, regardless of what Bonds did that afternoon.

Once Bonds hit the 73rd, the story was a no-brainer. I don't even remember how Carl found his phone number. It was probably listed. It's not like Bauman is a celebrity. Nonetheless, Carl called the Roswell home about an hour after the season ended and a rumored-to-be alien named Joe Bauman picked up the phone.

"More power to him," the 78-year-old Bauman told Carl. "I said the same thing when McGwire was chasing it, that records are made to be broken. I'm just happy it stood for 47 years. I always said if someone broke it, it'd be a left-handed hitter. They've got a little advantage, and I was right."

Bauman and his wife watched the game on TV specifically to see if Bonds could establish a new pro ball mark. He also watched Bonds hit 71 and the 72 two nights earlier.

A retired gas station owner, Bauman made more money at the filling station than playing baseball. He never reached the majors. He never even played at a higher classification of baseball. Carl didn't detect any sense of bitterness in Bauman. It had been 40 years since he'd been to a live major league game — his last was in Philadelphia — but that's mostly because he still lives in Roswell.

Besides, where would Bauman park his alien spacecraft if he came to a game?

"I've had some calls from friends and neighbors telling me they were sorry he hit it," Bauman said. "But I don't feel bad. It's an amazing feat. I know when I hit 72, I wanted to quit baseball because I didn't think there was anything more I could accomplish."

In 1954, Bauman not only hit 72 homers, but batted .400 with 224 RBIs, 456 total bases and 150 walks. His slugging percentage was .916. You can look it up. The home ballpark he played in wasn't a bandbox, either. The highest home-run total for a teammate was 12.

Of course, there's a Bauman connection to San Francisco. It's a bit sad, a little eerie. Two years ago, he was profiled and interviewed in a book entitled *"Baseball's Forgotten Heroes: One Man's Search for the Game's Most Interesting Overlooked Players."*

The author was Tony Salin, a free spirited taxicab drive who lived in San Francisco.

Salin died in late July.

Even if Barry Bonds had gone 0-for-5 in the final game, he would finish with an .851 slugging percentage — .004 points higher than the 81-year-old record set by Babe Ruth in 1920.

Slugging percentage is an under-utilized statistic that measures the power of a player. It's computed by dividing total bases into at-bats. For instance, a single or walk or hit-by-pitch is worth one base. A double is two bases, three for a triple and four for a home run.

With the first-inning homer and a single in the third inning (Bonds popped out in his final two at-bats of the season), Bonds finished with an .863 slugging percentage to shatter the .847 record of Ruth.

"That," Bonds admitted, "is the one I don't think is going to be broken."

The only person who ever slugged above .800 in a season was Babe Ruth. He did it twice. Nobody had come close since then. Any slugging percentage over .500 is considered very good, over .600 is outstanding, .700 is practically unheard of.

And Bonds shattered Ruth's record with an .863 percentage!

Bonds' final on-base percentage was .515, the highest in the National League since 1900 and the 10th highest in baseball history.

The crowd continued its chanting of "four more years" and "Bar-ry, Bar-ry" throughout the afternoon.

With the pennant race over and Mark McGwire's record broken, the soon-to-be free agent Bonds seemed more relaxed, smiling more, waving to the crowd more and enjoying what might possibly be the final game of his career in a Giants uniform.

"I'm glad I did it at home," Bonds said. "That was the key. Today's home run, I was more just in shock. You know, your chances of hitting a home run on someone who throws that slow is so slim. When I did, I was just like, 'what else can you give me, God?' Enough is enough."

Upon his final at-bat, Bonds' thoughts turned to Eric Davis. The classy 39-year-old veteran was given a nice pre-game tribute and played his final game, pinch-hitting in the seventh inning and flying to right.

"It's sunk in now, once you get through the ceremony," Davis said. "Everything has to come to an end. I'll come back in some capacity. It's not the last you'll see of me."

Danny Glover, Rob Schneider and Robin Williams were three celebrities in the clubhouse after the game. Williams got three baseballs autographed and shook Davis' hand. In classic form, Davis told him, "*nano nano.*"

"You know," Davis said, grinning as he looked at reporters, "from Mork and Mindy: *nano nano.*"

Eric Davis will be missed, big time.

Rich Aurilia singled in his final at-bat to finish with 206 hits.

Veteran Mark Gardner worked an inning of relief, which would turn into the final appearance of his career, and recorded the win.

Robb Nen saved his 45th game with a scoreless ninth inning, a 2-1 victory over the Dodgers, and the Giants finished with a 90-72 record — two games behind the Arizona Diamondbacks.

Over the final 30 games of the season, which many felt would decide the MVP, here are the numbers of candidates Bonds, Sammy Sosa and Luis Gonzalez.

Player	BA	OB	SLG	HR	RBI	BB
Bonds	.407	.611	1.119	13	21	29
Sosa	.413	.505	.875	11	23	16
Gonzalez	.277	.378	.578	6	16	14

Overall, the top three candidates for the MVP produced these numbers:

Player	BA	OB	SLG	HR	RBI	BB
Bonds	.328	.515	.863	73	137	177
Sosa	.328	.437	.737	64	160	116
Gonzalez	.325	.429	.688	57	142	100

On Monday morning October 8, Barry Bonds finished cleaning out his locker. Along with longtime friend and assistant Steve Hoskins, Bonds wheeled the famous $3,000 reclining chair from his corner in the clubhouse to his car.

The "I'm going to DisneyWorld" commercial, shot with his wife and three children, was already in circulation on TV. Bonds had a European vacation and trip to DisneyWorld on his itinerary. He was to squeeze in an appearance at Game One of the World Series, when he would throw out the first pitch and be presented the Commissioner's Historic Achievement Award.

The thoughts of Giants fans were squarely on where Bonds would play next season.

Bonds said he didn't want to think about baseball for a while. He just wanted to get away. He didn't even want to talk with his agent Scott Boras for at least a week.

"(Bonds) is our franchise player," Giants general manager Brian Sabean said. "He was before he did what he did this year. I do believe that Scott Boras has his best interests at heart because that's what Barry claims — as well as what we've seen throughout the Robb Nen negotiations. But it's still a situation that will be negotiated with a guy who is very good at what he does."

The last weekend, Bonds spoke candidly about how much he loves playing in San Francisco and how he's never been treated better by the media and fans here.

"This is my home," Bonds said. "It's been my home since 1968 when my dad came here. This will always be my home. It's nice to go places and the whole city is rooting for you. You walk into stores and you've got old ladies that don't even know anything about baseball, deciding to watch a baseball game and telling you what a great accomplishment this is and the things you're doing."

But little old ladies don't have extra millions to pay Bonds or pay the players around Bonds.

"Winning is going to come first for me," Bonds said. "That's going to be the key, putting a team together that's going to win and then I'll make my decision."

If he ends up in a new home, odds are Bonds will play in a ballpark more favorable to home-run hitters. Remember the media speculation documented in Chapter 3 that Pacific Bell Park was, "the House Built for Barry Bonds?"

Well, it wasn't built for offense. Two years after Pac Bell's debut, enough numerical evidence exists to prove the ballpark, without question, does *not* favor hitters and does *not* lead to additional home runs. Colorado's Todd

Helton calls it the worst for hitters in the National League. Consider the following numbers from 2001:

	HR	R	AVG
Giants hitters at home:	97	352	.256
Giants hitters on road:	138	447	.276

	HR Allowed	ERA	Opp. Avg.
Giants pitchers at home:	49	3.79	.251
Giants pitchers on road:	96	4.60	.266

A couple more points on Bonds' season. With the umpires enforcement of the so-called "new strike zone" in 2001, there were 2,432 *fewer* walks in baseball and Bonds still broke Ruth's 70-year-old record for walks in a season — another indication of just how often teams pitched around him.

Bonds averaged a homer every 6.52 at-bats in 2001. With that average, if he was able to hit instead of walk 177 times — and granted, that's impossible — he'd have hit an additional 27 homers — giving him an even 100 for the year!

The new strike zone also led to 235 *fewer* home runs. Roger Maris and Mark McGwire broke their records in the first year of expansion, when home runs were up. Bonds did it with homers down.

As for the theory that Bonds benefited from the newer, more hitter-friendly ballparks than have opened since 1998, note that Bonds hit three at Miller Park and only one at Enron Field.

Rob Neyer, the numbers expert at espn.com, analyzed Bonds' 2001 season and compared it to some of the other greatest individual years in baseball history in an October column.

Neyer ranked Bonds' 2001 season *the* greatest ever.

Within three weeks of the regular season, Bonds made good on his pledge by making a $100,000 donation to the victims of the World Trade Center tragedy.

Bonds also made good on his bet with Shawon Dunston and ordered him a CL 500 Coupe. In order to pay for it and stay "in my budget," Bonds told me he sold his Porsche.

The 97th World Series will be remembered as one of the greatest ever played, a seven-game duel between the Arizona Diamondbacks and New York Yankees that featured heart-stopping comebacks and heroic performances.

On November 4, the final game was started by Curt Schilling and Roger Clemens, the man who turned Schilling's career around in a Houston weightroom a decade earlier. It was Schilling's third start in nine days and seventh of the postseason.

Schilling left with a 2-1 deficit. Randy Johnson, less than 24 hours after throwing 104 pitches in the Game Six victory, relieved Schilling in the ninth inning. At the very eerie time of 9:11 p.m., the Diamondbacks started a rally in the ninth inning that would see them score two runs off the invincible Yankees closer, Mariano Rivera.

Luis Gonzalez (who fell short of Babe Ruth's total bases record by 36 in the regular season) knocked home the winning run with a bloop single to center, scoring Jay Bell and sending the state of Arizona into a state of euphoria.

Sitting in the rafters of Bank One Ballpark with my friend Eric Winter — after driving from San Diego to Phoenix when Eric called me at 9 a.m. to say he had an extra ticket waiting for me — I witnessed thousands of random people hugging and kissing. Later that night, Eric cracked the whip on me and told me to get back to writing this book the next day.

Exactly one week later, on November 11, citing burnout and mental fatigue, Mark McGwire sent a fax to ESPN to announce his retirement. He finished his career with 583 homers. I watched the report on my television, just hours after finishing the first draft to Chapter 11 of this book.

McGwire's retirement is yet another example of the cruelty of aging in baseball. The following players serve as reminders to Bonds' daunting task of maintaining his excellence as he turns 38 years old during the 2002 season.

Bobby Bonds

Year	Age	AVG	HR	RBI
1978	32	.267	31	90
1979	33	.275	25	85
1980	34	.203	5	24
1981	35	.215	6	19

Willie Mays

Year	Age	AVG	HR	RBI
1970	39	.291	28	83
1971	40	.271	18	61
1972	41	.250	8	22
1973	42	.211	6	25

Reggie Jackson

Year	Age	AVG	HR	RBI
1984	38	.223	25	81
1985	39	.252	27	85
1986	40	.241	18	58
1987	41	.220	15	43

Babe Ruth

Year	Age	AVG	HR	RBI
1932	37	.341	41	137
1933	38	.301	34	103
1934	39	.288	22	84
1935	40	.181	6	12

Mark McGwire

Year	Age	AVG	HR	RBI
1998	34	.299	70	147
1999	35	.278	65	147
2000	36	.305	32	73
2001	37	.187	29	64

Hank Aaron

Year	Age	AVG	HR	RBI
1971	37	.327	47	118
1972	38	.265	34	77
1973	39	.301	40	96
1974	40	.268	20	69
1975	41	.234	12	60
1976	42	.229	10	35

Aaron is the example that it can be done, although he benefited from a move to first base in 1971 and being a designated hitter the last two years of his career.

Barry Bonds finished the 2001 season with 567 career homers. With seven more, he'll pass Harmon Killebrew for sixth on the all-time list, 17 more passes McGwire for fifth, 20 more to pass Frank Robinson for fourth place and 33 more puts him into the 600-homer club.

Barring a major injury, he will pass them all in the 2002 season — two more Hall of Famers and McGwire is a sure-thing once he's eligible in 2006.

On November 13, Bonds filed for free agency.

On November 19, Bonds was the runaway winner of the Most Valuable Player award, getting 30 of 32 first-place votes and becoming the first player in baseball history to win a fourth MVP. Sosa received the other two first-place votes, both cast by Chicago beat writers.

"It's hard to tell your emotions on the actual day you win it," Bonds said. "But I'm excited. My family is excited. My kids are very happy."

Agent Scott Boras attended the press conference at 24 Willie Mays Plaza and handed out copies of the 38-page book his staff prepared to give potential teams courting Bonds. In the press conference, Bonds/Boras revealed their desire to chase some of the game's most astounding home run numbers:

660 — Willie Mays' career total (likely year: 2003).
714 — Babe Ruth's career total (likely year: 2005)
755 — Hank Aaron's career total (likely year: 2005 or 2006)
800 — why not?

If Bonds averages over the next five seasons the same statistics he's averaged the last five years — which is still quite a stretch because of how high those standards are — he would finish his career with the following numbers:

* 802 homers (the most ever).
* 2,092 RBIs (fourth-most ever).
* 3,033 hits (26th member of 3,000-hit club).
* 2,364 walks (the most ever)
* 2,303 runs (the most ever)

If he does, and I won't bet against him, Barry Bonds will be remembered, without a question, as the greatest baseball player of all time.

If he doesn't, if he just comes close, it's my humble opinion Bonds will go down as one of the four greatest players in baseball history: Ruth, Mays, Aaron and Bonds.

"My godfather thinks I can accomplish a lot of things in this game," Bonds said. "My godfather knows numbers very, very well. When he looks at my possibilities and what I can accomplish in a short period of time, his only thing is: 'you *have* to do it. You *have* to go for it. It's almost unrealistic to not (go for it) with the opportunities you've got.' "

Trust me, my laptop will *always* be down as Bonds chases history.

I'm not missing the show.

EPILOGUE

Staying home

"There wasn't any amount of money in the world to make me leave San Francisco. I was gonna stay. I wanted to be loyal and stick it out here. I wasn't going to give up. This is where I was raised. This is where I went to high school. This is my home. I'm a Giant for life."

Barry Bonds

On November 30, the Giants made their first contract offer to Bonds. It was believed to be four years and $64 million. No other team had publicly acknowledged making an offer yet.

On December 13, the Giants made their second contract offer to Bonds. It was believed to be four years and $72 million. No other team had publicly acknowledged making an offer yet.

On December 19, Bonds accepted salary arbitration from the Giants, a startling decision that prevented any other team from negotiating for his services and ensuring he would return to San Francisco for at least one more season. Both sides disclosed it was still their intent to sign a multi-year contract and avoid arbitration.

No other team ever publicly acknowledged making a contract offer to the greatest player of his generation, coming off the greatest offensive season in baseball history, whose goal is play another five years in pursuit of the most storied career records in baseball history, everything from 3,000 hits to 755 homers.

You heard that right: Just *one* team publicly admitted offering him a contract.

How could such a thing happen? It depends who you ask. Some teams, including the New York Yankees, were reportedly turned off by his personality, set their sights on former A's first baseman Jason Giambi and signed him to a seven-year contract for close to $120 milllion.

Most teams were undoubtedly worried about giving a long-term contract to a 37-year-old player. Some teams never had the financial resources to even attempt signing him.

Agent Scott Boras insisted all along that he fielded four-year and five-year offers from other baseball teams who insisted on keeping it quiet. The mystery teams didn't want to get their fans excited about possibly bringing in Bonds, then get disappointed when it didn't happen.

On January 14, the Giants and Bonds agreed to a complex five-year contract worth $90 million in present-day dollars, ensuring that Bonds will chase Aaron's sacred all-time homer record in a Giants uniform and try to deliver the city of San Francisco its first World Series title.

"There wasn't any amount of money in the world to make me leave San Francisco," Bonds said. "I was gonna stay. I wanted to be loyal and stick it out here. I wasn't going to give up. This is where I was raised. This is where I went to high school. I'm a Giant for life."

One of the happiest people was shortstop Rich Aurilia. He had the best year of his career in 2001 batting in front of Bonds and called his teammate to offer congratulations.

Bonds is 189 homers from breaking Aaron's record of 755. He needs to average 38 homers a year to break the record in five years. He needs to average 47 homers a year to break it in four years. Bonds filmed a commercial with Aaron in mid-January for an investment company. In the spot, Aaron tries convincing Bonds to retire from the game. The commercial allowed Bonds time to talk with Aaron and get to know him.

"I don't even know if I want to break his record," Bonds told me, as this book neared its final deadline. "Hank is an icon. But Hank told me, 'you get everything you can out of this game.'"

Bonds was gracious enough to allow me to watch him and Gary Sheffield in a normal offseason workout. For the past month, Sheffield was sleeping on an air mattress in Bonds' basement. Between sets in the weightroom, I asked Bonds if he ever received a congratulatory phone call from Mark McGwire.

Bonds shook his head no.

Three months after the season, Barry Bonds still had no idea how he did it. The season is mostly a blur. But as he looks at strength coach Greg Anderson and Flexing coachHarvey Shields, he knows this: "The two best years of my career are the two years they've been with me."

Once his playing days are over, Bonds will also receive a 10-year personal services contract with the Giants, similar to what Willie Mays and Willie McCovey currently have. Bonds will be paid a $100,000 annual salary, all of which will be donated to the Barry Bonds Charity Foundation.

"From the organization's point of view, the very first move we ever made, in late 1992, was to sign Barry Bonds to a six-year agreement," managing partner Peter Magowan said. "Many believe that was as good a signing as a club has ever had. I feel just as confident now about this signing over the next five years. If Barry can live up to everything that's been said about him, and expected of him, and lead us to what we have not as yet been able to achieve, which we hope we do, and that is bringing a World Series championship to San Francisco."

The signing was possible for two reasons: one, Bonds took less money in the early years of the contract; and two, Magowan agreed to let the payroll budget (originally at $70 million) expand to $73 million.

The $18.0 million average annual salary made Bonds tied for the fourth-highest paid player in baseball in average annual salary (although deferred money can make this confusion). The leader is Alex Rodriguez ($25.2 million), followed by Manny Ramirez ($20.0 million), Derek Jeter ($18.9 million) and Sammy Sosa ($18.0 million).

The details of the contract:

2002: $8.0 million base salary, $2.5 million signing bonus.
2003: $8.0 million base salary, $3.5 milllion signing bonus.
2004: $11.0 million base salary, $4.0 million signing bonus.
2005: $15.0 million base salary.
2006: $13.0 million base salary.
2007: $5.0 million in deferred money, plus interest, from 2002.
2008: $5.0 million in deferred money, plus interest, from 2003.
2009: $5.0 million in deferred money, plus interest, from 2004.
2010: $5.0 million in deferred money, plus interest, from 2005.
2011: $5.0 million in deferred money, plus interest, from 2006.

The Giants have the option to void the fifth year (2006) if the following does not occur: A, Bonds does not reach 500 plate appearances in the 2005 season; or B, Bonds does not reach a combined 1,500 plate appearances in the 2003-2004-2005 seasons, with 400 of those coming in the 2005 season.

"I wanted to make it fair," Bonds said. "Let me earn (the fifth year). I have no problem earning it."

It was a deal that made everybody happy. Bonds will get paid a salary that puts him with his peers. Boras delivered the five-year contract he wanted. The Giants won't have to pay more than $15 million any season, providing them the payroll flexibility to put a competitive team on the field each season with a chance to win a World Series.

"We've got a contract that allows us to pay him what he's worth and will allow us to win," Magowan said proudly. "I think we have the best team we've had in the 10 years we've been here."

Bonds felt the same way. As always, he was working out six hours a day, six days a week, eager for the 2002 season to begin and another chance to pursue his elusive World Series ring.

"Everybody knows my main goal is winning a World Series," Bonds said. "Whatever it takes, I'm willing to do it."